Georges Simenon Revisited

Twayne's World Authors Series

French Literature

David O'Connell, Editor

Georgia State University

TWAS 888

GEORGES SIMENON

By Phyllis Carlin. Courtesy of the artist.

Georges Simenon Revisited

Lucille F. Becker

Twayne Publishers
New York

Twayne's World Authors Series No. 888

Georges Simenon Revisited
Lucille F. Becker

Twayne Publishers
1633 Broadway
New York, NY 10019

Library of Congress Cataloging-in-Publication Data

Becker, Lucille Frackman.
Georges Simenon revisted / Lucille F. Becker
p. cm. — (Twayne's world authors series ; TWAS 888. French literature)
Includes bibliographical references and index.
ISBN 0-8057-4557-2 (alk. paper)
1. Simenon, Georges, 1903–1989. I. Title. II. Series: Twayne's world authors series. ; TWAS 888. III. Series: Twayne's world authors series. French literature.
PQ2637.I53Z582 1999
843′.912—dc21 98-33697
[B] CIP

This paper meets the requirements of ANSI/NISO Z3948-1992 (Permanence of Paper).

10 9 8 7 6 5 4 3 2 1

Printed in the United States of America

A Robert, pour moi le plus grand Bob

Contents

Preface

The present volume *Georges Simenon Revisited* is a return after 20 years to my literary biography, *Georges Simenon* (Twayne Publishers), enriched with new material and new insights into the author's life and work. At that time, Simenon was known principally as the author of detective novels, a genre relegated to the status of paraliterature, without recognition of the fact that even in his detective novels, baptized the "Maigrets," Simenon re-created the genre and transformed it into a viable literary genre in which he expressed some of the most important themes of the twentieth-century novel. At that time, too, the literary merits of his work were obscured by the sheer magnitude of his output: 573 works (190 potboilers signed with 17 pseudonyms, 358 novels and short stories signed Simenon, 25 autobiographical works), 30 series of articles published in the French press before and immediately after World War II, and a ballet scenario. Simenon was spoken about in terms of records, the hundreds of books written, the hundreds of thousands of books sold, the millions of dollars earned, the thousands of women he slept with, the number of novels adapted for the cinema and for television. All of this diverted attention from consideration of the "romans durs" or "hard (problem) novels," the major part of his literary production. For the cultural importance of Simenon's oeuvre derives not from its success in terms of financial ratings or of records established, but from its success in conveying to the reader insights into the human condition.

Simenon's romans durs, which are marked by an extraordinary blend of narrative skill and psychological insight, established him as one of the major French-language novelists of the twentieth century. The novelist Frédéric Dard observed: "Before Picasso, they painted differently. Before Trenet, they sang differently. And before Simenon, they wrote differently. Simenon leaves us much more than a body of work, much more than a style of writing. . . . He did not reinvent life, what he did was to show it to us. Before him . . . our feelings were kept under glass and we expressed ourselves in well articulated sentences. Since Simenon, we think with our senses, we perceive with our hearts . . . [His intuitive gifts] permitted him to tell all, life and death, men and their misery, love and grief."[1]

In the opening chapter of the book, I trace in Simenon's biography the major influences on his work, incorporating a great deal of biographical material that has come to light since 1977. The following chapters demonstrate the way in which Simenon transformed this biographical material into literature. The saga of commissaire Maigret is considered in chapter 2. Chapters 3 and 4, which analyze the romans durs, on which Simenon's literary reputation is based, center on the violent nature of aberrant human behavior and illustrate Thoreau's observation that "the mass of men lead lives of quiet desperation." Chapter 5 considers Simenon's narrative gifts and the "poetic line" or atmosphere of his novels, while the last chapter on film draws on the material in the preceding chapters to demonstrate the virtually insurmountable difficulty of translating Simenon's introspective novels into film.

It would be impossible to deal with Simenon's vast literary production within the scope offered by the present study. I have, however, discussed the essential elements of his art, illustrating my observations with selections chosen according to their importance within the body of his work, as well as those that conform to my own preferences. But each reader of Simenon has his or her own favorites, for Mauriac it was the last of Simenon's novels that he had read, for Simenon the last that he had written.

Acknowledgments

I am grateful to M. Jean Simenon as well as to Mme Ariane Sulzer of the Administration de l'Oeuvre de Georges Simenon for their kind and generous permission to quote from the works of Georges Simenon. I thank Mme Christine Swings, the administrator of the Centre d'Etudes Georges Simenon at the Université de Liège, for her valuable assistance. I am also grateful to Dr. Linda Connors, Head of the Drew University Library Acquisitions Department, for her invaluable contribution to the creation of the Georges Simenon Research Center at Drew University in Madison, New Jersey. The center contains Simenon's complete works in both French and English, as well as extensive secondary source material.

Chronology

1903	Georges Joseph Christian Simenon born in Liège, rue Léopold, 13 February.
1903	Family moves to 10, rue de Gueldre.
1905	Family moves to 1, rue Pasteur (today 25, rue Georges Simenon).
1906	Birth of Christian Simenon, Georges's brother.
1906–1908	Attends nursery school of Sisters of Saint-Vincent-de-Paul.
1908–1914	Student at Institut Saint-André des Ecoles Chrétiennes.
1911	Family moves to 53, rue de la Loi, where mother rents rooms to foreign university students.
1914–1915	Student at collège Saint-Louis.
1915–1918	Student at collège Saint-Servais.
1917	Family moves from rue de la Loi to rue des Maraîchers.
1919	Family moves to rue de l'Enseignement. Doctor informs Simenon that his father is seriously ill. He leaves school to be apprenticed to a pastry cook. Shortly afterward, he becomes a salesclerk in Librairie Georges and is fired after six weeks.
1919–1922	Works as cub reporter on conservative Catholic newspaper, the *Gazette de Liège,* for which he writes articles and short stories signed Georges Sim. Given his own column, "Hors du poulaillier" (from the hen roost), which he signs Monsieur le Coq. He also contributes articles and short stories to the paper *Noss'Pèron* and the blackmail sheet *Nanesse.* Frequents a group of young painters and poets calling themselves "la Caque" (the keg), who meet in a ruined house behind the Saint-Pholien Church. Writes his first novel, *Au pont des Arches* (using pseudonym Georges Sim).

1920 Engaged to Régine Renchon, nicknamed "Tigy." Enlists in army to finish military service as early as possible.

1921 Désiré Simenon dies. Writes another novel, *Jehan Pinaguet* (under pseudonym Georges Sim), not published until 1991. Spends 18 months in service near his home and continues to write for the *Gazette de Liège.*

1922 Leaves Liège for Paris. Becomes messenger boy to Binet-Valmer, chairman of the Ligue des Chefs de Section et Anciens Combattants, a far right-wing organization.

1923 Marriage to Régine Renchon (Tigy) in Liège on 24 March. Returns to Paris and begins to write short stories for *Le Matin* and other Parisian newspapers. Writes more than 1,000 of these stories in the next 10 years. Secretary to marquis de Tracy, travels with him to many of his châteaux, in particular the château of Paray-le-Frésil, renamed Saint-Fiacre and made the birthplace of Simenon's famous detective Maigret.

1924 Leaves service of marquis de Tracy; settles in Paris, where he begins to write potboilers, the first of which, *Le roman d'un dactylo,* was written in one morning on the terrace of a café.

1924–1934 Writes 190 potboilers under 17 pseudonyms.

1925 Spends the summer in Normandy. Brings back to Paris a cook, Henriette Liberge (renamed Boule), who will become his lover and remain with the family until her death. Rents an apartment Place des Vosges in Paris, where he associates with painters Derain, Soutine, Kissling, Foujita, Vlaminck.

1926 Spends the summer in Porquerolles.

1928 Buys his first boat, the *Ginette,* and spends the summer touring the rivers and canals of France. Beginning with the first issue of *Detective* magazine, 25 October 1928, and continuing through 1930, writes a series of articles and detective short stories, which he signs with pseudonyms. These include: *Les 13 mystères, Les 13 énigmes, Les 13 coupables,* later published under patronymic in book form by Fayard.

1929 Has larger boat, the *Ostrogoth,* built, on which he travels as far as Delfzijl in Holland. Travels to Norway and Lapland by regular boat. Returns to Delfzijl, the putative birthplace of Maigret, and writes the novel *Pietr-le-Letton,* the first signed with his own name.

1931 Publishes 12 novels (see bibliography for titles arranged chronologically). In February launches Maigret series with an "anthropometric ball" at the Boule Blanche in Montparnasse. Jean Renoir buys film rights to *La nuit du carrefour* and Abel Tarride to *Le chien jaune.* Publishes articles: "Escales nordiques," in *Le Petit Journal,* 1–21 March; "L'aventure entre deux berges," in *Vu,* 1 July.

1932 Publishes seven novels and two articles: "Au fil de l'eau," in *Le Figaro illustré,* 1 May; "L'Heure du Nègre," in *Voilà,* 8 October–12 November. Rents property, "La Richardière," in Marsilly near La Rochelle. Travels throughout Africa. Two film adaptations of Simenon's novels (see filmography section of bibliography for all film adaptations).

1933 Publishes seven novels. Tours Europe in summer. Publishes articles: "La caravane du crime," in *Détective;* "Sa majesté la douane," in *Voilà,* 18 March–29 April; "L'Afrique qu'on dit mystérieuse" (signed Georges Caraman), in *Police et Reportage,* 27 April; "Les grands palaces européens" (signed Georges Caraman), in *Police et Reportage,* 25 May; "Chez Trotsky," in *Paris-Soir,* 16, 17 June; "Police judiciaire," in *Police et Reportage,* 22 June; "Cargaisons humaines" (signed Georges Caraman), in *Police et Reportage,* 24 August; "Une première à l'Ile de Ré," in *Voilà,* 7 October; "Pays du froid" and "Les gangsters du Bosphore," written for *Police et Reportage,* unpublished when magazine folded.

1934 Publishes four novels and articles: "En marge de l'affaire Stavisky," in *Paris-Soir,* January–February; "A la recherche des assassins du conseiller Prince," in *Paris-Soir,* March–April; "Peuples qui ont faim," in *Le jour,* April–May. Rents a schooner, the *Araldo,* on which he tours the Mediterranean during the summer. Articles on this trip include *Mare Nostrum,* published in *Vu.* Sued by a hotel keeper in Libreville for defamation in *Le coup de lune.*

1935 Publishes three novels. Travels around the world: New York, Panama, Colombia, Equador, the Galapagos, Tahiti, New Zealand, Fiji, Australia, the Indies, Turkey, Egypt, the Red Sea. Articles on his travels in Central America, *En marge des méridiens,* published in *Marianne.* Series of articles on his travels, *Les vaincus de l'aventure,* published in *Paris-Soir,* 12–25 June. Additional articles published in *Le jour* and *Paris-Soir.* Seven articles, *Le drame mystérieuse des îles Galapagos,* published in *Paris-Soir.*

1935–1936 Publishes 12 articles, "Histoires de partout et d'ailleurs," in reactionary publication, *Courrier royal.*

1936 Publishes four novels. Sued for *Quartier Négre.*

1937 Publishes four novels and articles: *Police Secours* or *Les nouveaux mystères de Paris, Paris-Soir,* 6–16 February; *Long cours sur les rivières et canaux, Marianne,* later published under same title by Editions Dynamo, Liège, 1952.

1938 Publishes 11 novels and collection of short stories *Les sept minutes.* Buys house in Nieul-sur-Mer where his first wife, Tigy, would live until her death in 1985.

1939 Publishes three novels. Birth of son Marc.

1940 Publishes two novels. Organizes aid to Belgian refugees at La Rochelle. Settles in château de Terre-Neuve at Fontenay-le-Comte.

1941 Publishes six novels.

1942 Publishes seven novels. Writes autobiographical work, *Je me souviens.* Starts transforming *Je me souviens* into autobiographical novel *Pedigree,* published in 1948.

1943 Publishes collections of short stories: *Le petit docteur, Les dossiers de l'Agence O.*

1944 Publishes four novels and collections of short stories: *Signé Picpus, Les nouvelles enquêtes de Maigret.*

1945 Publishes three novels. Travels with family to the United States. Meets Denise Ouimet, who will become his second wife. Publishes articles, *Au chevet du monde malade,* in *France-Soir.*

1946 Publishes three novels; articles on Canada, *Le Canada,* for *France-Soir;* and articles on travels throughout the United States, *l'Amérique en voiture,* for *France-Soir.*

1947 Publishes seven novels and short stories: *Maigret et l'inspecteur malchanceux* (later *malgracieux*). Travels to Cuba, on his return, crosses desert by car and settles in Arizona. Death of Christian Simenon.

1948 Publishes six novels, including *Pedigree.*

1949 Publishes six novels and short stories: *Maigret et les petits cochons sans queue.* Birth of his second son, Jean, called Johnny, to Denise Ouimet. Settles in California.

1950 Publishes five novels. Divorced from Régine Renchon (Tigy) at Reno, marries Denise. Settles at Shadow Rock Farm, Lakeville, Connecticut.

1951 Publishes eight novels and short stories: *Un Noël de Maigret.*

1952 Publishes five novels. Returns to Belgium, where he is elected to the Belgian Royal Academy of Language and Literature. Sued in Belgium for *Pedigree;* loses suit and decides to forego writing future volumes. Travels to Paris, Milan, Rome, Brussels, Liège. Returns to Lakeville. Elected to American Academy of Arts and Letters. Elected President of Mystery Writers of America.

1953 Publishes six novels. Birth of daughter, Marie-Georges (nickname Marie-Jo).

1954 Publishes five novels and short stories: *Le bateau d'Emile, Nouvelles exotiques.*

1955 Publishes five novels. Returns to Europe with family. Named Chevalier de la Légion d'Honneur.

1956 Publishes four novels.

1957 Publishes three novels. Settles with family at Echandens, near Lausanne.

1958 Publishes five novels. Delivers speech, *Le roman de l'homme,* at Brussels Exposition Universelle. Presides over Brussels Film Festival.

1959 Publishes five novels. Birth of son Pierre.

1960 Publishes three novels. President of the jury of the Thirteenth Cannes Festival.

1961 Publishes three novels.

1962 Publishes four novels.

1963 Publishes three novels. Moves to mansion at Epalinges near Lausanne, his twenty-ninth home. Denise leaves for sanatorium after nervous breakdown and never returns to Epalinges. Simenon remains with three youngest children and Theresa, his companion.

1964 Publishes four novels.

1965 Publishes three novels.

1966 Publishes two novels. Bronze statue of Maigret erected at Delfzijl.

1967 Publishes four novels.

1968 Publishes five novels.

1969 Publishes three novels.

1970 Publishes three novels. Death of Henriette Simenon-André.

1971 Publishes four novels.

1972 Publishes two novels. Following aborted attempt to write a novel, titled "Victor," Simenon gives up writing fiction. Leaves Epalinges; moves to apartment in Lausanne.

1973 Doctor Honoris Causa Université de Liège. Buys a small eighteenth-century house next door to apartment house in Lausanne where he will live with Theresa until his death.

1973–1981 Dictates into tape recorder. 21 volumes of these "Dictées" published.

1974 *Lettre à ma mère* published.

1977 Establishment of Centre d'Etudes Georges Simenon at the University of Liège.

1978 Suicide of Marie-Jo Simenon, 16 May. Rue Pasteur renamed rue Georges-Simenon in November.

1981 *Mémoires intimes suivis du livre de Marie-Jo,* his last work.

1985 Death of Régine Renchon (Tigy Simenon).

1987 At Yalta, Crimea, U.S.S.R. meeting of the International Association of Crime Writers, the Prince Alexei Tolstoy Award for lifetime achievement in the crime writing field was presented to Georges Simenon.

1989 Death of Georges Simenon, 4 September.

Chapter One

Biography—A Remarkable Life

Every work of fiction must of necessity bear a relationship to the life of the author. The attitudes and behavior of the characters and the settings in which their actions take place reflect to a greater or lesser extent the experience of the writer. The degree to which a writer can subsume his own education, class, thoughts, and emotions into his fiction will vary; Simenon's novels are clearly inseparable from his biography. What may mislead the reader in Simenon's case, however, is the fact that he controlled the interpretation of his past through repeated interviews and autobiographical works, manipulating the facts to create the Simenon myth. For the biographer, the wealth of material furnished by Simenon can be a trap. It is too easy to follow his lead and to tell the story he wished to tell. And, in fact, biographers have generally accepted Simenon's version, with the notable exception of Pierre Assouline, who tells us that "Simenon did not so much invent or distort as construct his legend, model his statue, and forge his myth, to the extent that already halfway through life he was no longer in a position to distinguish between truth and falsehood, fact and fiction."[1]

It is possible, however, to separate to some extent myth from reality and, by studying certain autobiographical novels, to demonstrate the way in which Simenon's entire experience appeared in his work. "In truth," Simenon wrote, "I have no imagination. Everything is taken from life. In the course of my travels, I met so many different types of people, I shared the private lives of so many people, that I need only look for what I need in my memory. Occasionally, I draw my inspiration from an actual occurrence."[2]

Even as a small child, Simenon listened, observed, and absorbed everything around him. He was a voyeur, one who was fascinated by the dark side of life. He perceived from the very beginning that the human condition was characterized by dishonesty, fear, and guilt, and these were to lie at the heart of his fictional universe. The record of Simenon's childhood and adolescence can be found in the autobiographical novel *Pedigree,* a work in which we find adumbrated the themes and characters of his novels.[3] What he has done is to use his prodigious memory as an encyclopedia, borrowing from it a name, a tic, a gesture, an atmosphere. Using this material as a starting point, he goes beyond it, integrating it into a new reality, which is the novel.[4]

Pedigree is a roman-fleuve or saga; it is the chronicle of a liégeois family between 1903 and 1918 and is different from all of Simenon's other novels by reason of its length, its linear structure, its chronological sequence without flashbacks, and its absence of plot. The work concentrates on the portrait of a city, Liège, a class, and a family during the early years of the twentieth century, beginning with the birth of Simenon's alter ego, Roger Mamelin, on the same Friday the thirteenth of February in 1903 as Simenon, and ending with the armistice of 1918. Certain political and social events of the time are evoked—the Agadir crisis, anarchist bombings, general strikes, the German occupation, the armistice, the mine disaster at Souverain-Wandre, and the echoes of revolutionary intrigue brought to Liège by impoverished students from Eastern Europe,[5] but these are treated only as background material for what Simenon calls "the epic of ordinary people . . . the *chanson de geste* of those who do what they are told to do without knowing where they are going and who try all the same to go somewhere and who never give up, hoping and despairing and hoping again, through thick and thin" (quoted in Assouline, 303).

Pedigree is a re-creation of the landscape of personal memory, a work in which Simenon succeeds in imposing a whole lost world upon the reader.[6] "The childhood of Roger Mamelin," Simenon wrote, "his milieu, the setting in which he develops, are very close to reality, as are the people he observed. The events, for the most part, are not invented. But, above all, as far as the characters are concerned, I exercised the writer's privilege of re-creating reality, starting from composite material, remaining closer to poetic truth than to pure and simple truth . . . *Pedigree* is a novel, thus a work in which imagination and re-creation play the greatest role, but this does not prevent me from admitting that Roger Mamelin has a great deal in common with the child I once was."[7]

Simenon brings to life in *Pedigree* the whole sensory world of his childhood in Liège. His words capture the sounds, sights, tastes, smells, and textures of the city with its houses, streets, canals, and barges, the different seasons, and changes of climate. Here, as throughout his work, we find the Proustian triggering of memories by the repetition of sensory impressions from the past recaptured in the present along with the emotions and events that accompanied them. Certain cities in Simenon's novels, even those not so named, are in reality merely the topographical transposition of Liège with its alleys, its small shops, its church, and its town square (Assouline, 76). Through his sensations, one of the principal sources of his inspiration, Simenon never lost contact with the child and the adolescent he once was. "All of my novels are fantasies of my childhood," he said (quoted in Assouline, 76–77). Answering a journalist who asked him why it always rained in his novels, Simenon answered, "it rains in my novels because it pours in Liège 180 days a year."[8]

And then, surfeited with the sights, sounds, and smells of his native city, Simenon did what his alter ego Roger Mamelin had sworn to do, he left Liège forever. Paradoxically, the past he had fought to escape is the past to which he kept returning, reconstituting it through sensory evocations. "It is true that I also put my memories of Liège into other cities. It is clear that we absorb images, sounds, and life until the age of 17 or 18. As that is the part of my life that I spent in Liège, I absorbed a great deal. Since my profession consists of rendering what I absorbed, it is evident that there is a lot of Liège in what I render."[9] But, even more than Liège in and of itself it is the original experience of provincial insularity, of a stifling and unbearable milieu that Simenon acquired there and internalized in a universally applicable model. It is also the only place in which it is possible to put down roots.[10] While *Pedigree* is inseparable from Liège, the city is also present in the pseudonymous *Au Pont des Arches, Jehan Pinaguet,* and certain popular novels. It is the background for a number of novels clearly situated in Liège (*Le pendu de Saint-Pholien, La danseuse du Gai-Moulin, Les trois crimes de mes amis*) and in works in which Liège is not identified but which are totally or partially inspired by this city (*Les fiançailles de M. Hire, L'Ane Rouge, Crime impuni, Le locataire, Faubourg, Chez Krull, Chez les Flamands, Bergelon,* and the short story, "Le témoignage de l'enfant de choeur").

Writing in prose that is pictorial and tactile, Simenon in *Pedigree* does for Liège what the young Joyce did for Dublin: he evokes the city with such immediacy that we feel we've walked its streets and visited its markets, that we have seen, heard, and smelled its "sidewalks in the rain, the rumbling of the streetcars which jolt in the street, dawn over the marketplaces, the appearance of 'bouquettes' [liégeois crêpes] on Christmas eve and the warm wine to accompany them, the horse-drawn barges, fog over the canals, the wagons filled with vegetables, and the cries of the tradeswomen, the flowers in the open air stalls . . . the alleys filled with the smell of French fried potatoes, the casseroles of mussels, and the large glasses of beer . . . the odor of gin, of tar, of ginger, of leeks and cloves."[11] Many other obsessive images of Liège recur throughout Simenon's entire fictional oeuvre:

> . . . the cobblestones glistening with rain and the red and beige streetcars, the very dark, quiet neighborhood with its red brick houses that seem more self-contained than anywhere else, the Saint-Nicolas bell tower which marks out the hours, the *Pont des Arches,* which links outre-Meuse to the center of the city, the canal, the lock, the shop where the sailors come to drink, the towpath which disappears into the countryside . . . The glassed-in kitchen of Puits-en-Sock street . . . also the alleys that open onto that street and that have the smell of poverty. . . . The other alleys in the direction of the cathedral where half-clad girls lift up curtains and issue more or less explicit invitations.[12]

Against the backdrop of Liège during the early years of the twentieth century, Simenon portrays the life of the petite bourgeoisie, a class that would at last find its novelist just as the proletariat had found its own in Emile Zola more than a half-century before. Simenon's family came from the traditional petite bourgeoisie of artisans, merchants, and small businessmen, but when his parents moved into the new occupations of the modern petite bourgeoisie —his father as bookkeeper in an insurance firm, his mother as saleswomen in a department store—they did so with conflicting results. To offset the status represented by white collar rather than artisanal work—Désiré Simenon was the only educated member of his family—there was the concomitant loss of identity in working for others, often for lower wages than before.[13]

Despite their modest economic situation—they had only the "bare essentials," as Simenon's mother constantly proclaimed—Henriette Simenon clung to her class and its imagined superiority to the proletariat and the peasantry, both classes absent from Simenon's work. Simenon was imbued with the conservative, repressive ideology of the petite bourgeoisie that remained his throughout his life despite his professed disinterest in politics and his claims to being an anarchist. Simenon may have been apolitical, as he maintained, but with a distinctly conservative social agenda. Simenon's class detested intellectuals, the proletariat, and immigrants. Even as a child, he could feel his mother's fear of the proletariat, the previously invisible "other," who now seemed to threaten the status quo with its new demands for equity. In *Pedigree,* Simenon shows members of the petite bourgeoisie huddled behind their closed shutters as they watch striking miners march through their neighborhood during the general strike of the miners of

Seraing. "Their hobnailed shoes scraped the cobblestones or the asphalt. The men seemed to discover with amazement these neighborhoods where they never came and where fear had blocked the windows and the doors. . . . Some carried their children on their shoulders. Women stumbled, clutching to their breasts the edges of dark shawls with heavy wool fringes. The miners wore helmets of cuir-bouilli and people trembled behind their curtains as they watched them pass, their eyes in their hardened faces brighter than those of other men" (*Pedigree* 1:85).

In *Je me souviens,* the autobiographical work that was the basis for the novel *Pedigree,* Simenon makes palpable his mother's fear of déclassement by contact with those whom she considered to be her social inferiors as he describes trips to the market with her when he was a little boy. She would drag him quickly past the inns where, in the dark interiors, he saw peasants eating "enormous plates of bacon and eggs and slices of bread as large and thick as wagon wheels." For years, Simenon recalls, he was hungry for this "peasant food," which his mother scorned as she "slipped through this enchanted world, dignified, constantly counting, an eager child hanging on to her skirts."[14]

In the same work, Simenon admonishes his son never to forget his humble origins. "You live in a château, you have a park at your disposal . . . a distinguished governess follows your every step . . . I clutch hold of the fragile chain that links you to those from whom you are descended, the little world of little people who struggled in their turn—as tomorrow you will in yours—confusedly seeking a means of escape, a goal, a raison d'être, an explanation for good luck or misfortune, a hope for an improved condition and for serenity" (*Souviens,* 41). Thirty years later, in his *Lettre à ma mère,* written to his mother after her death, Simenon wrote: "All your life, you insisted on belonging to the world of people of small means. It would greatly astonish you to learn that, at my age, I draw nearer to it because I feel that it is my world also and because it is the world of truth."[15]

The fear of the working class as well as the xenophobia of the petites gens—their hatred of Jews and foreigners—can be explained not only by fear of difference, but also by a constant obsession with stability, a determination to maintain the status quo and avoid losing their place in a rapidly changing world. Simenon makes use of the petite bourgeoisie's reflexive stereotype of the Jew of popular tradition. The Jewish characters in his works embody centuries-old collective mental images: they are drug dealers, pimps, shady doctors, crooked lawyers, usurers, dishonest financiers, thieving bookkeepers.[16] In *Le fou de Bergerac,* Simenon moves anti-Semitism to an extreme level.[17] Here, the so-called madman of Bergerac, who is Jewish, is not only an international thief and murderer, assassinated by his own son—the odious scion of a detestable race—he is also a white slaver, supplier of flesh to brothels in South America where the "French girls are the cream of the crop."[18] Maigret "had had hundreds of people like Samuel to study in Paris and elsewhere. He had always done it with a certain curiosity mixed with embarrassment, not quite disgust, as if they belonged to a species different from that of the ordinary human race" (*Fou,* 115). The anti-Semitism of the Catholic petite bourgeoisie was also fueled by the church's teachings about a people rejected and different, condemned to be the horrifying symbol of the foreign and of the cursed. It was God's curse that doomed the Jews to wander the earth, persecuted by the people they encountered (Wardi, 242).

Simenon absorbed his mother's obsession with class divisions. The crisis leading to tragedy in many of Simenon's novels is produced when the protagonist breaks down class barriers. We see this situation in *Le déménagement,* when the protagonist, a member of the petite bourgeoisie, moves from his old apartment on the rue des Francs-Bourgeois in the Marais to a modern suburban apartment complex. Disoriented in this new milieu, he acts in an imprudent way that leads to his murder. In other novels, *La mort de Belle* for example, the tragic denouement is, in part, the consequence of a man's marrying out of his class.

While his writing enabled Simenon to cross the line between classes, his heroes, who are driven by a similar desire to escape, succeed or fail purely by chance. In many of his novels, Simenon attributed to his protagonists his own guilty perception that leaving one's class constituted an act of betrayal. When Maugras, the protagonist of *Les anneaux de Bicêtre* (see p. 73), observes a group of indigent old men at Bicêtre Hospital, he senses that their world of the petite bourgeoisie is the one to which he rightfully belongs. "He was born there. He more or less learned how to live there. And then he betrayed them," he reflects.[19]

In the novel *Le passage de la ligne,* a fictional transposition of elements of the author's life, Simenon traces the upward mobility of his protagonist, Steve Adams, who, like his creator, breaks through the class barrier. He does so three times; twice with the help of others, the third time by himself. Were it a traditional bildungsroman, the novel would have ended with Steve's having achieved financial and personal success, but Simenon goes beyond such a traditional denouement to reflect his own experience. At the end of *Le passage de la ligne,* Steve Adams, dissatisfied with his financial success as well as with his suitable marriage, decides to abandon everything; he leaves his wife and fortune to open a small antiques shop near Toulon, a return to the life of the petit bourgeois that is strangely premonitory of the last fifteen years of Simenon's life when he retired to a modest home. In the tight interweaving of Simenon's life and fiction, we find not only the influence of his life on his work but also the reverse—the unusual influence of his work on his life—and the ultimate blurring in his own mind of any distinction between the two.

Steve Adams's disquiet echoes faithfully the lifelong malaise at the core of Simenon's being, an anxiety that drove him from country to country and from dwelling to dwelling. Simenon changed residences 31 times during his life as he tried time after time to take possession of a place in the hope of taking possession of himself. "I spent my life leaving," Simenon stated in a television interview.[20] The theme of flight provoked by existential malaise is one of the basic themes in Simenon's oeuvre. In the novel *Malempin,* Simenon explains the cause of this malaise as the fear of unknown catastrophe lurking on the horizon: "For ten years, or rather twenty, perhaps thirty years," the protagonist remarks, "I have been walking around on tiptoe, hardly daring to take a deep breath! Because I learned that everything is fragile, everything that surrounds us, everything that we take for reality, for life: wealth, reason, peace of mind . . . Not to mention health! . . . And honesty . . ."[21]

The world of the petite bourgeoisie was that of practicing Catholics, and the Catholic liturgy pervaded Simenon's work. The festivals and holidays he describes in *Pedigree* are religious in nature. The atmosphere of Sundays in his parish would mark him forever; the rites of Sunday mornings, all of the memories and sensations of that day merge in his work. Sundays, exceptional days in every respect in Simenon's novels, are either days of pleasure, like the typical Sundays of the Donge family (*La vérité sur Bébé Donge*), or of crime, the "Sunday of the [Donge's] great drama,"[22] the attempted murder around which the novel is centered (see p. 85). The *Testament Donadieu* is divided into three parts titled "The Sundays of La Rochelle," "The Sundays of Saint-Raphael," and "The Sundays of Paris." It is on a Sunday morning that Hubert Cardinaud (*Le fils Cardinaud*) leaves mass with his young son, picks up the traditional cake, and carries it home by the pink string wrapped around the box, only to discover that in his absence his wife has run off with another man. In the novel *Touriste de bananes,* on board the ocean liner *l'Ile de Ré* somewhere in the Pacific Ocean, 30 days after leaving France, the protagonist knows that it is unmistakably Sunday by a certain change in the atmosphere:

> A real Sunday, a Sunday like every Sunday, even though one might have believed that, in this immensity in which the *Ile de Ré* was sailing, every day would resemble the others. . . . Why wasn't it a day like the others? . . . Why was there a smell of Sunday, a radiance, a Sunday idleness? Sunday mass was not enough to explain it, nor was the elaborate cake that was served at lunch. We had crossed half of the sea routes of the world and it was the same Sunday as everywhere else, a heavy, luminous, sluggish Sunday, a Sunday moreover that brought to mind certain village fairs.[23]

The sound of church bells announcing Sunday morning mass constitutes a leitmotif in Simenon's work. By a remarkable process of synesthesia, Simenon uses visual images to conjure up the sound of these bells, most notably in *Les anneaux de Bicêtre,* where the sounds of the ringing bells are perceived as rings detached from their source that fall away into the air. Simenon's work contains repeated references to the Catholic atmosphere of his youth, allusions to church buildings and liturgy, images borrowed from religion, where clouds look like angels, rooms smell like sacristies, and women are as cold as theological virtues.[24] The anguish of many of Simenon's characters may be attributed to their awareness that they exist in a world deprived of divine grace.[25] The maxim, "Comprendre sans juger" (understand without judging), at the heart of Simenon's philosophy of life—expressed as Maigret's moral code—might seem to reflect the church's understanding of and compassion for the sinner. Or it could also be identified with the church's teaching, "Let he who is without sin cast the first stone," or the concomitant "Judge not lest you be judged," which provides peace of mind to the guilty. In any case, despite the prevalence of religious images, religious questions per se are as absent from Simenon's work as are political considerations. Religion, said Simenon, is a question that is too personal, too intimate, to be dealt with in a novel (Parinaud, 407).

The Roger of *Pedigree,* like Simenon, was an altar boy; he served the mass at six o'clock in the morning in the Bavière Hospital. The early hour was not a problem in summer when it was already light outside, but the winter darkness filled the boy with fear: "I admit that I ran, keeping to the middle of the street, fearing the shadows."[26] Had he had a bicycle, he would have been able to escape any pursuers, but his mother, pleading poverty, refused his request. In a short story, titled "Le témoignage de l'enfant de choeur," Commissaire Maigret, the policeman hero of Simenon's Maigret saga, buys the coveted bicycle for an altar boy in whom he recognizes himself. Simenon explained that in his work he used the word altar boy not only in a literal but also in a figurative sense to describe a child brought up in accordance with the most conventional ideas. "That education marks you for life, even if you stopped believing {as I have} all you were taught long ago."[27] "[Catholicism} . . . begins with baptism, the catechism, first communion . . . Upon awakening, at the table before and after meals, at noon, in the evening. . . . 'I am guilty.' Because I was born a man, I am guilty, every day, at every hour . . . torn . . . between hope and despair, heaven and hell, between good and evil."[28] His religious education explains in large part the fear and guilt at the heart of Simenon's oeuvre, guilt he sought to expiate through the secular form of confession known as literature.

Pedigree is not only the narrative of a city and a class, it is also the story of Roger's (Simenon's) immediate family and extended family of aunts, uncles, and cousins. Various other inhabitants of Liège appear from time to time as they interact with the protagonists. At the center of the first two thirds of *Pedigree*—"A l'ombre de Saint-Nicolas" and "La maison envahie"—is Simenon's mother, the dominant influence on his life and work. Henriette Brüll Simenon (Elise Mamelin in *Pedigree*)[29] was of mixed German and Dutch parentage, the youngest of thirteen children "whom nobody had expected and who had turned up to complicate everything" (*Pedigree* 1:13). Her father had been a successful merchant before his alcoholism brought ruin upon him and his family and led to his suicide. The life of Simenon's mother "as a frightened unhappy little mouse had begun after her father's death when she was five and the family had left the large house by the canal at Herstal, where timber from the north filled sheds as big as churches" (*Pedigree* 1:13). She and her mother, from whom she inherited her inordinate pride, came to Liège. In order to camouflage their poverty, Henriette's mother would put empty saucepans on the stove when visitors arrived. Her daughter inherited her obsession with keeping up appearances. After her mother's death, left entirely on her own, she went to live with one of her wealthy married sisters, performing domestic chores in exchange for room and board. A few years later, she became a salesgirl in the Innovation Department Store and then left this position to marry Désiré Simenon. Unfortunately, her marriage did not bring the security she sought; it merely reinforced her conviction that she could count only on herself. Henriette Simenon suffered from the beginning from a fivefold handicap: economic (ruin and resultant poverty); moral (alcoholism and suicide); linguistic (Flemish mother tongue in a francophone city); physical (anemia); and familial (breaking apart of the family). Nothing thereafter could heal the original wounds.[30] She bore the memory of a past laden with problems, anxiety, and tragedy. Her background explains her desperate fear of poverty and her insatiable need for security.

It is unquestionably his mother's psychological inheritance that determined Simenon's anxiety and his lifelong search for equilibrium. Although he always believed that he took after his father, he realized ultimately that he resembled his mother even more. In 1976 he wrote: "I was sure that I took after him. I realize today, at my age, that I take after my mother every bit as much. Like her, I am much more sensitive than the average person. Even an event that basically has nothing to do with me is enough to disturb me deeply and, as they say, 'knock me down.' "[31] Like his mother, Simenon always felt instinctively that something terrible was always about to happen.

Simenon portrayed his mother as an excitable person, subject to nervous crises and gratuitous crying fits. "She suffers because of everything . . . she suffers through habit" (*Souviens,* 35, 37). She seems almost to take morbid pleasure in her own anguish. Simenon lends his mother's temperament to the mother of the protagonist of *Les quatre jours du pauvre homme*: "How she loved misfortunes! She would have knit them! She would have begged God to make them rain down on our heads."[32]

Henriette's humble manner and constant complaints hid an iron will that would let nothing stand in the way of her search for financial security. Her personal fears coupled with an awareness of the terrible fate awaiting the wives of miners killed in a mine disaster explain her determination to assure her security in the event of her own husband's death. When she asked Désiré to take out a life insurance policy, she was furious when he shrugged off her request, not knowing that he had applied for one and had been turned down because of the heart condition that was to cause his death at the age of 43, a premature death that explains Simenon's preoccupation with illness and mortality. Henriette then decided that she must provide for her own future and moved her family to a house on the rue de la Loi, which she converted into a boardinghouse for foreign students. In 1929, nine years after the death of Désiré, still motivated by a need for financial security, Henriette Simenon married a railway employee whose benefits included a widow's pension.

Henriette Simenon's second marriage was a severe blow to Simenon, who had idealized his dead father; his love for him became a cult. What Simenon considered to be his mother's betrayal inspired the novel *Le chat,* the most devastating portrayal of a couple in Simenon's work short of spousal murder. Very soon after their marriage, Henriette and her second husband began to distrust one another. He accused her, not entirely without reason, of being in a hurry to collect her widow's pension. "Together, in the large house without boarders," wrote Simenon,

> the sentences you exchanged . . . must have been terrible and expressed a profound hatred since, one day, you decided to stop talking to one another and to use scribbled notes when it was necessary to communicate. When I speak of hatred, I do not exaggerate. . . . when a man and a woman who live together, united by marriage, reach the point at which each one prepares his own food, each one has his own larder which is locked with a key, and waits for the kitchen to be empty to eat, how can you explain that? . . . You were both afraid of being poisoned. It had become a morbid idée fixe. (*Mère,* 91)

Simenon resented his mother and feared her brutal outbursts of anger. He felt that she was wrong to take in boarders and thereby deprive his father of a corner to call his own. The fact that Désiré's early death proved that she had been right, that she would otherwise have been left destitute, did not change his mind. His feelings toward his mother determined his misogynistic attitude toward women. Simenon's first wife, Régine Renchon, remarked: "I think that he was greatly influenced by his mother and for him it is she who represents all women . . . except for prostitutes."[33] The image of women is always linked to the fear of loss of identity through female domination, a fear paralleled by the concomitant desire for total fusion analogous to the one existing between the mother and the very small child.[34]

Henriette's temperament, her obsessions and ambitions, her tics, and even a few of her virtues are found in many of Simenon's female characters, but as we see in *Pedigree,* she is one of the few women in his work to be analyzed in depth. Women, in all of Simenon's other novels, with the exception of the eponymous *Tante Jeanne, La vieille,* and *Betty,* serve merely as catalysts to provoke the reactions of the males (Becker, 2481). Even the series of murderous, castrating mothers in the Maigrets are two-dimensional caricatures of a pathological psychological profile.[35] Victims of such women, men dominated by a stifling feminine environment, appear also in the novels *Les demoiselles de Concarneau, Le cercle des Mahé,* and *Le Coup-de-Vague.*

Insight into Simenon's feelings for his mother can be found in *Portrait-souvenir de Balzac,* an account of the life of Balzac that he wrote and narrated for French television in 1960. Simenon's discussion of Balzac serves as a catharsis for his feelings about his own mother: "It is said that the novelist is a man who never loved his mother or who never knew maternal love," Simenon remarked. "This might seem to be a gratuitous remark at first sight. However, could the need to create other men, to draw from oneself a host of different characters come from a happy man, integrated harmoniously into a little world made to his measure? Why persist in living the life of others if one is at ease and without conflict? Doesn't the child's peace of mind come from the mother's love for the child and the child's love for the mother?"[36] One must necessarily conclude that the most damning remark of all those Simenon attributes to Balzac echoes Simenon's own perceptions: "All of my misfortunes came from my mother; she ruined me by design and for pleasure" (*Balzac,* 233). A psychiatrist once commented that Simenon's psychological profile was that of "a small boy holding the hand of a mother who would always withhold her approval."[37]

In *Lettre à ma mère,* a poignant farewell written by Simenon to his mother three years after she died at the age of 91, he observed: "We never loved one another when you were alive, you know it well. Both of us only pretended" (*Mère,* 10). The work transcribes the thoughts of the 71-year-old author as he sits in his mother's hospital room attempting to understand the woman who has always remained a stranger to him. He no longer judges her: "I know now that there was never malice on your part, nor egotism. You were following your destiny" (*Mère,* 67). His mother, like her father and like most of her brothers and sisters, was the victim of heredity. Instead of the dependence on alcohol chosen by many of them, Henriette, the youngest, who had witnessed the struggle of the family and its progressive decay, decided that it was up to her alone to achieve her salvation. In a moving epitaph, Simenon pays final tribute to his mother: "You followed the course of your life with rare fidelity . . . you succeeded" (*Mère,* 114–15).

Simenon's allusion in *Portrait-souvenir de Balzac* to "a son Mme Balzac had, this time not sired by her husband, but by the châtelain of Saché, M. de Margonne"(*Balzac,* 210), reminds us of Mme Balzac's well-known preference for her ne'er-do-well bastard son Henri—on whom she doted to the exclusion of her other children—and brings us back to another reason for Simenon's feelings toward his mother, her undisguised preference for her younger son, Christian, born three years after Georges. Simenon spent the rest of his life seeking reasons for this preference. The feeling that he had been rejected by his mother and replaced by his brother proved devastating to him. While there are a few references to Christian in *Je me souviens,* he is excluded from *Pedigree,* where Roger is spared his brother's existence as Elise miscarries. But he is not spared his mother's complaints about the prolapse of her womb and her blackmail that, if he does not behave, an ambulance will come to take her away to the hospital. These threats, together with his father's illness and early death, explain Simenon's preoccupation with sickness and death.

Both mother and younger brother are summarily dispatched in a curious episode in *Les mémoires de Maigret.* Maigret's father befriended a local alcoholic doctor, who had killed his own wife and child in a botched delivery. The doctor seemed to have stopped drinking when Maigret's father, in a generous but highly improbable act of faith, engaged him to deliver his second child. The intoxicated doctor once again killed both mother and child. The litotes, "I was left an only child," which concludes Maigret's account of the event, is Simenon's settling of accounts with both mother and brother, free from the guilt that is cast upon the misguided father.[38] The unit of father and son as sole members of the family group, achieved in *Les mémoires de Maigret,* can be found in a series of novels in which the son is raised by the father alone, among them *Le déménagement* (Emile), *L'horloger d'Everton* (Ben), and *Les anneaux de Bicêtre* (René Maugras).

Chilling proof of Henriette's preference for Christian is, according to Simenon, the remark she made to him when he visited her as she lay dying in the Bavière Hospital: "What a pity it is that Christian was the one who died" (*Mère,* 107). Since Simenon is the only source for this information, one could presume that this statement—as well as other accounts of Henriette's rejection of her older son—might be distorted by the son's perceptions. But any doubts about the accuracy of Simenon's words, or about her preference for her younger son, are dispelled by Henriette Simenon herself. When asked in a television interview—at the time of Simenon's triumphant return to Liège in 1952—to speak about her famous son, she replied that he had always been difficult: "When you asked him to shut the door, he would say 'no.' " She then added: "You know I had another son, *he* was wonderful—so sweet, so thoughtful."[39] Even when Georges Simenon was at the height of his remarkable career, his mother would never give him the approval or love he sought so desperately.

Although absent from *Pedigree,* Christian is present in much of Simenon's work in the guise of the younger, weaker, wastrel brother, preferred by a mother who is jealous of her older son's success. The novel *Malempin* presents—together with many other autobiographical elements—the trio of a mother, a rejected successful older son (here a physician), and an adored good-for-nothing younger son. Guillaume Malempin, Christian's alter ego, goes from job to job, takes money from his widowed mother and brother, and steals from his employer. Despite this, his mother "uses every ruse imaginable to make . . . [Malempin/Simenon] help . . . (his) brother financially and to use (his) . . . limited influence on his behalf," maintaining all the while that "Guillaume is the great man in the family" (*Malempin,* 97, 98).

Christian Simenon's career, even when not measured against his brother's, was disastrous. He worked as a functionary in the Belgian Congo, where he led a dissolute, alcoholic life. Christian is most likely the prototype of the young "adventure's failures"[40] who populate Simenon's African novels.[41] In 1940, he returned to Belgium, joined the pro-Hitler fascist organization Rex, and participated in commando operations against communists, Jews, and members of the Belgian Resistance. He played a major role in a particularly bloody slaughter of 27 civilians, a rexist operation for which he was tried in absentia after the war and condemned to death (Assouline, 366). Terrified, he fled to France to seek his brother's help. Simenon offered three possible solutions—Christian could flee to fascist Spain or Portugal, surrender to the Belgian government, or enlist in the French Foreign Legion—and recommended the third. Two years later, Christian was killed in Indochina, a death for which Henriette Simenon blamed Georges and for which he, himself, felt responsible. He expiated his guilt in *Le fond de la bouteille,* written in 1948 soon after Christian's death. The novel, which provides remarkable insight into Simenon's attitude toward his brother, takes place in Tumacacori, Arizona, on the Mexican border. Patrick Martin Ashbridge (P.M.), a successful rancher and lawyer, returns home one evening to find his brother Donald waiting for him. Donald has escaped from Joliet penitentiary and wants P.M. to help him cross the border to join his wife and children, who are waiting for him in Mexico. P.M. has always worked hard and has achieved both financial success and a respected place in the community. No one among his wealthy friends suspects his modest origins. Now Donald's arrival threatens "his whole life, the security bought so dearly, with such persistence."[42] All this for a failure. Donald "had failed at everything! A weakling! A person who had never been able to look life in the face and assume his responsibilities as a man, as he had assumed his" (*Bouteille,* 35).

And yet, Donald had always been the preferred brother, his behavior excused because he was weak. "That's the excuse. . . . In that case, the weak one has all the rights" (*Bouteille,* 60). It was like the story of Esau and Jacob in the Bible, a story that he (P.M.) had never been able to understand. "Jacob was weak . . . Esau was strong, and it was Jacob who was blessed" (*Bouteille,* 184). The fraternal conflict goes as far back as Cain and Abel. "He had been taught about the curse that weighed down on the children of Cain" (*Bouteille,* 183). In that case, why has he always felt a vague malaise vis-à-vis his brother, P.M. wonders, "a feeling that, although difficult to define, is like guilt?" (*Bouteille,* 167–68). It is indeed guilt, and it motivates his subsequent actions. He sacrifices his own life as he helps his brother cross to safety in Mexico. P.M., Simenon's fictional creation, does what the author did not do—he saves his brother.

Christian was unquestionably his mother's favored son, but Georges was his father's. And, for his part, Simenon was ashamed of his mother's lack of dignity and of her hypocrisy, but he revered his father, his veneration intensified by his father's early death. Désiré's is the only name that remains unchanged in *Pedigree*—one does not tamper with the names of heroes and gods. The youngest child of a large Walloon family, Désiré is very different from Elise/Henriette. He seemed "to be accompanied always by music that he alone heard and with which his regular steps kept time. Beneath his mustache, his avid lips half opened in a vague smile that expressed complete inner contentment" (*Pedigree* 1:17). From his father, Simenon inherited the contemplative side of his nature, his feeling of kinship with the world. Like him, he is "sensitive to the quality of the air, to far off sounds, to moving spots of sunlight" (*Souviens,* 23). This sensitivity would enable Simenon to evoke an atmosphere in his works by conveying to the reader a few decisive sensory impressions.

Désiré is head clerk in a small insurance company. He erred in choosing fire insurance rather than life insurance when given the choice by his employer, because life insurance was very new at the time. Life insurance becomes the more lucrative branch by far, and Désiré's junior colleague earns much more than he. Henriette continually reproaches her husband for having chosen unwisely, condemning his family to financial hardship. But Désiré is happy, "happy in his household . . . happy in the street where he envies no one, happy in his office where he knows he is first" (*Souviens,* 23). "My father went to his office exactly as he would have gone to heaven," Simenon stated. "He was the Just. . . . Despite the mediocrity of our life, he was at peace with himself and with others. My mother and a few of her sisters always wanted more."[43] As Henriette furnished the model for Lecoin's mother in *Les quatre jours du pauvre homme* (see p. 10), so Désiré is the inspiration for Lecoin's father:

"Through his glasses, he looked straight in front of him, with a look that was both strong and kind at the same time, with the shadow of a smile on his features. . . . People who smile like that, with that kind of sweetness, are people who have given up once and for all, given up fighting or expecting anything from anyone" (*Quatre jours,* 35).

However nurturing the father-son relationship may be, the paternal figure, except for Maigret, is rarely dominant or even strong. At times, as in *Les anneaux de Bicêtre,* the presumed perfection of the father is questioned as the protagonist muses on his childhood: "He was fond of his father, no doubt. Nevertheless, the boy had begun to discover, somewhat to his distress, that his father was not intelligent, that his view of life was a restricted one, that his resignation and gentleness were perhaps merely stupidity" (*Bicêtre,* 99). An aphorism Simenon repeated in many of his novels, which echoes a remark he made to his mother—"There are only two types of people in the world: those who spank and those who get spanked (those who get kicked in the butt and those who kick). I do not want to be spanked"[44]—would seem to express his view of his father as a victim and his determination not to emulate him in that respect.

With very few exceptions, however, the theme of the father as friend and mentor, possessing the power to exorcise evil and despair, runs through Simenon's work. Simenon once stated that he noticed that most men have more memories of their father than of their mother and that paternal love was almost always stronger than maternal love. He added that many women do not even know what maternal love is.[45]

Désiré lends his dignity, his quiet courage, his family feeling, and his taste for a calm, regular, contemplative life to many of Simenon's protagonists, principally Maigret (Becker, 2481). It is Maigret's reassuring paternal presence that separates what Simenon called his romans durs, the non-Maigret difficult problem novels (the Henriette cycle), from the Maigrets (the Désiré cycle). Until the very end, writes Simenon, Désiré "kept his smiling serenity, he inhaled the joy of life wherever it presented itself as naturally as others breathe" (*Souviens,* 41).

Simenon tells not only the story of his immediate family in *Pedigree* but also that of two clans, the Walloon Mamelins (Simenons) and the Flemish Peters (Brülls), the numerous uncles and aunts and their spouses, and the scores of first cousins with whom he grew up. The Mamelins are pure Walloons, attached to their city and the working class Outremeuse district of Liège in which they live; they are "not people who move and who change occupations. They are suspicious of everything that moves. One is what one is, once and for all, employee, cabinetmaker, hatter, rich or poor" (*Souviens,* 16). They represent stability, integration into a neighborhood and into the artisanal petite bourgeoisie. They do not play important parts in Simenon's oeuvre. Only certain details of their occupations, their tics, or illnesses—such as aunt Cécile's dropsy—supply background material. The Mamelins are a tightly knit clan under the domination of the mother and are very different from the Peters, who are not united as a family and who are often set against one another by self-interest and jealousy. These restless, anguished, maladjusted members of his mother's family, seeking to escape through drink, vagabondage, and power, serve as prototypes for the protagonists of Simenon's romans durs. Elise notes that they are different from other people. "You know . . . it's rather as if we were strangers everywhere, all the members of our family," she says to her brother Léopold (*Pedigree* 2:134). Of Henriette's purported twelve siblings, only four play a role in *Pedigree* and appear in a series of novels in successive reincarnations.

Henriette's oldest brother, Léopold, who is 30 years older than she, remembers their former wealth and tells her stories about their enormous home in Holland, an hour's walk from the closest dwelling. "The canal, which goes from Maestricht to Herzogenbosch, passes in front of the house, much higher than the land, and the boats you see gliding past reach to the tops of the poplars and always, particularly when the wind fills their sails, seem about to capsize into the fields" (*Souviens,* 59). These barges that go by on the canal, higher than the land, are an image that recurs in a few of Simenon's novels, most vividly in *La maison du canal.*

At that time, Léopold was a handsome young man who was studying at the university. For some obscure reason, he sold himself to replace another recruit and while in service married the canteen girl of his regiment, a scandal that provoked a rupture with his family. The rehabilitation of a fallen woman, whether a whore or one with a sordid past—with varying degrees of success or failure—is a theme that appears in many novels.[46] According to Simenon, it was, in part, the desire to save his second wife, Denyse Ouimet[47], from her unsavory past that motivated his marriage.

After he left the army, Léopold worked at various odd jobs as he sank ever more deeply into alcoholism. Periodically, he would disappear without a trace for six months or a year at a time. Eugénie, his wife, would get a job and wait for him to contact her. When Léopold returned, he would put an ad in the newspaper to find her. She never reproached him; they would resume life together until he would disappear once again. One day, Léopold died of cancer of the tongue. This time, Eugénie knew he would never return and starved herself to death. "Eugénie, the canteen girl, had let herself die for love at the age of sixty, a few weeks after the final departure of Léopold, who had left so often before" (*Souviens,* 61). This great love would inspire one of Simenon's few portrayals of true love—without reference to sexual passion—in *Le grand Bob,* one of his finest novels.

Léopold, the alcoholic vagabond, is the prototype of those who totally scorn all social life and all socially acceptable behavior. For Simenon, "there is something great about that strength of character to accept daily humiliation, or rather, not to feel that humiliation"(Parinaud, 390). It is evident, he contends, "that the true tramp is a more complete man than we . . . He [Léopold] was a nonconformist. . . . The tramp is a man who lives without making any concessions, and who can live according to his own personal canons"(*Gril,* 11). In *Maigret et le clochard,* the tramp's refusal to judge or denounce a murderer confers a certain nobility on him that Maigret admires, despite his disappointment at not having the testimony necessary to arrest the guilty man.[48]

The antithesis of Léopold is Albert, the financially successful Brüll sibling, named Louis de Tongres in *Pedigree.* His fictional progeny will be the wealthy Terlinck (*Le bourgemestre de Furnes*), Malétras (*Le bilan Malétras*), and Eugène Malou (*Le destin des Malou*), all of them immured in their solitude despite their wealth and position.

Three of Simenon's maternal aunts were also to inspire cycles of novels. Aunt Maria (Anna Brüll in *Je me souviens,* Louisa Peters in *Pedigree*), who ruled over her household, had a grocery store/bar in Liège on the Coronmeuse quai where she provisioned the boatmen whose boats were moored above the locks. The memory of that neighborhood would remain stronger and more vivid for Simenon than that of the neighborhood in which he grew up:

> The Coronmeuse quai, and with it the canal, the port where one or two hundred canal boats, perhaps even more, stand side by side, at times ten deep, with laundry drying, children playing, dogs napping, an invigorating odor of tar and resin. . . . There is the old-fashioned store window, cluttered with merchandise, starch, candles, packages of chicory, bottles of vinegar. There is the glazed door and its transparent advertisement: the white lion of Rémy starch, the zebra of an oven cleaner, the other lion, the black one, of a brand of wax. . . . Above all, the unique, the

> marvelous odor of this house where nothing is unimportant, where everything is exceptional, where everything is rare. . . . Is it the smell of gin that predominates? Is it of the more insipid groceries? For they sell everything, there is everything in the store, barrels of American oil, rope, stable lanterns, whips, and tar for boats. There are jars of candy of an uncertain pink color and glass drawers stuffed with cinnamon sticks and cloves. (*Pedigree* 1:100–101)

Mixed with these odors is the smell of willows, since Uncle Lunel is a basketmaker. Lunel, like Léopold, has fled, but he has done so while remaining behind, taking refuge from the world in his deafness. In *Chez Krull, Chez les Flamands,* and other novels, including several Maigrets, Simenon will evoke this establishment, with domineering women like Aunt Louisa and withdrawn men like Uncle Lunel.

Another sister, Aunt Marthe, the one for whom Henriette worked when she was young, is the wife of a wealthy wholesale grocer, Hubert Schroefs (Jan Vermeiren). They live in a "huge house of white brick, just opposite the meat market, with the wholesale grocery store and the main entrance from which the trucks come out. And on the canvas covering of these trucks there is the name of my uncle in enormous letters" (*Souviens,* 117). Aunt Marthe will provide inspiration for a long line of alcoholic women who periodically go on binges, referred to as "novenas" in the family's lexicon, while Vermeiren's lineage will include the wealthy, arrogant, cruel individuals found in *Le riche homme, Le bourgemestre de Furnes,* and *Oncle Charles s'est enfermé.* A scene recounted in both *Je me souviens* and *Pedigree* is repeated in *Oncle Charles s'est enfermé.* Aunt Marthe, an alcoholic, has locked herself in her room, with a revolver. Elise/Henriette is called upon to get her out without incident; Henriette fails in *Je me souviens,* Elise succeeds in *Pedigree.*

Like Marthe, Félicie, the prettiest of Simenon's aunts and the sister closest in age to Henriette, is an alcoholic. "Poor Félicie, in truth the most unfortunate, also the prettiest, the most moving of my aunts, whom I still see leaning her elbows on the counter of her beautiful café in a pose filled with romantic nostalgia" (*Souviens,* 50). Félicie is married to the owner of a bar—a most unfortunate situation for an alcoholic—who torments and beats her and finally drives her mad. Roger is present when they take her in a straight jacket to the hospital—where she will die of delirium tremens—while her husband is led off to jail. The protagonists of two novels—*Malempin* and *Faubourg*—will witness a similar scene during their childhood. It is described in detail in *Faubourg*:

> There were many people in the house, aunts and uncles, also people he didn't know. They were speaking softly, mysteriously. You would have said that a crime had been committed. Then they heard a piercing female shriek, a cry of terror, and he saw his aunt . . . carried down the stairs by two male nurses. . . . During this time, his uncle, the one he had never seen before . . . sobbed, leaning against the wall, all alone in a shadowy corner of the corridor.
>
> For a year, when they passed in front of the house, his mother repeated to him:
>
> —He was your uncle. . . . But you must never speak of him. . . . Because of him, your aunt went mad.[49]

Alcoholism, the legacy of the Brülls, a form of self-destruction chosen by members of that clan to flee from themselves, is one of the principal themes in Simenon's work, from the first novel signed Simenon, *Pietr-le-Letton,* to the last, also a Maigret, *Maigret et monsieur Charles.* Not only his grandfather, but at least one of his uncles and two of his aunts became alcoholics in adolescence, unhappy secretive alcoholics. In *Quand j'étais vieux,* a journal that Simenon kept for the years 1960–1962,[50] he wrote that of all the dangers he ever ran, alcoholism was undoubtedly the most serious (*Vieux*, Preface, 1:i). "I have studied the question as only specialists have done, in the domain of criminology also. . . . Perhaps because I just missed becoming an alcoholic" (*Vieux,* 2:160). Even though he stopped drinking in 1949, he realistically always considered himself to be an alcoholic (*Vieux,* 2:166). There was no alcohol in the Simenon home; Désiré did not drink, and Henriette had a justifiable fear of alcohol. During his rebellious adolescence, Simenon drank, but it was not until he began the first Maigrets that he acquired the habit of drinking wine. "I was rarely drunk but I needed a pick-me-up as early as the morning, especially to write" (*Vieux,* 2:164). According to Simenon, however, it was only in the United States that he became an alcoholic:

> I am speaking of a particular, almost permanent state, in which one is dominated by alcohol, whether during the hours one is drinking, or during the hours when one is impatiently waiting to drink, almost as painfully as the drug addict waits for his injection or his fix. . . . If one has never known this experience, it is difficult to understand American life. The crowds cease to be anonymous, the bars cease to be ordinary, ill-lit places, the taxi drivers complaining or menacing people. From one end of the country to the other there exists a freemasonry of alcoholics. . . . It's another world in which certain preoccupations disappear, where the importance of things changes. (*Vieux,* 2:168)

While he drank heavily, particularly in Canada and the United States, Simenon did so only in spurts because he forced himself to abstain when he was preparing, writing, or revising a novel. His output of five or six novels a year on average left him very little time to let himself go.[51] Simenon escaped, but the alcoholism that had ruined the life of his maternal grandfather and many of his uncles and aunts, source of the fear that Henriette had instilled in him, came back to haunt Simenon in the person of his second wife Denyse, an irredeemable alcoholic. In his *Mémoires intimes,* Simenon charts the progress of her disease, the scourge of the Brüll family entering his life from without to poison his mature years. "Alas, D. (Denyse) is drinking more and more and I would be the last one to reproach her for it. Doctors have recognized for a long time that alcoholism is not a vice, but a sickness, which has to be taken care of like any other and is not something of which to be ashamed" (*Intimes,* 1136). Denyse's addiction is evident as early as in the novel *Trois chambres à Manhattan,* which celebrates their meeting and their passion. Alcoholism determines the actions of the characters in many novels,[52] and is endemic among the tramps in the Maigret series as well as among the expatriate failures of the so-called exotic novels.

Henriette's boarders would also serve as models for Simenon's fictional characters. Most of the racial or ethnographical clichés in Simenon's work seem to have come from his observation of his mother's boarders before 1914 (Assouline, 55). These young men and women came from Eastern Europe to study in Liège because it was the least expensive of the French-speaking university cities. Some of them were also there to pursue revolutionary activities. Frida Stavitskaïa, Elise's first boarder, belonged to a group of nihilists, and her father was a political prisoner in Siberia. Other boarders were Schascher, a timid redheaded Russian Jew, "so ugly that he scares children, so poor that he wears neither socks in his down-at-the-heel shoes nor underwear under his clothes" (*Pedigree* 2:141); Saft, a blond "real," as distinguished from Jewish, Pole; Bogdanowski, obese and insolent, of uncertain nationality; Lola, remote and sensual; and Mlle Feinstein, vulgar, narcissistic, and a gifted mathematician: "She is nasty (she caught Elise overcharging her boarders for their coal) . . . she is envious of everyone because she is ugly, because she is Jewish, because her father was born in a ghetto on the Russian border, an old Jew with a long beard who, over there, humbly skirted the buildings" (*Pedigree* 2:110). These foreign students or their counterparts appear in eight of Simenon's novels,[53] their earliest appearance dating from the first Maigret, *Pietr-le-Letton* of 1931.

Pietr, the Lett, is described as a typical Northern type. Commissaire Maigret had studied several of the sort, all of them intellectuals, and those with whom he had associated during his brief career as a medical student had baffled his Latin nature.

> He remembered one of them, among others, a thin blond Pole whose hair was already sparse at the age of twenty-two, whose mother was a charwoman in his country, and who, for seven whole years, took courses at the Sorbonne, without socks on his feet, eating nothing but a piece of bread and an egg each day. He could not buy the written courses and he had to study in the public libraries. . . . he had hardly finished his studies when he was offered an important professorship in Warsaw. Five years later, Maigret saw him return to Paris, as dry and as cold, in a delegation of foreign scientists and he dined at the Elysée Palace.[54]

While the first two-thirds of *Pedigree* are dominated by the figure of Elise, the third part, *Quand les lampes se sont éteintes,* presents a highly detailed portrait of Roger. "When I wrote *Pedigree*," Simenon observed, "I had a second reason for doing so . . . when it was finished, I said to myself: 'I've finally finished with all those people. Now that I have put them into a book in the flesh, they no longer encumber me and I am going to be able to write about new and different characters'. . . . [However] I never completely got rid of Roger in *Pedigree* for we are one to a certain extent. Other than in *Pedigree,* I never put myself into my novels"(Parinaud, 388). Perhaps Simenon believed what he said, or perhaps he was seeking to cover his tracks, or perhaps his professed divorce from his characters represented an attempt to assuage his own guilt by seeking absolution for his guilt-ridden doppelgängers—writing was for Simenon a means of purging his inner demons. What is not in question, however, is the fact that Simenon never ceased to externalize his own psyche in his novels. All of his protagonists are incarnations of the author at different stages of his life; from the avid young man in revolt against the stifling mediocrity of his milieu and desperate to succeed to the middle-aged man of humble origins who has risen in the world through his own efforts and who now perceives the meaninglessness of his achievements.[55]

The sexual voraciousness of his male protagonists is also Simenon's. We can find in the third volume of *Pedigree* the origins of his sex addiction. Roger has always been ashamed of his mother, of the way she treats her boarders, of her constant whining and complaining, of her calculating treatment of others depending on their social status, of her lack of pride, and of her hypocrisy. Coupled with shame is the feeling of impotence experienced by the small boy before the domineering woman, and the desire to free himself. His mother's emasculating nature will leave an indelible imprint on him and affect his judgment of all women, whom he will regard as adversaries. Consciously or unconsciously, they try to enter into a man's inner, private life. While Roger's humiliation takes the form of an inferiority complex, he begins to adopt an increasingly aggressive attitude toward his mother. Roger's rebellion against Elise occurs at the same time as his sexual awakening and causes a psychic crisis that will have a profound effect on the portrayal of women and sexuality in Simenon's work. Woman is considered to be both the enemy and the desired object. In order to be possessed, she must also be humiliated to be brought down to the level of the male. Therefore, he wants a woman who has been soiled (Parinaud, 217). That is why there are so many men in Simenon's work who are impotent other than with whores, many who even marry whores, and others who become infatuated with fallen women. Impotence, a manifestation of failed manhood, leads to murder in both the romans durs, among them *La mort de Belle,* and the Maigrets, among them *Maigret tend un piège.* Sexuality in Simenon's work is always described with the pitiless crudity of his adolescent vision.

Simenon's sexual compulsion has often been compared with Casanova's, and there are certain similarities between the two men. The lives of both were a search for the maternal warmth they did not receive. Both lost their virginity at a young age—Casanova at 11 to a priest's sister, Simenon at twelve and a half to a 15-year-old young girl. "Sex," wrote Casanova in his *Memoirs,* "is a part of the story, but only the vehicle for a deeper knowledge of the human condition."[56] Simenon also maintained that his sexual compulsion was merely the need for contact that only sexual relations could satisfy. "How could I have created dozens, perhaps hundreds, of female characters in my novels if I had not experienced these adventures that lasted for two hours or ten minutes?" (*Homme,* 426). But there is a vast distinction between Casanova's and Simenon's sexuality. Casanova was past master at the art of seduction—he had affairs that lasted for varying periods of time and he liked his women to be intelligent. "Without speech, the pleasure of love is diminished by at least two-thirds," he wrote (Smith, B4). Simenon's sexuality was purely physical. Throughout his life, spurred on by his insatiability, he frequented innumerable whores. His repeated allusions to his two-minute encounters with many thousands of whores resemble adolescent record keeping. In almost every novel, there is a sexual deviant, whether nymphomaniac, satyr, sexual pervert, child/woman, or instinctive woman who responds in the fashion of an animal. Significantly, there is no real eroticism in Simenon's novels, sex is more or less mechanical. The high point of sensuality in the entire oeuvre would seem to be Maigret's gastronomical pleasures.

The sexual confusion and guilt resulting from Roger's troubled relationship with his mother leads to a masochistic desire to be punished. He is obsessed by the need to sink further and further into vice. His despair leads to what might be called moral suicide—he steals from his grandfather's cash register, he sells black market merchandise, he makes illegal liquor, he frequents German soldiers and whores and delights defiantly in his shame. Like Frank Friedmaier—one of Simenon's most antipathetic creations and the protagonist of the wartime novel *La neige était sale*—he seeks to avenge himself on a world that did not permit him to remain pure. Yet, even during his worst moments of debauchery, Roger longs for something better. "It seemed to him that all that was needed was an effort made once and for all, and then there would be no more bastards, life would be beautiful and clean, as harmonious as certain memories, and you would no longer have the impression of constantly floundering about in filth." He feels that his life is somewhere else, he doesn't know where, but he decides that he will keep on looking for it (*Pedigree* 3:134). Roger is the prototype of the young men in Simenon's work who feel the need to escape from the pettiness and meanness of their milieu and to lead violent lives, like Emile in *Les suicidés;* the Roger who longs for purity and order will be the inspiration for Alain Malou in *Le destin des Malou.* Like all adolescents, Roger is driven by his sexuality and, at the same time, is ashamed of it, his guilt made all the more acute by a Catholic education that equates sexuality with sin. Not only the teachings of the church but also all traditional ideas of right and wrong are upset in wartime when, in order to survive, parents encourage their children to lie and to cheat. Simenon's unconventional ideas of morality may well stem from his adolescent experiences during the German occupation of Belgium during World War I.

It is Désiré who finally saves his son. One morning Roger returns home after a night of debauchery and learns that his father has had a heart attack. As he enters Désiré's room, it seems to him that his father is silently transmitting the message: " 'You see, son. I have saved you.' For Roger is saved, at present, he is sure of it" (*Pedigree* 3:192). All the problems that had seemed insurmountable are now solved. He will not have to endure the humiliation of certain failure at his exams because his father's illness furnishes him with a perfect excuse to drop out of school. The important theme of paternal salvation in *Pedigree* is found in many of Simenon's novels, among them *L'Ane Rouge, Le fils,* and *La neige était sale,* and is implicit in all of the Maigrets. Désiré, the father, forgives all trespasses and has the ability to exorcise the evil possessing the son. Roger draws back from the edge of the precipice; he will enter the world and seek a place in society. "I am going to be a man, I promise you," he tells his father (*Pedigree* 3:191). The leitmotif of Simenon's work, "It is a difficult job to be a man," attests to the difficulty of this endeavor.[57]

In an interview with Brendan Gill, Simenon said: "I was born in the dark and the rain, and I got away. The crimes I write about—sometimes I think they are the crimes I would have committed if I had not got away. I am one of the lucky ones. What is there to say about the lucky ones except that they got away?"[58] It is Simenon's awareness of the thin line separating the criminal from "those who got away" that governs his refusal to pass judgment. He wants his readers to realize that they, too, could be driven to the limit and, as a result, to ask themselves the question: "Why he and not I?"

Pedigree ends with the armistice of 1918. Roger is almost 16 years old. The details of Simenon's remaining years in Liège can be found in the novels *Les trois crimes de mes amis, Le pendu de Saint-Pholien,* and *L'Ane Rouge.* In the first two, Simenon tells about a clique of young poets and painters calling themselves "la Caque" (the keg), who met in a ruined house behind the Saint-Pholien Church where they "feverishly sought intense excitement, any kind of ecstasy, of the body, of the senses, of the mind, by any means imaginable and even using artifices, by meticulously codified formulas that resembled those of sexual maniacs."[59] Under the influence of alcohol and drugs, Joseph Klein, one of the members of "la Caque," hanged himself one Christmas eve on the portal of the Saint-Pholien church, a death that Simenon believes he and his friends could have prevented. In *Le pendu de Saint-Pholien,* "la Caque" becomes "les Compagnons de l'Apocalypse" and a murder is added to the suicide. Before killing himself, Klein murders another member of the group with the passive compliance of the others. Simenon finds absolution in the novel for his own guilt when he has Maigret pardon the young men involved. Several of the members of "la Caque"—not all as Simenon stated—were to fail. Their fate was one of the reasons why failure became an obsession with him. Looking back on his life at the age of 72, Simenon wrote: "I knew too many of them in my adolescence, then later on during my early years in Paris, then even later on, and even today. I was afraid of becoming one of them for years. . . . The failure, for me, is the man who had great ambitions in one field or another, who was enthusiastic, who sacrificed everything, and who, one day, years later, realized that he hadn't arrived anywhere" (*Homme,* 415). In truth, Simenon's fear of failure seemed to go all the way back to his initial failure to win his mother's love and respect, a failure that never failed to haunt him.

Two other men with whom Simenon associated at that time, Hyacinthe Danse and Ferdinand Deblauwe, ended their unsavory careers as murderers, both motivated by the defection of the whores for whom they pimped. Deblauwe shot his rival, and Danse bludgeoned to death his mother as well as the whore. Simenon wondered whether the time in which they lived could serve as an explanation for their crimes. "Are there periods of more intense ferment, or moments when unhealthy currents flow? . . . I am inclined to believe it, above all since, in the youth I knew, I find in all of my friends, only less accentuated, the very thing that made criminals of those I mentioned. What gave us that taste for fallen women, the most disgusting love affairs . . . that unhealthy exaltation between two glasses of wine? . . . Wasn't it the fault of the war that we lived through as children without understanding it and that marked us without our realizing it?" (*Trois crimes,* 115). The ubiquitous lawlessness of wartime attracted Simenon to the criminal world and almost all of his novels, both romans durs and Maigrets are built around murder or murder deflected, that is to say suicide.

And during those years in Liège he walked constantly, the luxury of the poor that was always to provide him with the solitude and the sensory stimulation necessary for the creation of his works. "I wandered, for the most part early in the morning or late at night, through the crowded working-class streets or the greenery of the hills. I was hungry, yes, hungry for everything, for traces of sun on the houses, for trees and faces, hungry for all the women I passed. . . . I was hungry for life, and I wandered through marketplaces gazing here at the vegetables, there at the multicolored fruit, elsewhere again at the displays of flowers. 'Big nose,' yes . . . for I was inhaling life through my nostrils, through my every pore, the colors, the lights, the odors and noises of the streets" (*Intimes,* 700–701).

After leaving school, Simenon unsuccessfully tried various occupations for brief periods until he became a cub reporter in 1919 on the *Gazette de Liège*—a conservative, Catholic newspaper—where he remained until December 1922. He also collaborated on two other newspapers, the

Walloon *Noss'Péron* and the satirical *Nanesse.* While Simenon's childhood provided the themes and characters and many of the plots of his novels, his experience as a journalist broadened his knowledge of people and different social milieus; the situations he encountered provided material for his novels. Journalism was also an excellent apprenticeship for the future novelist in other ways; it taught him to grasp the essential detail and to write quickly. As a reporter, Simenon said,

> I found myself behind the scenes, face to face with harsh reality and, for four years, I was going to see the other side of the picture, to discover the hidden forces behind the life of a city. There was no lack of human material . . . 50,000 frantic spectators who are thrilled by a boxing match or a political meeting; the automobile or streetcar accident that transforms several lives; the bloody drama that shatters families; the prowler, the thief, the pallid hoodlum, the drug addict in desperate need of a fix; the politician who comes to solicit votes; or the decent man in search of a decoration, of the chairmanship of some organization or another, of something, or anything that will take him out of his mediocrity.[60]

Simenon graduated rapidly from cub reporter to his own column "Hors du poullaillier" (from the hen roost), consisting of humorous short articles, which he signed Monsieur le Coq. These articles alternated with columns of straightforward news reporting signed Georges Sim. Other than a few potboilers and early short stories written under pseudonyms, they are the sole examples of humor in an entire body of literature that stresses the difficulty of life. The subject matter—which includes strikes, predictions about the end of the world, the rise of the dollar against European currencies, the Charlie Chaplin mania, the servant problem, feminist orthography, and unfavorable trade balances[61]—illustrates the adage, "The more things change, the more they remain the same."

Although Simenon wrote extensively about all aspects of his life and work, he was uncharacteristically reticent about 17 articles he wrote for the *Gazette de Liège,* titled "Le péril juif," articles that repeated the violent anti-Semitism of the infamous "Protocols of the Elders of Zion." This scurrilous work, originally published in czarist Russia to foment pogroms against the Jews as a means of channeling and redirecting the discontent of the populace, was disseminated throughout the world. Simenon's articles were uncovered by the Belgian journalist Jean-Christophe Camus. When Camus asked for Simenon's comments in the matter, the author maintained that it was a question of two or three articles he was assigned to write. Camus agrees that *La Gazette de Liège* was indeed a right-wing, anti-Semitic, Catholic journal, and that Simenon was given the assignment, but finds that Simenon far exceeded any demands made upon him.[62] Simenon's silence about and subsequent disavowal of these articles show once again how deftly Simenon engineered his legend.

L'Ane Rouge, a thinly disguised fictional version of Simenon's early days as a cub reporter, reveals a not uncommon urge on Simenon's part to psychically disrobe and show himself as he really is in an attempt to receive from the reader, here recast in the role of the mother, the unconditional love the mother is supposed to give to the small child. Jean Cholet, the protagonist of the novel, is a 16-year-old cub reporter who works for a Catholic newspaper, the *Gazette de Nantes.* The editor-in-chief of the publication is the kind, understanding M. Dehourceau, the fictional counterpart of Joseph Demarteau of the *Gazette de Liège.* Simenon wrote that Demarteau was the third in the series of four men—following Désiré and the Walloon poet Joseph Vrindt and preceding the marquis de Tracy—who gave him his chance and saved him from himself. Simenon was certain that without the director of the *Gazette de Liège* he would never have become a journalist.

While many of the elements are autobiographical—Jean Cholet's profession, his sexuality, his excessive drinking, his feelings of suffocation in his family, and his need to break away—the story departs from Simenon's life as Jean sinks completely into vice, justifying his debasement by his superstitious belief that "it was necessary to get down to rock bottom! It was the only way to finally extricate oneself. Once at the bottom, in one way or another, it would end."[63] As in Simenon's case, the miracle of salvation comes with the death of Cholet's father. "The miracle was to gather everyone around him in this concert of infinite indulgence. . . . It was really a liberation! Jean hiccuped, coughed, unable to catch his breath. They turned to him. A hand was placed on his shoulder. 'You must be a man.' . . . Now everyone was nice to him! They were going to put him back on the right track. The past was wiped out" (*Ane,* 205). In what appears to be a gratuitous debasement of an idol, Simenon has Cholet's father die in a brothel. The only satisfactory answer to this strange turn of events can be found in Simenon's need to justify his alter ego's immorality, as if to say: " 'You see, I was no worse than my father who was, above all, a good man who succumbed to a human weakness'. . . . Simenon absolved himself of guilt by identifying with his kindly but weak father."[64]

The return of the prodigal son at the end of *L'Ane Rouge* is not autobiographical. In 1922, Simenon left Liège for Paris and, except for his triumphant return in 1952 when he was elected to the Belgian Royal Academy of Language and Literature, and his visit to his dying mother in 1971, he never returned to his native city. "I realized that only what you have lived yourself can be transmitted to others through literature. I had to know the world from every angle, horizontally and vertically . . . know it in all its dimensions, come into contact with countries and races, climates and customs, but also to penetrate it vertically . . . have access to different social strata, to be as much at ease in a tiny fisherman's bistro as at an agricultural fair or in a banker's living room" ("Romancier," 88–89).

During his first six months in Paris, Simenon worked as an office boy for Henri Binet-Valmer, a writer and president of an extreme right-wing political movement to whom he had been recommended by Demarteau—a frustrating, demeaning job that he gave to the protagonist of *Les noces de Poitiers.* He returned to Liège briefly in 1923 to marry Régine Renchon (rebaptized Tigy by Simenon), an artist who represented stability and protection from solitude and failure, a fate he feared. She appears in the guise of the tolerant, understanding wife cum mother, whose seeming ability to see into her spouse's soul is unbearable to the weak male (*La main, La mort de Belle*). Neither this marriage nor his second were to keep Simenon from his lifelong pursuit of women that, by his own calculations, ran to as many as four whores a day.

Upon their return to Paris, Simenon became the secretary of the marquis de Tracy, the fourth among the men whose moral support saved him from ruin.[65] He traveled with him from château to château as he managed his estates. Without the marquis's knowledge, Tigy would follow them and stay in hotels nearby, a situation transposed into *L'aîné des Ferchaux.* The provincial aristocracy appears in four of the Maigrets.[66] In the so-called *Les mémoires de Maigret,* Tracy's château de Paray-le-Frésil becomes the château de Saint-Fiacre, where Maigret was born, and the estate manager Pierre Tardivon—whom Simenon admired—would take on the role of Maigret's father, the bailiff of Saint-Fiacre.

In the early twenties, Simenon began submitting stories to the newspaper *Le matin,* edited at that time by Colette. She told him that his stories were too pretentious, that he should avoid striving for literary effect and make his work simple by paring it down to what was absolutely essential. When Simenon followed her advice, which he feels was the most useful literary advice he ever received, his stories were accepted for publication. At this time, he also began to write pulp fiction. The 190 popular novels that he wrote under 17 pseudonyms from 1924 to 1934 can be divided into three basic categories—crime, love, and adventure. These potboilers were, for Simenon, an apprenticeship in his craft.

Simenon and Tigy moved into an apartment on the Place des Vosges in 1924, where they were to live intermittently for seven years. They spent their summer vacation in 1925 in Normandy, the setting for several Maigrets and romans durs.[67] It was in Normandy that they met Henriette Liberge, a 17-year-old farm girl, whom they hired as a maid and took back with them to Paris. Rechristened Boule by her employer, Henriette Liberge was to become Simenon's mistress as well as his maid and remained with him for 40 years, sharing more of his life than any other woman, until he was forced by his second wife's jealousy to part with her. He sent her to his son Marc's home to care for his children, and she remained with Marc until her death.

Until the outbreak of the Second World War, Simenon traveled continually with Tigy, his travels furnishing the material for many articles and novels. On his first boat, he followed the canals of France from north to south and from east to west, and later brought to life the world of canals, of barges, and bargemen in *L'écluse No.1, Le charretier de "la Providence,"* and *La veuve Couderc.* The island of Porquerolles in the Mediterranean, where he spent the summer of 1926, and where he would return many times, furnished the setting and atmosphere for *Cour d'assises, Le cercle des Mahé, Mon ami Maigret,* and the remarkable short story, "Sous peine de mort."

In 1929, Simenon commissioned the building of a large boat, the *Ostrogoth.* In keeping with his extraordinary gift for self-promotion, he hosted a three-day party to celebrate the christening of the boat by the Curé of Notre-Dame at the Square du Vert-Galant. Later on, Simenon had his fictional policeman write in his putative memoirs—*Les mémoires de Maigret*—that he received an invitation to this party and that it went on for three days and nights (*Mémoires,* 28). Simenon, Tigy, and Boule traveled on the *Ostrogoth* as far as Delfzijl in Holland, the purported birthplace of the Maigret novels, now home to a commemorative statue of the celebrated policeman, built in 1966. *L'assassin, L'homme qui regardait passer les trains, Maigret et l'affaire Nahour,* and *Un crime en Hollande* all take place in Holland. From Delfzijl, he and Tigy went on alone by regular boat to Norway and Lapland. The atmosphere of the trip north from Stavanger in the south of Norway, when the boat stopped at all the tiny ports of the Norwegian coast, is re-created in *Le passager du "Polarlys"* and is evoked in *Le voyageur de la Toussaint.*

Simenon traveled throughout Africa in 1932. Three years later, on an extended voyage, he visited Panama, Colombia, Ecuador, Tahiti, the Galapagos, New Zealand, Australia, Fiji, the New Hebrides, Turkey, and Egypt. He used a few of these landscapes as background for several of his novels, but, rather than exotic adventures they became, in effect, settings for the presentation of his usual characters and themes.[68] "Local color," Simenon remarked, "exists only for people who are passing through. And I hate being a tourist. I am not seeking the sense of being abroad. On the contrary, I am looking for what is similar in man, the constant" (*Vieux* 1:88). In several series of articles inspired by his travels, Simenon rid himself of what he didn't want to put into his novels, the picturesque and "some more or less philosophical or political cogitations" (*Vieux* 1:91).

Simenon began to tire of the hedonistic life they were leading in Paris and spent longer and longer periods away from the capital. In 1932, he rented a small château, "La Richardière," in Marsilly in the countryside outside of La Rochelle, and, in 1938, bought in Nieul-sur-mer the house that he had dreamed of. "I called it a grandmother's house, because its atmosphere was the one that, when I was very young, I dreamed of finding during my vacations in the country."[69] When he divorced Tigy, he put the house in her name, and she remained there until her death. It was in the "grandmother's house" that Tigy, who had never wanted children, agreed to have a child. Prompted by the fear of war and the uncertainty prevailing in Europe, Simenon atavistically went back to his native Belgium for the birth of his first son, Marc Christian Simenon, on 19 April 1939. The family returned to Nieul-sur-mer a few months later.

In his *Mémoires intimes,* Simenon wrote that La Rochelle was one of the cities in the world he loved the most (*Intimes,* 1003). Everything about the city pleased him, its light like that in Vermeer's "View of the City of Delft," its sounds and smells, and its streets covered with arcades that sheltered the pedestrian from the rain, the Café de la Paix on the Grand-Place, where Simenon would play cards and which would become the haunt of the homicidal hatter in *Les fantômes du chapelier.* Nine other novels are situated in whole or in part in La Rochelle and environs, more novels, in effect, than in any setting other than Paris.[70]

After the invasion of Holland, Belgium, and Luxembourg by the Germans in 1940, Simenon went to Paris to the Belgian Embassy to offer his services but was told to go back to La Rochelle, where he would be more useful helping Belgian refugees. Only two of Simenon's novels, *Le train* and *Le clan des Ostendais,* both inspired by his experiences with refugees in La Rochelle, are set against a background of war. This may be explained by the fact that, except for this brief period as head of Belgian refugee services, Simenon had no meaningful contact with the war. It did not interfere with his life; he continued to write, enjoy his family, and fraternize with members of influential Franco/German society. However, in the police dossier compiled after the war on his wartime activities, it was less his associations than the success of the movies based on his books that weighed heavily against him. From 6 February 1942 to 8 April 1944, eight films based on seven of Simenon's novels and on one short story[71] appeared on the screens of occupied France, a number unequaled by any other writer at that time; five of them were produced by Continental, a German film company with a French front.[72]

Concerned with the risk of being tried as a collaborator, Simenon decided to leave France, troubled by his vivid memories of the heated atmosphere at the end of World War I. In the last chapter of *Pedigree,* Roger witnesses a frightening scene—a group of men undress and shave the head of a woman who had slept with Germans. She flees, "to the boos of the crowd, livid and frozen in the drafty streets" (*Pedigree,* 3:217). It was indeed time to leave!

In 1945, Simenon left France and the risk of retribution for a fresh start in North America. He went first to francophone Québec and settled his family there. During a business trip to New York, he met Denyse Ouimet, who had been recommended to him as a bilingual secretary. "For the first time in my life I was about to experience what people call 'passion,' a real fever, which some, including psychologists and doctors, consider to be a sickness," he wrote (*Intimes,* 837). Just as one must be open to infection, Simenon—with all ties cut to France, virtually starting anew in a foreign country—was open to anything that could change his life. And then Denyse appeared. Simenon, like his protagonist François Combe in *Trois chambres à Manhattan*—the fictional transposition of his fateful meeting with Denyse—was a man adrift who had severed his ties with his past. The novel closely parallels Simenon's description of the actual events in his autobiographical *Mémoires intimes*—the aimless wandering from bar to bar through the streets of the alien city, the heavy drinking, and the sexual intensity and concomitant jealousy. Denyse/Kay had a lurid past and was not hesitant about sharing all of the details of her sexual adventures with her lover. For his part, Simenon clung to the old-fashioned notion of male virility and female virginity: "I have a deep need for 'exclusivity,' not just in the present but in the past of a woman," he wrote (*Vieux* 3:123–24). Thus the happy ending of *Trois chambres à Manhattan,* one of the very few in

Simenon's oeuvre, takes on a different hue in light of *Lettre à mon juge,* the novel that followed it. Both tell the same story of an obsessive sexual relationship. Charles Alavoine, the protagonist of the second novel, is also jealous of his lover's past, but, unlike Combe, he is unable to make peace with her former persona and kills her. Much later, in his *Mémoires intimes,* Simenon dispelled the myth of abiding passion that he had created in *Trois chambres à Manhattan*: "Unlike love, which we called it for want of a better name, passion also feeds on violence. I was sure by now that she was purposely trying to exhaust my patience to get me to treat her brutally" (*Intimes,* 854).

Denyse accompanied Simenon back to Canada as his secretary. Soon the pretense was dispensed with entirely, and the Simenon household became a ménage à quatre, Simenon, Boule, Tigy, and Denyse. The disparate group set out in two automobiles across the United States, staying for months at a time in Florida, California, and Arizona, the setting for three of his American novels, *La Jument Perdue, Le fond de la bouteille, Maigret chez le coroner,* the second half of the novel *Crime impuni,* and a series of articles titled "L'Amérique en auto." When Denyse became pregnant—their son Jean, called Johnny, was born in 1949—Simenon divorced Tigy and married her. Tigy was given custody of Marc with the proviso that she and Marc never live more than six miles away from Simenon.

In 1950, Simenon bought Shadow Rock Farm in Lakeville, Connecticut, where he lived until 1955, Tigy nearby but always invisible.[73] A daughter, Marie-Georges (nicknamed Marie-Jo), was born there in 1953. The nine American novels situated on the East Coast[74] all contain Simenon's major themes of solitude and alienation, but introduce a new one that Simenon found to be distinctly American, the overwhelming need to belong. His trip to Belgium in 1952, when he was elected to the Belgian Royal Academy of Language and Literature, as well as visits to Paris, Milan, Rome, and Liège, could have influenced his decision to return to Europe three years later. His departure, however, was to be expected—Simenon had spent his entire life in flight. By 1955, he had been in the United States for more than nine years, five of them in Lakeville, a long time for Simenon. Further, his marriage to Denyse was deteriorating. And so, once again, like so many of the protagonists in his novels, he uprooted himself in search of a new life.

From 1955 to 1957, the Simenons lived on the French Riviera. Then, attracted in large part by Switzerland's favorable tax structure, they settled near Lausanne in a magnificent château, Echandens, where their son Pierre was born in 1959. During those years, Simenon's marriage became an ordeal; the couple's relationship was marked by constant bouts of alcoholic rage and violence, interrupted only by Denyse's stays in a psychiatric clinic. In 1963, Simenon moved to an enormous mansion that he had built at Epalinges, but Denyse lived there for only a few months before she left definitively for the clinic in 1963. Simenon remained at Epalinges until 1972, together with his three youngest children and Teresa, Denyse's former Italian maid who became Simenon's lover and remained his devoted companion until his death. In a curious illustration of life imitating art, Simenon transformed Teresa into Madame Maigret, Simenon's archetypal ideal woman[75]—the completely devoted wife/mother, who exists only to serve her mate and who asks nothing but his presence in return. Teresa embodied the love he had always sought: "For me, an old man who has had the time to think and reflect, love is silence first of all. It is the ability to stay together in the same room without speaking, each one conscious of the other's thoughts . . . it is a hand that unconsciously seeks the other's body in sleep, not for sexual reasons, but only for contact. . . . [It is] complete spiritual and physical contact. It is thinking of the same things together, experiencing the same reactions, and seeking the reflection of these emotions in the other's eyes" (*Homme,* 582).

Simenon and all of his family, except for his sons, have their counterparts in his fictional characters. Even in his memoirs, he tells only of his sons' activities and of his love for them, but he never attempts to understand or to explicate their personas. Only Marie-Jo, his beloved daughter, appears in one of his novels, *La disparition d'Odile.* Marie-Jo, sensitive and vulnerable, haunted by what she called "Madame Angoisse" (Madame Anguish), suffered more than her brothers from the violent quarrels of her parents and made several unsuccessful attempts at suicide. The novel, written after one of these attempts, tells the story of the thwarted suicide of the protagonist Odile (Marie-Jo), a young woman stifled by the weight of existence and unable either to establish meaningful relationships with others or to carry any project to its conclusion. She has manic-depressive tendencies, at times she feels the need to assert herself and to demonstrate her exceptional qualities, and, at other times, she is overwhelmed by feelings of humility and self-disgust. In a vain attempt on Simenon's part to forestall Marie-Jo's tragic destiny, he ended the novel on a positive note; recovered both in body and in mind from her suicide attempt, Odile is bravely starting a new life.

But no novelist can contrive happy endings in real life; Marie-Jo killed herself in 1978. Simenon was devastated by her suicide. Had it not been for Teresa, Simenon maintained, he would have done the same. In his *Mémoires intimes,* his last work, written two years after the tragedy, Simenon sought to understand Marie-Jo's death and to apportion responsibility for it. Was her suicide attributable to the influence of her disturbed, alcoholic mother, to her father's excessive love for her, or to her incestuous love for him? Was her death perhaps the result of genetic fatality, an excessive sensibility passed down either from the Brülls through her father or inherited from her psychologically ill mother? "All sorrows can be borne," Isak Dinesen once said, "if you put them into a story or tell a story about them," but at the most tragic moment of his life, Simenon had no more stories to tell.

In 1972, Simenon left Epalinges and moved, first to an apartment in Lausanne and then, only with Teresa, to a modest eighteenth-century house where he lived for 15 years until his death. That was the longest time Simenon ever spent in one dwelling. He announced at the same time that he would no longer write novels because of recurring bouts of dizziness resulting from his Ménière's disease and also because he felt that, after 50 years, he had become a slave of his characters. "All of my life, I was preoccupied with others and tried to understand them. Now I am trying to understand myself" (*Homme,* 440–41). No longer able to write a novel but still obsessed by the need to express himself, Simenon dictated into a tape recorder the shattering *Lettre à ma mère* and 21 other works, which he called *Dictées.* A comparison of these dictated memoirs with his novels provides useful insight into Simenon's genius as a novelist. He covers much of the same material in both genres, but when he talks about himself without going through his characters, he does it badly. Only through an intermediary, as in his portrait of Balzac, for example, does he really succeed in expressing himself.

Simenon spent the last years of his life in a modest house much like his childhood home in Liège. There, without distraction (what Pascal called "divertissement"), he was left face to face with the void at the heart of all human existence, the destiny promised by Pascal to the man without God. "What are my novels?" Simenon asked. They are "stories of men like me who lived different lives. But didn't they all, like me, in the end find themselves confronting nothingness?" (*Traces de pas,* 116).

Chapter Two

"Maigrets"—Novels of Crime and Detection

Simenon's earliest pseudonymous potboilers included detective stories as well as tales of adventure and romance. Encouraged by the success of his first detective novel, *Nox l'insaisissable,* published in 1926 under the pseudonym Christian Brulls, Simenon turned increasingly toward the genre and wrote three series of short stories for the magazine *Détective.*[1] These were followed by several works in which Simenon experimented with various aspects of detective fiction; commissaire Maigret makes his first appearance in *La maison de l'inquiétude* of 1929, signed Georges Sim.[2]

Simenon proposed a series of Maigret novels to Fayard, one of the publishers of his pseudonymous potboilers. He signed a contract with them in 1929 for six detective novels to be signed with his own name. That number would grow to nineteen under Fayard's imprint. Simenon presented these novels as a transition between the popular novels he had been writing and the more serious literary works to which he aspired, and for which he did not consider himself ready. Not knowing at that time how to shift the action from one location to another, he created a character, a policeman, who could move about with the freedom and ease enjoyed by the protagonist of the picaresque novel. Simenon launched this first Maigret series with an enormous party, an "anthropometric ball," so-named for the police department of anthropometry where lawbreakers are stripped, measured, and photographed. All of the Parisian celebrities were invited to what was, in essence, a superb publicity stunt, the invitations reading, "Georges Simenon has the honor of inviting you to the Anthropometric Ball, which will be held at the Boule Blanche to celebrate the launching of his detective stories"(*Mémoires,* 28).

While Simenon originally intended to stop writing detective novels after fulfilling his contract to Fayard, he returned to his policeman hero and wrote over the years a total of more than 100 novels and short stories featuring Commissaire Maigret, often trying out in them themes and situations he would use later in his more serious works. Like Arthur Conan Doyle, who found himself unable to free himself of his detective

Sherlock Holmes, Simenon submitted to the pressure of his readers—and perhaps to the demands of the extravagant lifestyle he had adopted—and resurrected Maigret throughout his writing career. Ironically, as had also been the case with Conan Doyle, it was the great number and success of the "Maigrets"—a word that has passed into current usage to designate Simenon's detective novels—that distracted readers and critics from the quality of his other work. Over the years, Maigret has become disassociated from his creator and has taken on an independent existence. Readers tend to see him as a historical figure rather than as a creature of fiction. Through movies and television, Maigret has become a symbol of a literary genre, and in this way he has overcome the limitations of this codified genre to assume a more universal character, occupying a place among the great fictional detectives of literature like Doyle's Sherlock Holmes, Hugo's Javert (*Les Misérables*), and Dostoyevsky's Porfiry Petrovich (*Crime and Punishment*).

Before considering the Maigrets, it is necessary to define the detective novel in order to demonstrate how Simenon used its conventions to create a new type of fiction, transforming its rules and techniques to express some of the most important themes of the twentieth century novel, guilt and innocence, solitude and alienation (Becker, 2485). In working toward what he would later define as the "pure," or quintessential novel, Simenon brought a crucial innovation to the genre—he sought not so much to unmask and punish the criminal as to understand him. At times, as is often true in the detective novel, the plots of the Maigrets are lacking in verisimilitude, but they captivate the reader by their sense of mood and their character interplay. While Simenon did not alter the basic social conservatism of the genre—the job of the policeman is to punish deviant behavior and maintain the status quo—his Maigret was a new kind of hero, with a newfound concern for the psychological and social determinants of crime; his actions inspired an appreciation for the operations of the homicide division of a metropolitan police department.

While the detective novel has been defined in many different ways, most agree that it is a fictitious prose narrative of an investigation that ultimately reveals to the reader how, by whom, and, occasionally, why the crime was committed. It is a novel because it is a fictional story in prose in which the author seeks to arouse the reader's interest by the portrayal of passions, or of customs and manners, or of unusual events. What makes it specifically a detective novel is that it is the fictional account in prose of an investigation that, although not always conducted by the police, does lead eventually to the discovery of the criminal. The detective novel is made up of two contradictory but complementary elements, a mystery and an investigation, both of which satisfy two basic human emotions, fear and the need for security; the crime elicits the fear that gives rise to the investigation; the investigation, in turn, serves to alleviate the fear. The author of the detective novel must devise the mystery and the investigation at the same time; he must set up a mystery for the investigation and invent an investigation for the mystery, with each one influencing and acting on the other.[3] Every detective novel, writes Michel Butor, is built on two murders, "the first, which is committed by the murderer, merely provides an opportunity for the second, when the murderer himself becomes in turn the victim of a pure and elusive killer, the detective; the detective who puts him to death, not by any of the vile methods he himself was reduced to using, such as poison, dagger, gun with silencer, silk stocking that strangles, but by the outpouring of truth. . . . The detective is the son of the murderer, Oedipus, not only because he solves a mystery, but also because he kills the one to whom he owes his official standing, the one without whom he would not exist in that capacity."[4]

Crime, particularly murder, mystery, and investigation have figured prominently in literature from the very beginning, for every murder mystery poses symbolically the eternal problem of good and evil. The hunting down of evil and the triumph of good satisfies a profound metaphysical need and each expression of the conflict between good and evil reflects the needs of a particular time and a particular place.

Detection, with or without metaphysical overtones, also plays an important role in ancient legends. In his *History of the Detective Novel,* Hoveyda maintains that Archimedes was one of the first great detectives. The king of Syracuse had given gold to an artisan to fashion a crown for him. Later, he learned that the artisan had stolen a part of the gold and replaced it with silver, but he was unable to prove it. Archimedes, like the scientific detective Sherlock Holmes more than 2,000 years later, took the matter in hand. Knowing that a body will displace its own volume of water, and that density equals weight divided by volume, he had two crowns made, one of silver, the other of gold, each one weighing the same as the one delivered by the artisan. He then immersed the silver crown in a bucket of water, which overflowed. The artisan's crown displaced less water than the silver crown, but the solid gold crown displaced still less than the others. Archimedes' investigation had proved the artisan's guilt.[5]

The essential components of the future detective novel were already in place at the end of the eighteenth century in works that were very different from one another. The Gothic novel, which was designed to provoke fear, appeared at that time in England. It was built around adventures that were replete with frightening crimes and evil characters. It was necessary to combine the emotional appeal of these works with the intellectual appeal of works designed for a more sophisticated public—Voltaire's philosophical tale *Zadig,* for example. The eponymous hero here is a forerunner of the scientific detective. In a remarkable demonstration of the powers of deduction, in a chapter titled "The Dog and the Horse," Zadig describes with great precision the lost dog and horse of the king that he has never seen, basing his conclusions on tracks that each had left behind. It was not until the second half of the nineteenth century, however, with the arrival on the scene of the criminal investigator, whether private detective or policeman, that there appeared a literary genre that specialized in crime and detection.

An important influence on the evolution of the detective novel was the memoirs of Eugène-François Vidocq, published in 1828. Vidocq, who began his career as a criminal and wound up as head of the French Sûreté, the first large urban police force that would become la Police Judiciaire or Criminal Investigation Department, provided the inspiration for Balzac's Vautrin who, similarly, metamorphosed from convict (*Le père Goriot*) into director of the French Sûreté (*Les illusions perdues*). Vidocq, the ambiguous figure of the criminal who is also a hero, is at the heart of an important theme in much detective fiction, the identity between the criminal and the detective—the criminal representing the id, the detective the superego—a theme that figures prominently in the Maigrets and explains in part Maigret's great compassion for those who cross the line into murder.

Thus, the detective novel, which postulates the existence of a hidden secret to be uncovered, was born during the height of romanticism with its glorification of the forces of darkness and mystery and its fascinating mythology of the criminal. Romanticism exalted the superman, whether bandit or policeman, both of whom were outside the normal order of society, and both of whom possessed the extraordinary perspicacity and energy that would characterize detective literature, a literature dominated by the figure of the superior man, so different from Simenon's humanly fallible, bourgeois Maigret.

In the post-romantic period, detective novels changed, giving the powers of reason precedence over the powers of darkness. Although

Poe's *The Murders in the Rue Morgue* is considered by many to be the first detective novel, it was actually preceded by Balzac's *Une ténébreuse affaire,* perhaps the archetype with its investigation, suspense, and unexpected developments. It was Poe, however, who created the detective novel that glorified the intellect and showed that all mysteries can be solved by pure intelligence. He established a format that is still popular. It would begin with a seemingly insoluble mystery. Then, a series of witnesses and suspects would appear who would throw out false clues. Finally, by careful reasoning, the detective would arrive at the correct, irrefutable, enlightening, and completely unexpected conclusion. In Poe's *The Murders in the Rue Morgue,* the inexplicable grisly murders that occur in a locked, upper-story room, accessible only through a tiny window, are solved by his detective Dupin, who discovers that they were committed by a vicious orangutan on the loose in Paris. Poe was the first to understand the dramatic impact of ratiocination, centering the interest on the detective's investigations rather than on the criminal affair. His detective novel is basically optimistic for it postulates that reason can find the answer to all problems and that there is a specific cause for every event. In short, it reassures us and dissipates our fears by affirming that there is no insoluble mystery in the universe.

Poe's influence spread from England to France thanks to Baudelaire, who had translated all of his works into French. Among his French disciples, Poe's real successor was Emile Gaboriau, the creator of Inspector Lecoq. A policeman rather than an amateur detective, Lecoq grasps the workings of the criminal mind, for he, like the nonfictional Vidocq, started out as a criminal before moving over to the side of the law. Lecoq's method of "psychological identification" has him shed his own ideas in an effort to understand the thought processes of the criminal, much as Maigret will do in Simenon's novels.[6]

We find then in the works of Poe and Gaboriau the prototypes of the investigators of the detective novel—the dilettante private eye and the police inspector—as well as of the French and the Anglo-American schools of detective writing (Benevenuti, 14). The English, like Poe, concentrate on the progress of the investigation, seen as a complicated cat-and-mouse game between the detective and the criminal. The French, on the other hand, emphasize atmosphere rather than inquiry and focus on human relationships, whether between the victim and the murderer or between the murderer and the detective. *The Murders in the Rue Morgue* set the pattern for the problem or puzzle type of detective novel, but the genre achieved great popularity only when Arthur Conan

Doyle adopted Poe's formula and applied it in his novels centered on the eccentric amateur detective Sherlock Holmes and his constant companion and witness, Dr. Watson. Conan Doyle's novels are contemporary with the first major advances of modern science. Science brought with it the promise that man would eventually solve all of his problems by applying the scientific method to them. Sherlock Holmes, with his microscopic vision and his impeccable reasoning powers, has been called the scientific detective—his success is based on unerring observation, complete concentration, and encyclopedic knowledge. What was essential here was the elimination of chance, the exclusion of all obscurity, and the triumphant affirmation of determinism.

The puzzle or problem mystery inherited from Conan Doyle reached the peak of its popularity in England in the 1920s and 1930s, a period known as the golden age of the detective novel. Agatha Christie, the best known practitioner of the genre, perfected the format. Governed by rules,[7] the novel generally centered around a murder committed among a fairly close-knit group of people, all of them considered to be suspects. The British "puzzle" mystery presented an innocent, optimistic view of society and man and took place in a fictional world of country estates filled with servants and weekend guests, so different from the real world of Simenon. Here, the detective, an amateur like Doyle's Sherlock Holmes or Christie's Poirot, interrogates the suspects, checks their alibis, and searches for other clues. At the end, he gathers the suspects together, describes what he has observed and deduced, and points to the guilty party. Reduced to a formula, Agatha Christie's work, the prototypal English detective novel, is a rather lifeless objective study of the crime with a view to disproving the alibis of the suspects.

Concurrent with the success of the English puzzle novel, Simenon perfected a detective novel that was much closer to the realistic social novel. Although he maintained for the most part the basic formula of crime, inquiry, and solution found in the classical detective novel, he came closer to the pure novel by his presentation of believable characters in an everyday, realistic setting. Simenon's Maigrets center on the character of Maigret, or of the criminal as seen by Maigret, focusing the reader's attention on the psychological workings of the plot rather than the rational or mathematical ones. It was for this reason that, when Simenon first proposed his detective novels to Fayard publishers, they were loath to consider publishing them because, as they stated: "It's not a detective novel! It's not a real puzzle! It's not a chess game; it isn't even a good novel because there are neither good nor bad people, there is no love story, and it almost always ends badly. . . . [Furthermore], your detective is nondescript and not particularly intelligent. You see him seated for hours in front of a glass of beer! He is painfully ordinary!"("Romancier," 94). It was, however, precisely this "nondescript and not particularly intelligent" detective, conducting investigations that relied on instinct, intuition, and empathy rather than rational deduction, who would prove to be one of the most popular detectives in the history of the genre.[8]

Maigret's role, unlike that of Holmes or Poirot, is to understand intuitively rather than to reason. His insight into the human condition reveals much more than does physical evidence. Maigret's indulgent attitude reflects his moral code, summed up by the maxim "Comprendre sans juger" (understand without judging). It is strikingly different from the indifference, incomprehension, and disdain that characterize the behavior of the majority of those entrusted with law enforcement. His repeated disputes with his superiors about procedure emphasize his decency and his independence as opposed to their vindictive sense of justice. In *Une confidence de Maigret,* the commissaire explains: "Coméliau (the examining judge) is not a bad man. It is the result of the idea he has of his function, of his duty. In his eyes, since he is paid by society, he must show no pity for anything that threatens to disturb the established order. Serenely, he separates the good from the bad, incapable of imagining that some can be placed in a middle ground."[9] As time passes, Maigret finds himself more and more at odds with younger, more educated men, members of a new generation of powerful policemen who prize theory over intuition, experience, and personal contact with the murderer and his crime.

Maigret's infinite understanding and compassion can be traced to a need Simenon felt in his youth:

> When I was fourteen . . . I wondered why there did not exist a type of doctor who would be both a doctor of the body and of the mind, a sort of doctor who, knowing an individual, his age, his physical characteristics, his potentialities, could tell him to enter on one course or another.
>
> It was virtually psychosomatic medicine that I was formulating. That was in 1917, and it was in that frame of mind that I created the character of Maigret. For that is what Maigret does, and this is why it was necessary for Maigret to have completed two or three years of medical studies. . . . Maigret is for me a mender of destinies. (*Gril,* 48–50)

Maigret's ability "to live the lives of every sort of man, to put himself inside everybody's mind," remains constant throughout the Maigret novels, but his role as mender of destinies is, in effect, limited to understanding and sympathy.[10] His final confrontation with the murderer allows only for the consolation of confession but comes too late to alter destiny.

Maigret's methods, too, are consistent throughout the novels, although there is a change in emphasis from the early novels, where Maigret is solely a sympathetic witness, to the later works in which he occupies the entire novel and his reactions rather than the case at hand hold the reader's attention. This change is underlined by the use of Maigret's name in the titles of all of the 51 novels in the third cycle of Maigrets, which were published by Presses de la Cité between 1947 and 1972.[11] There, Maigret takes over the role of the novelist. Like Simenon, he seeks to find the man hidden beneath surface appearances; like Simenon, he writes down the principal elements of a case on an envelope; like Simenon, he finds that as a case proceeds he begins to resemble the characters. Brigid Brophy has stated that Simenon made Maigret a detective rather than a novelist because the detective is the only one who can actually approach the murder victim. Maigret has the novelist's passivity—while other detectives sit and think, he sits and imagines.[12]

In an interview with Roger Stéphane, Simenon himself pointed out the resemblance between the detective and the novelist: "In a criminal investigation, as in a novel, there is a very bad moment when you do not know how everything will come out. You begin to sense the truth, but you are still not sure, and then you say to yourself, if I don't get it in the next five minutes, everything will vanish into thin air and I will not arrive at the truth. . . . Basically, nothing resembles a novel more than a police investigation."[13]

One of the earliest Maigrets, *Le charretier de la "Providence,"* introduces the reader to Maigret's methods—or absence of methods—which remain virtually unchanged in all of the novels. It demonstrates that what is important for Maigret in the investigation of a crime is not who did it, or how he did it, but why he did it. The novel opens in characteristic fashion with notations on the weather, in this case the rain that has been falling steadily for two days when Maigret begins his investigation at lock number 14 connecting the Marne and the lateral canal. The body of an elegantly dressed woman without identification papers has been found in a stable for cart horses, which can be reached only by a narrow path. Since his arrival on the scene, Maigret has been familiarizing himself with a world that is completely new to him, that of canals and inland water transportation. As is customary during the first stage of all of his investigations, Maigret soaks up the atmosphere surrounding the murder, here that of a local café, inhaling "a distinctive odor, the nature of which was enough to mark the difference between this and a country café. It smelled of stables, harnesses, tar, and groceries, oil and gas."[14] By triggering the reader's olfactory and, to a lesser extent, other sensory memories, Simenon is able to evoke familiar places and scenes, creating thereby the distinctive atmosphere that characterizes his work.

Sitting in the café, Maigret observes all that is going on around him as the barges continue peacefully on their way from lock to lock pulled by horses on cart tracks that run on either side of the canal. The details of daily life found here, as in all of the Maigrets, give an illusion of reality to the novels and invite the reader to suspend disbelief, even when the plots strain credulity. Local color, thus, is not ancillary, but is an essential component of the works. Maigret's ruminations—despite his protestations to the contrary, Maigret thinks as well as feels—are interrupted by the arrival in the café of the owner of a yacht, Sir William Lampson, who identifies the dead woman as his wife Mary and affirms that she had left the yacht a few days before.

The next day Maigret is joined at the lock by Inspector Lucas, who will become a familiar figure in the Maigret entourage. Lucas informs him that the Englishman lives only for whisky and women, that Madame Negretti, one of the women on board, is his mistress, and that his companion Willy Marco, is a well-known swindler and is also the lover of Mary Lampson. When Willy is also found strangled, the second stage of Maigret's inquiry begins. At this time certain events become clearer, a few of the characters come to the forefront, and the reader is led to believe that he is independently reaching the same conclusions as Maigret. Trusting to intuition, but, it must be added, also having made certain prior mental calculations, Maigret questions Jean, the carter of the barge, the "Providence," that had been in the vicinity at the time of the murders, and accuses him of having killed Marco. Jean throws himself into the lock basin, where he is crushed between two barges. He is rescued and taken to the hospital but flees in order to die in the stable of the "Providence." Maigret, in the meantime, has taken his fingerprints and discovers that he was formerly a physician who had in all likelihood killed his wealthy aunt to satisfy his wife's taste for luxury and had spent fifteen years in prison for the crime.

Maigret returns to the stable for the customary final confessional *scène à deux,* in which Maigret helps the murderer to understand that he is basically not guilty. For Maigret, echoing Simenon, men are weak rather than evil, they struggle and kill to escape from unbearable pressures. Since the dying carter is unable to speak, Maigret speaks for him while the man confirms his statements by blinking his eyelids. Then Maigret begins a long monologue as he reconstructs the events leading up to the murder of Mary Lampson. After his release from prison, Jean saw his wife, who, despite her promise to wait for him, was now living with Sir Walter Lampson under the name of Mary Lampson. The carter felt the need to bring down to his level the elegant woman who had betrayed him. He took her to the stable where she stayed for three days, afraid of Jean and ashamed of her past actions. Finally, no longer able to stand such a life, she rebelled, and he killed her rather than permit her to leave him again. In order to divert suspicion from himself, Jean stole a sailor's hat, which he planted in the stable, but was then forced to kill Willy because he had witnessed the theft. When he felt Maigret closing in on him, he attempted suicide.

Maigret explains to Lampson why Jean fled the hospital. "A man without ties . . . a man who cut all links with his past, with his former personality . . . must hang on to something. . . . He had his stable . . . the smell . . . the horses . . . the burning hot coffee swallowed at three in the morning before walking until evening. . . . His burrow as it were . . . filled with his animal warmth. . . . There are burrows of all sorts. . . . There are those that smell of whisky, eau de cologne, and women. . . ." (*Charretier,* 242–43). As he speaks, Maigret feels the same sympathy for the worthless, alcoholic aristocrat before him as he does for Jean, for Lampson is as much alone, as much at a loss as Jean. This ability to understand is Maigret's outstanding virtue; it stems from his belief that he who murders is an unfortunate being, for "every man is capable of becoming a murderer if he has sufficient motivation."[15]

Le charretier de la "Providence" is one of many Maigrets in which the murderer is portrayed as worthy of pity. Maigret gradually develops an understanding of the criminal's miserable existence and empathizes with him. Following his lead, the reader tempers his harsh judgment of the murderer and is transformed from accuser to one who forgives. But too often such concentration on understanding the criminal makes the reader lose sight of the victim; a conspicuous oversight in *Maigret et le tueur.*

The novel opens on a cold rainy night as Maigret is called to the scene of a murder. A young student, Antoine Batille, was killed after leaving one of the shady bars he frequented in order to tape record conversations for his collection of "human documents."[16] The question arises as to whether he was killed because he had recorded a compromising conversation, particularly since his last tape was of a conversation between art thieves outlining a projected robbery. But this is a false trail, common currency in detective novels but virtually nonexistent in the Maigrets. Maigret feels intuitively that the murderer would resent having his crime attributed to someone else, and, to set a trap for the killer, he has the newspapers announce that Batille was killed by the thieves. As Maigret anticipated, the murderer writes to the newspapers to protest and telephones Maigret. Little by little, he unburdens himself to Maigret, the secular confessor. The final confession, contrary to all police procedure, takes place in Maigret's apartment, where Madame Maigret had received him earlier in Maigret's absence. Such improbabilities run through many of the Maigrets, although to a lesser extent than in most detective fiction. The strength of the narrative permits Simenon to persuade the reader to willingly suspend disbelief and accept the implausibility of the venue for the confession as well as the strangely unfounded confidence of Madame Maigret, a policeman's wife. When asked whether she was frightened to be alone with a murderer, Mme Maigret answers: "I knew that I wasn't in any danger" (*Tueur,* 175). We learn that Bureau, the assassin, suffers from a psychological compulsion to kill—his first murder was that of a child when he, himself, was only 14 years old. He wanted to be caught, as Maigret had intuited, in order to receive treatment for uncontrollable impulses. During Bureau's confession, the reader is lead by the author to sympathize with the killer rather than with the innocent young victim.

Maigret would have liked to have Bureau treated for his illness, but the young man is condemned to 15 years in prison. The judge deplores the lack of institutions where a man like Bureau can be treated and kept under surveillance at the same time. Here Simenon anticipates the need for forensic psychology, a branch of criminology that is only now gaining in importance. It consists of selecting a person who has committed a crime and profiling him, taking into consideration why he did it, what is behind his crime. Is the criminal legally responsible for his behavior, or might he be considered legally insane? If so, is he in need of treatment, how should he be handled, is he dangerous or only sick? And, finally, is prison appropriate or should the criminal be sent to a psychiatric hospital?

The fallacy of Maigret's motto, "understand without judging," lies in the fact that this understanding implies forgiveness for all, whatever the nature of the crime. Furthermore, Maigret is not always true to his stated principles: he pardons selectively, as illustrated in *Maigret tend un piège,* a novel in which he empathizes with the serial killer but is hostile to the killer's mother, the cause, according to Maigret, of his crimes.

The novel opens, as is customary, with observations about the weather; here it is a sweltering 4 August when the "hot air that seemed to rise up out of the softened asphalt, the scorching stones, and the Seine itself, which one half expected to be steaming like water on a stove," permeates Maigret's office on the Quai des Orfèvres.[17] The problem facing Maigret is formidable. In recent weeks, there have been five murders in a very small area of the eighteenth arrondissement of Paris. The pattern followed in each of the attacks has been identical: the victims, all women, have been stabbed to death, their clothing slashed to pieces. All that they have in common is their short, stocky build and the district in which they were murdered. Maigret asks a distinguished psychiatrist, Dr. Tissot, for advice. Tissot's response is characteristic of the psychological generalizations that are generally found in the pseudomedical, pseudopsychological discussions between Maigret and his friend, Dr. Pardon. Tissot states that among all the murderers with whom he is familiar there is one constant, a need to assert themselves, because almost all of them have been considered inferior in their own circle. He adds that this common characteristic convinced him that the majority of crimes, particularly repeated crimes, are a manifestation of wounded pride. What Tissot and his colleagues still do not understand is the process by which long-suppressed humiliation suddenly erupts into crime, but they believe that those who commit such crimes are driven by a need to be caught because they cannot bear to think that those around them still think of them as ordinary, harmless individuals. Thus, if someone were to take credit for the crime and be arrested in his place, the criminal would feel frustration at losing his claim to distinction.

Dr. Tissot's counsel leads Maigret to risk another murder, as he pretends to have arrested the criminal and then sets up one of his policewomen as a decoy in the murder area. Maigret counts on Tissot's assurance that maniacs, like most criminals, nearly always use the same technique, down to the smallest detail. The murderer does indeed attack the policewoman, who grabs a button from his jacket before he runs off. The expensive button, a type of clue found frequently in detective novels but rarely in the Maigrets, allows Maigret to track down the murderer, an interior designer named Moncin, and arrest him. The discovery of the killer so early in the narrative is contrary to all of the rules of the detective novel, but, for Maigret, it is not the identity of the criminal that is important, but the reasons for his crime.

Another crime of a similar nature is committed on the night of Moncin's arrest, but with some variations. Presuming that either Moncin's mother or wife committed this murder to save him, Maigret reconstructs Moncin's psychological crisis in a confession by proxy, a familiar structural device in the Maigrets. He tells the young man that his mother had been ashamed of his father, a butcher, and had brought him up as if he were a prince. She was there to protect and take care of him in any eventuality, but he had to pay for this protection with submissiveness. He was her property, and he was not permitted to grow up to be a normal man. When he was 24, his mother chose his wife, a woman she thought she could control but who turned out to be as domineering and as possessive as she. "You hadn't the courage to be a man. You weren't one," Maigret continues. "You needed them, the atmosphere they created around you, their attention, their indulgence. And that was precisely what humiliated you. . . . A plan for asserting yourself came into your mind." Maigret notes further that Moncin could not distinguish himself in his career, where he was a failure; nor could he kill his mother and wife because he would be the prime suspect. Since the action had to be something outstanding to satisfy his vanity, he turned to women in the street, using the knife because he needed "some furious, violent gesture" (*Piège,* 176, 179). He needed to destroy and to feel that he was destroying. He didn't rape his victims, because he was impotent, but tore their undergarments to shreds. Ironically, his crimes did not free him from the domination of his wife and mother, one of whom had killed the sixth woman to protect her property. While both were capable of this action, it was the wife who acted, thereby winning the final round in her match with her mother-in-law.

If Maigret extends pity and understanding to the male criminal, it is often at the expense of his female victims. In the Maigret saga, women either drive men to murder or kill, or provoke their own murders. The attitudes and behavior of males are conditioned by their disastrous relationships with females. The sons in the Maigrets are dependent on domineering mothers. When they marry, the mother continues to dominate them as she watches her daughter-in-law with deadly jealousy.

Maigret's inability to empathize with women is shown by his differing reactions to the male and female conspirators in *Maigret se défend.* At the beginning of the novel, Maigret's friend Dr. Pardon asks him whether he ever encountered a "pure" criminal, one who was evil for the sake of evil. Maigret, who "had always resisted believing in pure evil,"[18] replies that what seems to be evil at first sight becomes understandable as the facts become known. The remainder of the novel serves to prove this thesis. On returning home, Maigret finds a summons to appear before the préfet de police. He asks Maigret to resign because of a complaint he received from a high government official whose niece has charged him with sexual abuse. At first glance, this would seem to be the example of pure wickedness postulated in Pardon's theoretical question, for evil could be the only explanation for the desire of an obviously sane girl to harm Maigret. Maigret centers the ensuing investigation on an exploration of personality, trying to understand the criminal rather than to solve the crime. The reason for her actions slowly comes to light, reaffirming Simenon's thesis that crime is not so much willful sin as the product of sickness or unbearable pressure. Maigret discovers that the girl had been driven to this action by blackmail. Her abortionist had seen Maigret across the street from his office, where Maigret had been staking out a gang of jewel thieves. Because he feared that Maigret was watching him and would discover not only the nature of his practice but also the bodies of several victims buried in his garden, he had devised the bizarre plot to discredit the policeman. Maigret's inquiry reinforces his belief that he who murders is an unfortunate being. Maigret is able to feel the inner torment of the mentally ill murderer and says that he will perhaps be a witness for the defense when his crime comes to trial. On the other hand, Maigret feels only anger and contempt for the young girl who was forced into the plot through blackmail.

Maigret's hostility to homosexuals mirrors his feelings for women. When Couchet (*L'ombre chinoise*) disinherits his homosexual son, the action pleases Maigret, particularly because it drives the young man to suicide. The homosexual Philippe Mortemart in *Maigret au Picratt's,* described with all the clichés used by homophobes, is treated more harshly than murderers, and is told that he "doesn't have the right to soil the earth."[19] His very prejudices serve to make Maigret a fully developed, completely believable human being.

The psychological makeup of the victim interests Maigret as much as that of the criminal. "I will know the murderer when I know the victim well," he stated.[20] Simenon writes that one of the branches of criminology least known to the general public is victimology, that is to say, the responsibility of the victim in crimes (*Vieux,* 2:149), eight out of ten of whom, as Maigret states, were responsible for their fate.[21] In *Maigret à Vichy,* it is the victim who proves to be guilty, the murderer virtually innocent. In this novel, Maigret is in Vichy to take the waters, an excuse for this Parisian policeman—80 percent of his cases take place in whole or in part in Paris—to detect outside of the city. Hélène Lange, a middle-aged woman whom Maigret had seen on several of his walks, is murdered. Little is known about her except for the fact that she received substantial checks every three months and left Vichy to cash them in different cities. Hélène's sister, Francine, tells them that her sister had a lover years before in Paris, but she then leaves Vichy hurriedly before the police can question her further, seemingly terrified by a telephone call she received. Police surveillance of the public telephones leads to the arrest of Louis Pélardeau, who, following the pattern of the Maigrets, confesses to the murder and then explains the unlikely series of events that lead up to his act.

Years before, Pélardeau had been Hélène's lover. When Francine became pregnant, Hélène told Pélardeau that she was pregnant with his child, and left Paris with Francine. When the child was born, the birth certificate listed Hélène as his mother. Ever since then, she had taken money from Pélardeau ostensibly to support the boy—who had in reality died many years before—telling him that it was not suitable for him to see the boy until he came of age. Pélardeau met Hélène by chance in Vichy where he, like Maigret, had come to take the waters, and demanded news of the son who had become his raison d'être. When she would not reply, he seized her by the throat in a fit of anger and strangled her involuntarily. Here, the victim, who had goaded her murderer beyond endurance, is more villainous than he, and Maigret expresses the hope at the end of the novel that the decent, albeit incredibly naive, Pélardeau will be acquitted.

Maigret is similarly disinclined to bring to justice the murderer of the wine merchant in *Maigret et le marchand de vin,* a man whose psychological compulsion to use his power and money to humiliate those dependent on him would identify him as a natural victim. The merchant is one of a number of strong successful men in the Maigrets who provoke jealousy and frustration in those around them. The wine merchant had surrounded himself with people whom he despised. Every sexual encounter represented an attempt to defile his partner and to assert his dominance. When his secretary had asked him why he went out of his way to make people hate him, he answered that he did so because he could not make them love him, and that he preferred hatred to indifference.[22]

The murderer seeks to approach Maigret, circling closer and closer in an effort to be caught. This recurring theme in Simenon's detective novels presupposes that the murderer is most often driven by a need to expiate his guilt through confession, a Catholic view of human nature that is consistent with Simenon's early education. At the same time, Maigret begins to understand, or rather to feel intuitively, the psychological background of the crime. His choice of clues is revealing in this respect, for he never looks for fingerprints, traces of blood, or footprints. Nor does he attempt to interrogate witnesses to pinpoint the exact moment the crime occurred. For Maigret, a clue is a gesture, a word spoken inadvertently, a look that he intercepts. His clues are a gradually developing awareness of the pressures exerted by a particular atmosphere that drive an ordinary human being to murder. Solving a crime for Maigret does not involve discovering the criminal's method but attempting to relive the psychological crisis that provoked the crime. Putting himself in the criminal's place, Maigret asks himself whether he would make a certain gesture or say a certain word if he had committed the crime.[23] Simenon presents the precise psychological detail that makes the murderer an understandable human being. To emphasize that the traditional hunt of the "whodunit" is unimportant for Simenon, he frequently reveals the identity of the murderer at the beginning of the novel, devoting the remaining pages to the psychological analysis of the criminal that will convince the reader of the inevitability of his crime. As we discover the truth in these novels, we pity the murderer.

This is true in the case of the wine merchant's murderer, who had been a failure all his life. His desperate act is the last resort of an ego threatened with disintegration. Having committed a murder, he has become important for the first time. Maigret understands that men of his sort are terribly sensitive. "They long to talk, to make themselves understood, and yet they don't really believe that there is anybody capable of understanding them" (*Marchand,* 211). When Maigret and the murderer finally come face to face, the latter reveals that he killed his employer because he had robbed him of his self-respect. The wine merchant had degraded him to the point where he was ashamed to be alive. Humiliation, then, can be added to the limited range of human emotions—fear, jealousy, hate, lust—that drive Simenon's characters to murder.

There are very few members of the criminal class in the Maigrets, since Simenon's interest lies not in them but in the ordinary human being who is driven to crime. In the putative *Mémoires de Maigret,* the commissaire reflects that the young Simenon told him he wasn't interested in professional criminals. "Their psychology doesn't present any problem. They are people who are doing their job, and that's that" (*Mémoires,* 20). There is even a certain bond between the policeman and the professional criminal. Except in very rare cases, the policeman is entirely devoid of hatred or even of ill will. But he is also devoid of pity in this strictly professional relationship. Paradoxically, a sort of family feeling often springs up between the policeman and his quarry:

> The prostitute of the Boulevard de Clichy and the inspector watching her are both wearing cheap shoes and both have sore feet from the kilometers of pavement they've covered. They both put up with the same rain, the same icy wind. . . . It's the same with the pickpocket who slips through the crowd at the fairgrounds. For him, a fair or any gathering of a few hundred people represents not pleasure . . . but a certain number of wallets in unsuspecting pockets. The same is true for the policeman. And both of them recognize equally well at first glance the self-satisfied hick who will make an ideal victim. (*Mémoires,* 111–12)

At times, a certain closeness is established between the policeman and his prisoner, stemming perhaps from the fact that for weeks, sometimes months, the policeman and the culprit have been almost exclusively preoccupied with one another. "The officer works unceasingly to delve more deeply into the past life of the guilty party, tries to reconstruct his thoughts, to anticipate his slightest reflexes. Both of them are playing for very high stakes. And when they meet, it is in circumstances dramatic enough to dissolve the polite indifference that presides over human relationships in everyday life" (*Pietr,* 165).

There are a few gangs of violent criminals who terrorize with shootouts and bursts of violence, such as the American mafiosi in *Maigret, Lognon et les gangsters* or the so-called Picardy gang of Czechs who kill, torture, and steal in *Maigret et son mort*. But these murderers are exceptions and different from the usual criminal in the Maigrets. In the 1920s and 1930s—and all of the Maigrets, whatever their supposed date, take place in that period—there was an implicit understanding between criminal and policeman not to use a gun if at all possible. Holdups were meticulously planned and stylishly executed, and the police department had files on each criminal's tastes, habits, and compulsions. The police could put a mark on virtually every holdup; it was like a silversmith's mark.[24] In previous years, the police could also rely on an elaborate network of informers in bars, brothels, cafés, hotels, and among concierges to keep tabs on habitual criminals, a system that has broken down in a society marked by anarchy in crime and the anonymity of criminals.

Freddie the safecracker (in *Maigret et la grande perche*) belonged to the old breed of professional criminals. The police called him "Alfred-le-triste" (sad Freddie) and the newspapers tagged him "the burglar on a bike." Freddie had once worked for a safe manufacturing firm, but he now worked for himself, cracking the safes he had once installed. Maigret had always felt a certain affection for Freddie, whose career he had followed for years. It was for this reason that Freddie's wife, who also knew Maigret from her days as a prostitute, came to the commissaire for help when her husband stumbled upon a dead body on one of his routine safecracking jobs. Maigret determines that the body was that of a dentist's wealthy wife, who had been killed by her mother-in-law when she wanted to escape the woman's terrifying domination. The murder was in fact her third; she had already killed her husband, who was squandering their estate, and her son's rich first wife, also for her money. This woman, to whom Simenon lends his mother's terror of poverty, is the most evil in all of Simenon's oeuvre. She killed for money, the most unacceptable motive for murder in Maigret's canon and was even prepared to poison her son to prevent him from revealing anything to Maigret. By solving the murder, Maigret, a policeman, permits Freddie to continue to break open safes in the hope of realizing his dream to retire to the country on stolen money.

Maigret is employed by society to arrest the criminal, not to judge him. Simenon explained why he transmitted his own attitudes to Maigret:

> I have maintained excellent contacts with the Paris Police Judiciaire: many commissaires have told me their stories. Do you know that when a criminal finally confesses after hours of interrogation, he doesn't feel humiliated, but, on the contrary, liberated? . . . [The criminal] is relieved and thanks the commissaire, he is grateful to him. Links are forged between the policeman and the guilty party. When the guillotine still existed, one-third of the condemned asked the commissaire to come to the execution. It is this link that was forged between them that represents liberty. I am sure that when . . . doctors remove the weight of a hallucination from a sick person, he must also have similar feelings of deliverance, of gratitude. (*Gril,* 56)

The worst humiliation for a man, according to Simenon, is to feel rejected by human society. Maigret represents a forgiving society, identifies with the criminal, and, by understanding him, gives him back his self-respect after the confession, permitting him to a certain degree to be reintegrated into the community (*Gril,* 55).

When Maigret has finally helped the criminal to effect a catharsis through confession, he must turn him over to the judicial process and the insensitivity of judges and juries. Simenon often expressed his dismay at the "archaic quality of the French Penal Code, with laws that take no heed of our medical knowledge, particularly in the matter of the degree of responsibility of the criminal," adding that the first Maigrets were "imbued with the sense, which has always been with me, of man's irresponsibility. It is because of this feeling that Maigret does not judge but attempts to understand" (*Vieux* 1:144). The fundamental optimism at the heart of the detective novel is tempered in the Maigrets by Simenon's ineluctably pessimistic view of the human condition.

Maigret separates completely the policeman's job from that of the judiciary. "In any event, our role has never been to judge. It is the business of the courts and juries to decide whether a man is guilty or not and to what extent he can be considered responsible. . . . But the fact remains that there is a moment in which we must make a decision fraught with consequences . . . for, in the end, it is according to our investigation, from the elements that we have put together, that the magistrates, then the jurors, will form an opinion" (*Confidence,* 13–14).

In order to emphasize the irrelevance of everything that occurs once the dialogue between Maigret and the criminal has ended, Simenon takes Maigret to court only once (*Maigret aux assises*) to follow up a case in which he was involved. Maigret would have preferred to remain apart from these last rites to which he has never become accustomed and which depress and discourage him.

> In his office on the Quai des Orfèvres, he was still at grips with reality, and, even when he was drawing up his report, he could still believe that his sentences stuck close to reality.
>
> Then months passed, sometimes a year, if not two, and he found himself closed in the witness room one fine day with people he had questioned formerly and who were no longer anything but a memory for him. Were these really the same human beings, concierges, passersby, merchants, who were seated with empty expressions on the benches of the sacristy?
>
> Was it the same way, after months of prison, at the prisoner's bar?
>
> Suddenly you are plunged into an impersonal universe where everyday words no longer seem to be used, where the most ordinary facts are expressed by hermetic formulae. . . . Even today, he knew that he was giving only a lifeless, schematic reflection of reality. Everything he had just said was true, but he had not made the weight of things felt, their density, their movement, their odor. . . . Everything was falsified here, not through the fault of the judges, the jurors, the witnesses, the penal code or the procedure, but because complicated, living human beings suddenly were summed up in a few sentences.[25]

Maigret reflects that he is given only a short period in which to penetrate a new milieu, to hear from 10 to 50 people about whom he had previously known nothing and then, if possible, to distinguish truth from falsehood. He is continually reproached for doing the work of his men, leaving his office and going out to visit the scene of the murder, but this is indispensable for an understanding of the crime. The examining magistrate is at an even greater disadvantage, for he sees the accused only in the neutral atmosphere of his office, where they are reduced to two-dimensional beings detached from their private lives. What can the magistrate discover in this very limited time? Maigret wonders. After that, in court, the matter is presented in a few strokes, and the only admissible evidence is impersonal.

As he waits to give testimony, Maigret's discouragement grows. The case concerns a young man named Meurant who has been accused of the murder of his aunt and a four-year-old child. The aunt's throat had been cut, the child suffocated, and the gold that had been kept in the bottom of a Chinese vase had disappeared. Gaston Meurant, the accused, had visited his aunt regularly, while his brother Alfred, a ne'er-do-well, came only when he needed money. Responding to an anonymous telephone tip, Maigret had found Gaston's jacket covered with blood.

Maigret knows that Meurant is innocent despite all the circumstantial evidence against him. Meurant had always wanted a family but his wife deceived him by marrying him without telling him that she was unable to bear children. Maigret had seen men, in appearance as calm, sweet, and self-effacing as Meurant, who became violent when driven too far. He knows, however, that a man like Meurant, who loved children as much as Maigret does, and who also suffered because he had none of his own, would never have killed a child.

Maigret secures Meurant's acquittal and, in an almost criminal betrayal of his role as defender of the law, knowingly fails to avert Meurant's murder of his wife's lover, the real killer of the old woman and child. This abrogation of legal justice is not the only way in which the novel differs from the conventional detective story. The atrocity of the murder of an old woman and a four-year-old child, the blood stains on Meurant's suit jacket, and the activities of Meurant's brother would have been of prime importance in a traditional detective novel. Here they are incidental to the examination of the life and character of Meurant, a man who would have preferred to be unjustly convicted of murder rather than to have the failure of his domestic life revealed in public.

The incidental nature of the inquiry in *Maigret aux assises* is common to all of the Maigrets; the detection aspect is their least important feature. But that is generally true of the best detective novels; we do not read them simply because they remain faithful to a genre. What attracts the reader is that they recreate the genre in unexpected ways, skillfully employing digressive elements that divert us from the sameness of the plots and the lack of suspense, leading us to continue reading with pleasure until the denouement with its inevitable solution of the crime.[26] The most important of these digressive elements in Simenon's detective novels is the person of commissaire Jules Maigret of the Police Judiciaire, who is not only the sole protagonist of the novels but also their focal point. All of the characters in Simenon's work, other than Maigret, are nothing more than a thousand and one literary variations on the theme of failure.[27] Simenon's use of free indirect style throughout the works enables the reader to hear superimposed on one another the voice of the narrator and the voice of Maigret, permitting the reader to observe Maigret's actions and also be party to his thoughts.

Each novel adds to our knowledge of Maigret's life, his biography, his habits, tics and manias, his personal and professional lives. Intimate notations and details scattered throughout the Maigret cycle make him a completely believable human being and trigger a sense of recognition from one novel to the other. "For me, a man without a past is an incomplete man," Maigret remarks in *Les mémoires de Maigret* (56), an ingenious apologia written 20 years after the first Maigrets, where the roles of author and protagonist are reversed, and it is Maigret himself who tells about his life and career. We learn that Maigret's father, the last in a long line of tenant farmers, was the bailiff at the château of the count of Saint-Hilaire in Saint-Fiacre. Maigret's humble origins account for his sympathy for the little people and his attitude towards the rich. In his "memoirs," Maigret also tells how his mother died in childbirth when he was eight years old, how he was brought up by an aunt in Nantes, how his father's death from pleurisy at the age of 43 (the same age at which Désiré Simenon died) forced him to abandon his medical studies after two years, how he went to Paris not knowing what career he would pursue, and how he met commissaire Jacquemain of the Police Judiciaire (Sûreté at that time) who determined his choice of a profession.

Thirty years later, commissaire Maigret returns to his native village, in *L'affaire Saint-Fiacre,* after he sees an anonymous note, the provenance of which is never explained, stating that a crime will be committed during the first mass on All Souls' Day at the Saint-Fiacre church. The police at Moulins who received the note had thought it a joke, as did the Paris police to whom they forwarded it. Because they did not know Maigret's background, his fellow officers were surprised to see him act on the basis of such a letter. In Saint-Fiacre, Maigret finds that the whole world of his childhood has deteriorated. The countess is a demented old lady who keeps gigolos, and her son, a good-for-nothing playboy, is about to be arrested on a bad check charge. "He certainly had no illusions about mankind. But he was furious that his childhood memories should have been sullied! Especially the one of the countess, whom he had always seen as noble and beautiful, like a storybook character."[28]

When the first mass ends, Maigret notices that the countess is immobile, and when he approaches her he realizes that she is dead. In her missal, he finds a phony newspaper article stating that her son had committed suicide after publicly announcing that he was ashamed of the scandals provoked by his mother. The article had obviously been planted by someone who knew of her heart condition and counted on the article to bring on an attack. "Maigret felt personally attacked by the case, sick at heart, disgusted. . . . He had never imagined that he would find his native village in this condition" (*Saint-Fiacre,* 83). Maigret's indignation is another quality that sets him apart from the traditional detective, for, unlike the latter, he is never coldly removed from the case at hand. Each one becomes a personal matter to him; his reactions set the mood of the novel.

The criminal is apprehended, but not by Maigret, another violation of the rules of the detective novel, which specify that the detective must be the one to solve the murder. It is the countess's son who redeems himself by discovering that the bailiff and his son had been robbing the countess of her money and property and had killed her when they feared her new gigolo would get in their way.

Maigret's early years in Paris, his courtship and marriage, and his life in the police department are dealt with in detail in *Les mémoires de Maigret.* He describes his various assignments in the streets of Paris, the central market, the docks, the crowds, the department stores, and the brothels that preceded his promotion to the Quai des Orfèvres; a promotion he earned not for his police work, but for agreeing to the cover up of an accidental murder committed by the daughter of one of the wealthiest, most powerful industrialists in France (*La première enquête de Maigret*).

But Maigret is not presented as a traditional hero; all of Simenon's works emphasize his simplicity and bourgeois characteristics. Maigret is a white, middle-class Frenchman, a civil servant in a position of social power who lives modestly on his salary. "He embodies the social norm from which his criminal adversaries all deviate. . . . [He is] a privileged member of a uniquely privileged minority, a solid bourgeois, a comfortable, reasonably secure member of the urban middle class."[29] Maigret has what is essentially a live-in servant in the person of his wife, Madame Maigret, who represents Simenon's concept of the ideal woman (*Traces de pas,* 157). She is an old-fashioned bourgeois housewife and the most unliberated of women. Her role is to prepare meals that her husband will rarely eat, to get up before him so that he can be served coffee on awakening, to bring him his slippers, and put his newspaper beside his armchair. Madame Maigret is an expert cook and can prepare Maigret's favorite dishes better than any chef.[30] When he returns home, at no matter what time of the day or night, Mme Maigret waits for him behind the closed door and knows just when to open it for him. She is responsive to his moods and reacts accordingly. She knows how to stay in her place, she is good-natured and in excellent health. He calls her Madame Maigret, she calls him Maigret. Their rare outings together consist of a movie once a week and dinner with Dr. Pardon and his wife once a month. The women are quiet during the meal and then retire to a corner where they speak softly and knit. The Maigrets spend occasional weekends in an inn at Morsang-sur-Orge and, later on, at their home at Meung-sur-Loire where Maigret fishes, naps, plays cards, and Madame Maigret takes care of the house or embroiders. Madame Maigret poses a problem for filmmakers who find it difficult to portray such a one-dimensional character on-screen. Her role of a woman sacrificed to her husband's male chauvinism and his profoundly egoistic character can pass in the novels, but in films a negative portrayal of Maigret as husband would dramatically tarnish the legendary character of the commissaire.[31]

Maigret's physical appearance is established in *Pietr-le-Letton,* the first novel of the series:

> He did not resemble the ordinary policeman. He did not have a mustache nor did he wear heavy-soled shoes. His clothes were well cut, of fine wool. He also shaved every morning and his hands were well groomed.
>
> His build was plebeian. He was enormous and bony. Hard muscles stood out beneath his jacket. . . . Above all, he had his very own way of planting himself in a spot that had even displeased many of his colleagues.
>
> It was more than self-assurance, but it wasn't pride. He was like a solid block and everything had to break against it. . . . His pipe remained clenched in his jaw. (*Pietr,* 17)

Notations of Maigret's physical strength and infinite curiosity about people and things abound in the series. There emerges from all of this a picture of a quiet, unexcitable man who detests hurry, a stolid, peaceable figure who inspires confidence.

Maigret exerts unquestioned authority both in his apartment on the rue Richard Lenoir and in his other home, the Police Judiciaire on the Quai des Orfèvres. In Simenon's work, we see for the first time the day-to-day operations of an urban police department, particularly those of the homicide division. Richard Cobb has described the changing pattern of the clientele at the Police Judiciaire during the week as gleaned from the Maigrets. Monday is the busiest day for whores and pimps, and Wednesday for counterfeiters, who are replaced during the summer months by housebreakers and cat burglars. Murderers in crimes of passion can be seen early in the morning or late at night, particularly late Saturday night or early Sunday morning, together with elderly provincial couples, parents, either of the assassins or the assassinated, who have come to Paris by the night train. Saturday night belongs to young punks while Sunday is quiet in the Police Judiciaire but not in the morgue, where we find the victims of crimes of passion.[32]

Simenon returns repeatedly to aspects of Maigret's professional life that have become part of the Maigret legend; his cherished pot-bellied stove in his office and the all-night sessions at headquarters, interrupted by countless trays of sandwiches and beer ordered from the Brasserie Dauphine. "Those nights, which eight times out of ten ended with confessions, had finally acquired their rules, even their traditions, like plays that are performed several hundred times" (*Clochard,* 157).

Maigret is the first detective in the history of the genre to be surrounded by a whole team of collaborators. The story of Maigret's investigation is constantly interrupted by the reports of those who are working behind the scenes. Maigret's associates, carefully differentiated, make up a continually reappearing cast of characters. Among them are Janvier, the faithful, devoted to his wife and ever increasing brood of children; Torrence, who, although killed in *Pietr-le-Letton,* is resurrected by the author and returns to help Maigret in subsequent investigations; Lapointe, the youngest, who can pass for a student and who is always sent out to interview middle-aged maternal women; Lucas, the associate with the greatest ability, whose only problem is that his profession is written all over his face; Lognon, whom certain people call "Inspector Ungracious" because of his cranky air but whom Maigret refers to as "Inspector Unfortunate" because he seems to have a gift for bringing misfortune on himself; Inspector Fumal, whose lack of formal education stands in the way of promotion; Dr. Paul, the police surgeon; and Moers, the ballistics expert. Throughout the investigation, these secondary characters furnish the data that are required to make Maigret's inquiry go forward.

Maigret's life, his staff, his friends, his gourmandise, his sorrow at being childless, his constant head colds, all contribute to make him a completely believable human being. The reader rapidly identifies with him not only because of his appearance, his way of life, his values, and his purposes but because of the recognition of the superior qualities of the cultural stereotype that he embodies. Maigret conforms to the image of the Frenchman as skeptical, tolerant, and worldly-wise (Porter, 217).

It is not only Maigret who provides the reassurance of a cultural stereotype, it is also the second protagonist of the series, Paris, as tightly linked with Maigret as is London with Sherlock Holmes. Although 20 percent of the Maigrets take place in the provinces or abroad, Maigret, the Parisian policeman, is unimaginable without his city. Simenon makes use in the novels of cultural references designed to prompt recognition by means of the same suggestive images used in tourist brochures (Porter, 218). He brings to the reader his Paris of the thirties with its blood puddings and brioches; the former central market (les Halles); onion soup, chestnut vendors, and anglers on the banks of the Seine; book dealers along the quais; bistros with zinc bars; Notre-Dame and the Ile Saint-Louis; the Place du Tertre and the Place des Abbesses; the Moulin Rouge and Montparnasse; the Boulevard Saint-Michel and the Boulevard Rochechouart; the odors of café au lait, warm croissants, anisette; the small cafés and the large elegant cafés of the Champs-Elysées; the rue Mouffetard and the Place Blanche; the whores and the drab hotels of Pigalle; the train stations; the Quai des Orfèvres and the Sacré-Coeur (Becker, 2501). It is a pre-World War II Paris that remains the same even in those of Simenon's novels that supposedly take place in the fifties and sixties.

Maigret is one of the few harmonious characters in all of Simenon's work. He is wise and understanding. He knows that it is impossible to understand men completely, but he accepts them as they are. He is astonished by nothing and never moralizes. His wisdom restores faith in life. He is an ordinary bourgeois policeman, a hero only in terms of the definition proposed by Simenon: "The hero is the person who has the courage to make a good thing of his life."[33] Maigret's reassuring presence constitutes the major difference between the Maigrets and Simenon's other novels, the so-called romans-durs or hard novels. Many of the same themes are repeated in both types of novel, and Simenon often takes up subjects in the Maigrets that are more serious than those in the others. Despite this, in the Maigrets, Simenon only takes us to the threshold of tragedy, which he crosses in the romans durs. This is due to the reassuring presence of Maigret, the father figure, who convinces us that there is an order and a structure to life. In the other novels, there is no Maigret to whom the protagonist can confess, there is no one to understand or with whom to communicate, leaving him immured in his solitude, stifled and suffocated by repressed confessions (Becker, 2488).

Chapter Three

"Romans durs"—Novels of Crime and Deviance

The constant subject of Simenon's romans durs, or "hard" problem novels, the novels on which his literary reputation is based, like that of the Maigrets, is the violent nature of aberrant human behavior. Like the prototypal crime novel, the romans durs are novels of deviance. The deviant individual is one who differs markedly, for example in social adjustment or sexual behavior, from what is considered normal or acceptable to the group of which he is a member. Simenon's modernity lies in his recognition that the deviant, the criminal of one sort or another, is an appropriate and even representative man for our age.

All of Simenon's novels, whether detective or dur, are built around psychological investigations that are carried out in the Maigrets by the detective, the novelist's alter ego, and in the others by the novelist himself. In the Maigrets, Simenon observes the characters from a distance and then slowly closes in, while in the others he focuses directly on a character from the beginning and then delves deeper and deeper into his psyche to reveal what neither he nor the reader suspected previously. In the Maigrets, Simenon starts with a given situation that he examines in order to discover the psychological imperatives behind it; in the romans durs, he gradually builds up the pressures leading to the final tragedy (Becker, 2488–89).

Both the Maigrets and the romans durs, like detective and crime novels, make use of the same basic time frame; both juxtapose present and past events. The detective novel explores the past to determine the causes of the crime at the same time as it relates in the present details of the investigation that is taking place; the crime novel recounts events occurring in the present, even as it delves into the past to effect an in-depth analysis of the protagonist (Butor, 250–51).

Distinctions between the Maigrets and the romans durs are like those that exist between detective and crime novels. The detective novel begins in chaos and ends in closure, with the defeat of the criminal; the criminal is cast as a scapegoat whose detection and expulsion reestablish order and harmony. The essential point in the detective novel is not so much the punishment of the criminal but the exculpation of the rest of the characters, and, by extension, of the reader. Such closure cannot exist in the crime novel, for in the crime novel the killer can be found inside any one of us, the supposedly innocent.

Simenon's is a criminal universe, inhabited by psychologically marginal characters whose behavior is characterized by sexual deviance, revolt, flight, crime, attempted murder, murder, and suicide. Only 12 of the 117 romans durs are free of the violence that pervades his oeuvre.[1] The violent actions of the characters are, for Simenon, "tragic consequences of the fact that for many men and women life is sometimes, if not nearly always, unendurable. In the moment of crisis, they are driven to affirm themselves and, human society being what it is, they can do so only through murder, rape, arson, suicide, and the rest of the catalogue of crimes"(Gill 1953, 41). Thus the importance of the chance event that upsets the character's equilibrium and drags him into deviant behavior. Simenon is fascinated by problems of violence, alienation, and guilt and by the sight of human beings driven to their limit, compelled by passion and circumstance to damage others and themselves. But, whatever his crimes may be and whatever their origin, Simenon's protagonist, like Albert Camus's Meursault (*L'étranger*), is essentially guilty of not being like others; he possesses an indefinable quality that sets him apart and impels him to cross the line into murder and suicide that most people are able to skirt. What is remarkable in the romans durs is that, with a seemingly limited cast of characters and themes, Simenon has been able to populate and animate an entire universe.

The young men of Simenon's early novels, like the young Simenon himself, are high-strung, troubled, ambitious, anguished, pathologically sensitive, desperate to live intensely and to change their status in life. Two of Simenon's fictional counterparts, Roger (*Pedigree*) and Jean (*L'Ane Rouge*) turn back from the brink, each saved, like Simenon, by his father's early death from heart disease. For a third, Gérard Auvinet of *Les noces de Poitiers,* the birth of a daughter brings deliverance. But, in a pattern that is repeated from novel to novel, the characters are powerless to avoid the tragic defeat that Simenon most feared for himself. Like Marcel Viau (*Au bout du rouleau*), they are, as the title of the novel indicates, at the end of their tether after a lifetime of violence and failure. Viau, a weak, unstable character and a social misfit, makes a futile attempt to commit suicide when the police arrest him for past crimes; a second attempt in his jail cell succeeds.

The life of Emile Bachelin (*Les suicidés*), another of Simenon's desperate young men, was also marked by violence from the very beginning. When he is forbidden by her father to pursue his relationship with his daughter, Emile retaliates by burning down their house. He then elopes with the girl to Paris where they live in poverty, as Emile unsuccessfully tries his hand at various illegal activities, including blackmail—a criminal activity repeated in many novels.[2] Finally, seeing no reason to go on living, the young man successfully carries out the first part of their murder/suicide pact but bungles his suicide, as he has failed at everything throughout his life. "Look! *He's* alive . . ."[3] remarks the concierge, who plays the role of the chorus, in the final words of the novel.

De Ritter, the protagonist of *Faubourg,* also ultimately commits the violent crime that was his destiny. Driven by strange compulsions he does not himself understand, De Ritter returns to the town he had fled more than 20 years before, accompanied by a young prostitute named Léa. Although he had intended to spend only a short time in the town, he suddenly and unexpectedly decides to stay. But this desire, like all of his desires, is only fleeting, for he has never really known what he wants. As soon as he succeeds in marrying his rich, loving cousin, he becomes uneasy because "he [is] a victim . . . he would have been a good little boy if life had not taken it upon itself to fling him into adventure" (*Faubourg,* 166). He becomes jealous of Léa and finally kills an 18-year-old schoolboy who is infatuated with her, thereby giving in to the act of violence that has always been his destiny.

Maudet (*L'aîné des Ferchaux*) is another impatient young man, "impatient to live, to enjoy to the full everything life has to offer. But, above all, impatient to dominate."[4] Maudet's childhood had been intolerable, and he had sworn to escape the mediocrity he saw all around him. When he hears that a certain Dieudonné Ferchaux needs a secretary for a well-paying, glamorous position involving travel, Maudet, who is down on his luck in Paris, convinces his young wife Lina to accompany him to Caen to apply for this position.

From their very first meeting, Ferchaux and Maudet are drawn to one another, for reasons that become clearer as the novel progresses. Ferchaux finds in Maudet a strength almost equal to the one that helped him overcome almost insuperable odds in his youth, while Ferchaux personifies for the younger man the power and riches he hopes to obtain. They also seem to be drawn together by the magnetic force of destiny; they need one another and each feels instinctively that the other will serve as the instrument of his fate. This couple represents one of the strangest attempts made by Simenon's heroes to conjure death, for, by uniting, they are struggling against a type of extinction, "for the young man, death by suffocation in a mediocre and absurd life, for the old man, sinking into the implacable exile of solitude."[5]

At first, Maudet admires everything about Ferchaux, particularly the older man's ennui, "an immense, icy boredom, the boredom of a man who has seen everything, known everything, who has lost all of his illusions and who finally knows how infinite is human solitude" (*Ferchaux,* 103). What Maudet does not discover until later is that this is a pose; Ferchaux's glory belongs to the past, he can go no further. He now lives in desperate fear of solitude. When Maudet recognizes Ferchaux's weakness, there is a reversal in roles between master and disciple.

The narrative of the relationship between the two men is interwoven with an adventure story that demonstrates Simenon's skill as a storyteller. Maudet and Ferchaux, together with Maudet's wife, flee the police who are pursuing Ferchaux, and, as the police get closer to them, they abandon Maudet's wife and sail for South America. The second part of the novel takes place in Panama, where the two men have settled. Ferchaux is old and sick. He is busy dictating his memoirs, afraid that he will die before finishing them. It is only since he began them that he has become so frightened of death. Maudet, who is becoming more and more disgusted with the old man, is growing restless. Constantly straining toward the future, he knows that "his contact with people and things could only last as long as was necessary to draw out their substance, as it were. When there was nothing else to take, it was necessary to move on" (*Ferchaux,* 236). That was why he had abandoned Lina and that is why Ferchaux must now disappear. He has lived too long with the old man and there is nothing else to take from him but his money. "He was forced to follow his path as Ferchaux had followed his. . . . It was a necessity, a duty" (*Ferchaux,* 236).

At times Maudet would have a certain feeling that something had to be done. "It was when he felt removed from the surroundings in which he found himself, as if in a dream" (*Ferchaux,* 277). This dreamlike state, which separates many of Simenon's characters from reality as they commit their crimes, is a manifestation of their fundamental alienation. They wonder whether they have really lived or whether they have spent their lives lost in daydreams. One day, as if in a trance, Maudet senses what he must do as he hears that during westerly gales headless bodies of old people are frequently washed up on the beach. This is the work of the sellers of shrunken heads—white heads sell better than colored heads and heads of old people are most in demand because they have more expression and also dry faster. And so Maudet kills the old man and leaves the body for the old drunken seller of heads while he takes off for an unknown destination. Although he steals all of Ferchaux's money, Maudet's motivation was not solely theft, for he also had a desire for freedom in order to complete his journey to the limits of his possibilities (Richter, 84).

While Simenon describes the condition of the individual in society and interprets deviant or psychotic states of mind, he does not move, as does Dostoyevsky in *Crime and Punishment,* in mystical regions where spiritual truths are being considered; for Dostoyevsky, the murder committed by Raskolnikov and the interrogation he suffers at the hands of Porfiry are no more than steps on the road to redemption through suffering. Only once in his oeuvre does Simenon enter into this metaphysical realm of divine Grace, the kingdom of God's mercy as distinguished from his justice; only in *La neige était sale* do we find moral redemption through suffering.

The protagonist of the novel, a young man named Frank Friedmaier, lives in the corrupt atmosphere of wartime and occupation similar to that experienced by Roger in *Pedigree.* Frank's childhood, however, was even more tragic and sordid than that of Roger; he grew up in his mother's brothel, not in a boarding house, and without benefit of a father. The occupier would seem to be German and the occupied country eastern European, but Simenon did not explicitly identify them in this novel because he was trying to address the eternal, universal problems of Good and Evil.

Frank externalizes his self-hatred in violent action. He kills an enemy soldier on a dare and watches indifferently as a young violinist is arrested for the crime. He also kills an old woman, who had been kind to him when he was a child, in order to steal watches as barter for the green pass of the enemy. And then he seals his pact with the devil; he lures Sissy, a young girl who loves him, into his bed and changes places in the darkness with his friend, a bully, thief, and murderer. The plot misfires, and Sissy runs out into the snow barefoot, screaming Frank's name. "It did not matter, Frank had done what he wanted to do. He had rounded the cape. He had seen what was on the other side. He had not seen what he expected to see. No matter . . . he was on the other side of the turning and he had nothing in common with them any more" (*Neige,* 88).

The scandal is hushed up as Sissy is cared for by her father, Holst, a member of a clandestine resistance movement and the only man Frank has ever respected. Frank continues to court danger, flagrantly flaunting his green pass, his revolver, and his affluence. "He wanted fate to take notice of him" (*Neige,* 122). One morning, "fate gives him a gift," he is arrested by the authorities for certain criminal activities, of which, ironically, he is innocent (*Neige,* 214). He refuses to answer their questions but agrees to confess to the crimes he has actually committed, provided that Holst and Sissy be permitted to visit him. During the visit, they speak very little but they understand one another. Sissy, who still loves him, forgives him. And Holst, who knows of all of Frank's crimes, still is able to pardon as he tells Frank that "it's a difficult job to be a man" (*Neige,* 214). The difficulty of maturing emotionally to become a man is a leitmotiv in Simenon's work.

Holst's forgiveness, Simenon tells us, is the paternal pardon that grants peace and wipes out solitude, a major theme in his work. But, Holst's pardon, with its implicit sacrifice of his own daughter, goes far beyond human forgiveness to reach the divine absolution found in the miracle plays of the Virgin of the Middle Ages. Like Théophile, in Rutebeuf's thirteenth-century *Le miracle de Théophile,* Frank has sold his soul to the devil; he has suffered both mental and physical torture, confessed, and repented, and Holst, like the Virgin, has redeemed his pledge. Frank has spent his "season in hell"[6] and, at the end, embraces death as the "sublime and possibly only safe way of witnessing to a human absolute—a state of ecstasy and fulfillment" (Raymond, 141). As Frank is led away to be executed, it begins to snow and the clean snow, representing his expiation and purification, covers the dirty snow of his sins.

The revolt of Simenon's young men, however ill-conceived and violent it may be at times, represents a passionate refusal to accept a limited, mediocre life and the monotony and ugliness of the existence they see around them. They are driven to action and violently oppose anything that stands in their way. It is almost as if they were destined for revolt from birth. In this respect they differ from an even larger group of older men whose revolt comes later on in life after they have spent years living according to the rules of society. The desperate struggles of the young give way in the later novels to the disenchantment of the middle-aged. Gobillot, the 45-year-old lawyer in *En cas de malheur,* speaks about the defining characteristics of these older men. "Sunday, when our eyes met for the first time, he knit his brows as he looked at me as if he discovered something different about me, what I am tempted to call a sign . . . an invisible mark that can only be detected by the initiated, only by those who bear it themselves . . . who have lived a lot, seen a lot, tried out everything themselves, who, above all, have made a great effort, reached or almost reached their goal. I do not think that one can be so marked before a certain age, the mid-forties, for example."[7]

A pattern is common to all of the novels that are centered around middle-aged men who flee their milieu after years of conformity. Each has established a modus vivendi that permits him to function in society until an accidental occurrence disturbs the precarious balance that has been established, causing him to break with the life he has led and triggering a series of reactions that often lead to murder, suicide, and madness. In *Novembre,* it is the father's seduction of the maid; in *Les complices,* it is the crash of a school bus caused by the protagonist's carelessness; in *La main,* it is the death of a friend in a snowstorm; and, in *La cage de verre,* it is the suicide of his brother-in-law that starts the protagonist on the desperate path to the murder that has always been his destiny. And the few whose break does not lead to violence return armed with the desperate knowledge of the meaninglessness of existence, knowledge that gives them the strength to survive.[8]

Before their awakening, the lives of these men are characterized by a mechanical repetition of gestures and actions, almost as if ritual had the power to exorcise the misfortune that might otherwise overtake them. Simenon describes this unvarying routine of daily life in the opening pages of each novel. Dave Galloway, the watchmaker of Everton, "followed the routine of every evening, or more exactly of Saturdays, which were a little different from other days. . . . He no longer noticed that every day he went through the same motions, in the same order, and that it was this, perhaps, that gave him so peaceful and reassuring an aspect."[9] Steve Adams, in *Le passage de la ligne,* describes his father as belonging "to that train compartment that carried to London, every day at the same time, people belonging to the same class as he, with similar professions, who were leaving behind them more or less similar houses and families. Each morning on the way in, each evening on the way back, they greeted one another with a gesture as restrained as a Masonic greeting."[10] For fifteen years, Doctor Hans Kupérus of Sneek (*L'assassin*) "insisted that the same gestures be performed at the same times and that all the rites of a well-organized life be observed."[11]

The first few pages of *Le bourgmestre de Furnes* trace in half-minute segments Terlinck's occupations at the end of the business day. Similarly, in the opening pages of *Le bilan Malétras,* Malétras automatically pulls his cigar case out of his pocket, repeating the same scene that has been taking place at the same time for years. Sticking out his chest, Malétras fingers his vest, takes a gold cigar-cutter in the form of a guillotine out of his right vest pocket, and extracts an expensive gold lighter from another pocket. After lighting his cigar, he replaces the articles in his pockets, emits a deep sigh, leans back a little in his chair, and watches the smoke rise with half-closed eyes. M. Monde (*La fuite de Monsieur Monde*), Bergelon (*Bergelon*), Loursat (*Les inconnus dans la maison*), and Charles (*Oncle Charles s'est enfermé*) have similarly established routines that permit them to live automatically, thereby obviating the need to examine the meaning of their lives or to make an existential choice.

The break seems at times to occur spontaneously, but this is only because the reasons are not readily apparent. The crisis, in actuality, is the culmination of a situation that has been developing subliminally for a long time. Alavoine (*Lettre à mon juge*) is unaware of this slow maturation:

> There was just a moment when I began to look around me with different eyes and I saw a city that seemed foreign to me, a pretty city, very light, very clean, very bright, a city in which everyone greeted me with affability.
>
> Why then did I have the feeling of emptiness? . . . What was I doing there, in a small, peaceful city, in a pretty comfortable house among people who smiled at me and who shook my hand familiarly?
>
> And who had established that daily routine that I followed as scrupulously as if my life depended on it? What am I saying! As if, from the beginning of time, it had been decided by the Creator that that routine would inexorably be mine.[12]

Often a specific event causes the protagonist to deviate from his habits and daily routine. Terlinck (*Le bourgmestre de Furnes*) compares this awakening to a scene familiar to the citizens of Ostend. "They would bring a child who had never seen the ocean, whom they had blindfolded so that his first impression would be stronger. Once on the jetty, they abruptly removed the blindfold and the child would look at this infinitely vast horizon with anguish, he would quake at the knees, as if he were losing his footing, as if he felt himself being drawn into the abyss of the universe. Finally, panic-stricken, he would clutch hold of his father's legs, his mother's skirt, and burst into tears."[13]

In *L'homme qui regardait passer les trains,* Kees Popinga's break with routine, occasioned by a chance encounter, leads him into murder and madness. He is a drab, little man who lives in a stable, well-ordered, logical universe where everything, including his wife, is of the finest quality. He has, however, dreamed of adventure. Night trains symbolized another life for him. "In them he sensed something strange, almost depraved. . . . It seemed to him that people who leave in that way leave forever."[14] Precisely because Kees has felt such yearning, he follows a rigid routine, fearful that nothing could stop him any longer were he to give way on a single point.

One evening, Popinga meets his employer, Julius Coster, in a bar where he has been drinking heavily. Coster informs him that he has embezzled vast sums of money and that, as a result, the firm is going bankrupt. Popinga will be losing not only his job but all the savings that he had invested in the firm. Coster tells him that he is going to simulate suicide and then take off to join his mistress, Paméla, in Amsterdam. Suddenly, Popinga grasps a truth he has always suspected, that the orderly, logical world in which he lives is a collective lie, upheld by universal, tacit agreement. He feels a desperate need to know what else life has to offer and to do everything that propriety had previously forbidden. At the age of 40, he resolves to live as he pleases, without worrying about laws and customs, for he has discovered that no one else really takes them seriously.

Popinga now takes a train to Amsterdam, one of the trains he had always longingly watched go by, and goes to Paméla's hotel room. When she laughs in his face and humiliates him by refusing to grant him the favors she so freely bestows on everyone else, he strangles her. From Amsterdam, he takes the night train to Paris, where he will be able to fulfill all the desires he has suppressed for too long. He has adventures in Paris with automobile thieves, prostitutes, and pimps, loses his money to a confidence man, wanders from one furnished room to another, attempts a second murder, and, after an abortive suicide attempt, winds up in an insane asylum, where he decides to write "the truth about the Kees Popinga case" to convince himself that his experiences were not meaningless (*L'homme qui regardait,* 257). When the doctor asks him to produce these memoirs, Popinga gives him only blank pages. The truth that he has been unable to set down is that one cannot change one's life or live one's dreams, a message that is repeated throughout Simenon's work, earning him the appellation of "novelist of useless flight."[15]

Popinga's descent into madness, which parallels that of another murderer Hans Kupérus (*L'assassin*), is the type of conclusion for which Simenon has been faulted. It has been suggested that he often tacks on arbitrary, hasty, violent conclusions to otherwise well-constructed novels (Brophy, 67). It can also be argued, however, that such brutal responses reflect reality and may well be expected from a person who discovers that his entire life has been a sham, and that nothing justifies his existence. It is unusual to find in Simenon's oeuvre the occasional older man who does not surrender to madness, murder, or suicide but returns from his search for self-knowledge with an acceptance of his own limited humanity, fully cognizant of the void at the heart of all human endeavor. When M. Monde, Simenon's version of Everyman, resumes the life he had sought to flee, he does so with the serenity of those who have decided to look squarely at themselves and at others, accepting their limitations and inadequacies, those who have "laid all ghosts and lost all shadows."[16] And he is unable to tell those around him about this change in him, for his discovery is one that each man must make for himself, it is a truth that cannot be transmitted.

Malétras (*Le bilan Malétras*) had also planned his days minutely. "It wasn't a mania, it was a hygienic measure. He needed to lay out the days in that way, to divide them into blocks of time, he was convinced that it was thanks to that precaution that he maintained an unshakable equilibrium."[17] But his balance is upset when he strangles his young mistress in a fit of anger and finds that he has nothing to fall back on but self-awareness. As he takes the measure of his life, he finds that he has lived for more than 60 years without wondering why he did one thing or another or where he was going or whether his actions had any meaning. Further probing leads to the conclusion that nothing has meaning, that there is only one truth—"whatever a man does he is alone in life and in death;" nothing is important but the "thread of his dream" (*Malétras,* 176, 213). Like M. Monde, he intimidates those around him who are unable to understand a man "who is sufficient unto himself, coldly surveying others as a goldfish looks out at men through the sides of his bowl" (*Malétras,* 221).

The flight of two of Simenon's protagonists is not away from their milieu, but a burrowing into their surroundings. When his wife had abandoned him and their infant daughter 18 years before the opening of the novel,[18] Loursat (*Les inconnus dans la maison*) had cut himself off from the world and his legal profession and had shut himself up in his study, drinking four bottles of wine daily and reading the contents of his vast library in a haphazard manner. His only contact with his daughter Nicole, who had grown up without supervision, had been at mealtime. But Loursat is forced in middle age to reevaluate his life when he hears a pistol shot one night and discovers a body in his attic. By his actions, he had become a stranger in his home and knew nothing about what was taking place there. He now learns that Nicole is the leader of a band of rich adolescents who have been stealing for thrills, that their loot is stored in his attic, and that the dead man is a criminal who had been blackmailing them. A culprit is needed by the police, and Emile Manu, Nicole's lover and the only poor member of the band, is arrested. Loursat, angered by this injustice, decides to undertake the defense of this young man, who has been as humiliated by his poverty as Loursat was by his wife's departure. It is at this point that the novel begins to resemble a detective novel as Loursat makes inquiries in order to unmask the murderer. But the plot is merely a means to explore Loursat's character as he acquires insight into himself and sees that it was not his wife's abandonment but his own fundamental estrangement from others that had kept him on the outskirts of life: "The truth was that Loursat had never tried to live."[19] Armed with this knowledge, Loursat stops drinking to excess, unmasks the real culprit, and secures Emile's acquittal. The story of Loursat's return, which strains credulity, is one of Simenon's most affirmative conclusions. Not only does he come back from his self-imposed alcoholic retreat, but he also assumes the role of redresser of wrongs.

Humiliation, one of the most powerful stimuli for action in Simenon's oeuvre, triggers off Charles Dupeux's exile within his own home (*Oncle Charles s'est enfermé*), as it had that of Loursat. But Charles's retreat lasts for only five days. It begins when he returns home one day, goes up to the attic, and locks himself in. In brief flashbacks, Simenon reveals who Charles is and why he has acted in this way. He is an ordinary man, husband and father in a dysfunctional family, and office worker who is continually humiliated by his brother-in-law and employer, Henri. One day, Charles discovers by chance that Henri had encouraged the debauchery of his wealthy associate years before, knowing that such excess would be fatal to someone with his fragile constitution. The proprietress of the brothel where he would take the young man before he died has been blackmailing Henri ever since.

Charles has locked himself in the attic to think at leisure about what to do with Henri's secret and also with a windfall of 500,000 francs he has accumulated by stealing money and stocks from Henri over the years. Charles resolves the problem of the money easily. He decides to leave it hidden in the attic, for he concludes that life with the 500,000 francs would be exactly the same as before, perhaps in a more comfortable house but with the same difficult family. Henri inadvertently provides him with a solution to the problem of what to do with his knowledge of Henri's crime when he offers to buy Charles's silence, a bribe

Charles refuses to accept. He wants Henri to be as victimized and humiliated as he has always been and believes that Henri's inability to understand his refusal will produce this effect. "He alone prevents his brother-in-law from tranquilly enjoying his fortune and position! . . . And what made it even worse, precisely, was that he was so humble, so unobtrusive, so much a minor employee and poor relation!"[20] Charles has discovered the revenge of the underdog; saying nothing, "to make his brother-in-law die from fear, little by little" (*Charles,* 198).

Criminal or antisocial behavior most often cause Simenon's middle-aged protagonists to break with their former lives and customary behavior, but occasionally the catalyst precipitating their reactions is illness. This happens in two of Simenon's finest novels, *Les anneaux de Bicêtre* and *Les volets verts.* Illness as a stimulus for self-appraisal is not an uncommon theme in literature—two precursors of Simenon are Tolstoy, *The Death of Ivan Ilitch,* and Thomas Mann, *The Magic Mountain*—but never has the vanity of human existence been demonstrated with such unbearable rigor as in *Les volets verts.* All of the author's major themes can also be found in these novels—the ineradicable influence of childhood on the psyche, guilt at having betrayed one's class and youthful ideals, solitude, exile, alcoholism, futility of flight, and sickness of the body as a metaphor for sickness of the soul.

In the opening pages of *Les anneaux de Bicêtre,* the first sound heard by the newspaper publisher René Maugras as he comes out of a coma is the ringing of church bells, perceived by him as in a childhood memory as concentric rings of sound. We learn that Maugras was felled by an attack of hemiplegia at the Grand Véfour restaurant during a monthly luncheon reunion of a group of distinguished men, all of whom have achieved great success in various fields. He was brought to Bicêtre Hospital, where the routine of a large hospital and the medical details of illness and recuperation provide the framework for the inner drama at the heart of the novel. Although his mind has remained unaffected, half of Maugras's body is paralyzed and he cannot speak. Astonishingly, he is not depressed. On the contrary, "he could swear that he had never before enjoyed such serenity," for it has permitted him to give in to the temptation to stop struggling.[21] With the lucidity born of proximity to death, he considers the world surrounding him to which he no longer belongs, to which he has never really belonged, wondering whether it was ever worth the trouble it entailed. "What was the point of living? Several times . . . he had experienced the same sense of emptiness, even when he was making the greatest efforts and achieving the most tangible success" (*Bicêtre,* 50). Like Simenon, himself, Maugras questions whether others actually believe in their roles, whether they are really satisfied with themselves, or whether their activities, like his own, are merely a form of escape. In his state of semiconsciousness, in the emptiness of his drugged illness, he attempts to "evaluate with all possible detachment what was left of 54 years of a man's life" (*Bicêtre,* 86), and his pitiful inventory, which includes his drunken father, two unsuccessful marriages, and an unloved daughter, proves to him that life is meaningless (Becker, 2496). The Catholic writer François Mauriac remarked that it is novels like *Les anneaux de Bicêtre* that succeed, where Christian sermons have failed, in convincing us of the vanity of life.[22]

Maugras's bitter conclusion is reinforced by the humiliations to which his body is subjected and by his feelings of desperation, outrage, and helplessness as he is reduced by sickness to the status of an object. The one dramatic episode in the novel serves to intensify these feelings. His lungs fill with fluid and must be aspirated:

> An instrument forces his jaws apart, and a tube is thrust down his throat. He feels it going down. He would like to signal to them that he is choking, that he cannot bear it any longer, that he cannot breathe. . . . Those 10 or 15 minutes were the most unpleasant he has ever experienced in his life. He had really felt like an animal and he realized that he had behaved like one too, first by struggling, then, as he lay inert, by staring at each of them in turn with wild eyes . . . He was so tired! He had been tired for an eternity . . . and he had kept going all the same in spite of the temptation to let himself drift, to stop struggling, to give up once and for all. . . . They had hurt him badly, and above all they had taken away the little confidence he had left in himself and in man's potentiality. (*Bicêtre,* 92, 94)

As he lies impotent in his bed, Maugras can think of only two moments in the past—the time he thought he was dying was the third—when he seemed to have found a meaning in life, two moments during which he had felt "in harmony with nature. Twice he had almost been absorbed into nature. Nature had pervaded his whole being. He had become part of it. And both times he had been afraid" (*Bicêtre,* 185). Both of these experiences had been linked to water, sunshine, heat, and fresh smells. One took place on a Sunday in the country as he and his first wife lay stretched out on the sand on the banks of the Loire among the rustling reeds, sleepy from the heat and the wine they had drunk.

"Everything smelled good, the reeds, the earth, the river. The wine also, after it was cooled in the water, had a flavor he never again tasted. He chewed on a blade of grass, lying on his back, his hands under the nape of his neck, his eyes fixed on the blue sky traversed occasionally by a bird in flight. . . . His whole body was filled with peace and well-being" (*Bicêtre,* 154–55).

The second intimation of eternity took place on a boat going to the island of Porquerolles:

> When the boat slid away from its moorings, he stood in the bow, leaning over the transparent water. For a long time he was able to see down to the bottom and for the space of half an hour he lived in music, as though at the heart of a symphony.
>
> That morning was like nothing he had ever experienced since. It was his great discovery of the world, of a boundless, radiant world of bright colors and thrilling sounds. . . . He had often been back to the Mediterranean seacoast. He had seen other seas equally blue, trees and flowers that were more extraordinary, but the magic had gone and of all his discoveries, this was the only one to have left a trace.
>
> Was twice in a lifetime enough? (*Bicêtre,* 158)

Maugras spends several months in the hospital, his physical recovery symbolic of his spiritual and emotional convalescence. He will return to his former life, knowing that for him there is nothing else but with the self-knowledge he lacked formerly. He has reached no great conclusions, only an acceptance of his own flawed but exemplary human self.

At the beginning of *Les volets verts,* "the great Maugin," an aging French actor, is told by a specialist that, at the age of 59, he has the heart of a 75-year-old man. The doctor's diagnosis elicits a great cry of weariness that Maugin had been holding back for so long. "I am tired. T-i-r-e-d! Tired to death. . . . Do you understand?"[23] To the taxi driver who asks him where he wants to go after he has left the doctor's office, he replies: "Anywhere! Anywhere else! Nowhere!" (*Volets,* 47).

The novel traces the last weeks of Maugin's life, interwoven with flashbacks into his past. He had fled from a sordid background—his mother was the town whore and his father an alcoholic—and had worked all his life to become the greatest actor of his time. Now, confronted with death, he finds that it is all unimportant, that he feels no pleasure at having achieved his goals. Simenon maintained that neither the goal to be reached nor success are of any importance, but that it is

> solely the energy we expend, and above all the enthusiasm we expend to reach it that count, no matter what the goal may be. . . . I believe that this is more or less the case with every man who reaches or approaches his goal. He notices quickly that there was only one interesting thing: the pursuit of that goal. And, once having reached the goal, he is faced with a void. Consequently, why should he remain at any post to play the role of a marionette? He now has but one objective: to find simple, down to earth joys . . . to cultivate his garden or to fish . . . It all amounts to the same thing: to find nature once again and everyday life. (Parinaud, 383)

Maugin retires from acting to spend the time left to him fishing at St. Trophez. One day, he catches his foot on a fishhook and it becomes infected. The infection spreads rapidly throughout his body and the doctors are unable to operate because of his heart. In his delirium, Maugin has a dream in which he is on trial, a dream that reflects the guilt at the core of Simenon's being. As the great actor appears before his judges, he recognizes that:

> He was guilty, without the shadow of a doubt. He knew it. He had, in a way, known it all his life. At least he had felt that he was somehow out of line, that something was wrong, something out of gear, something he was more or less consciously struggling against. It was as though he had been swimming with all his might against a violent current to reach some invisible goal, the mainland, or an island, or simply a raft.
>
> He blushed, ashamed. For he had been big and strong. . . . Yet, he had arrived nowhere. He had not attained his goal. . . . What was it that he had been guilty of? Was it to have chosen the wrong goal, to have wanted to be Maugin, always Maugin, a Maugin more and more important? He was going to explain the reason to them, and they would understand.
>
> He had done that in order to escape. Yes! To escape, that was the word. He had spent his life trying to escape. . . . He had fled. . . . Lord God, how many things he had fled from, and how tired he was!
>
> Was that it, at last? Was it the rule to remain, to accept?
>
> Or was he guilty because he had spent his life looking for something that doesn't exist? (*Volets,* 214, 215, 218)

Maugin's feelings of guilt and alienation are common to Simenon's protagonists. They illustrate Albert Camus's premise that, if no one is completely guilty, no one is completely innocent either. It is for this reason that Simenon's spokesman Maigret refuses to judge. And that is why the author himself feels infinite compassion for his characters, in effect the same compassion he seeks for himself on the part of the reader.

As Maugin takes stock of his life, he finds that the long road he traveled has led nowhere. "He had climbed the road too fast, and his heart could stand no more, missed a beat. . . . His body stiffened, as though he were trying to hold himself on his head and his heels, and suddenly he was filled with shame, felt tears welling up, couldn't find his hands to cover his face," as he stammered, just before dying. "Excuse me nurse. . . . I've dirtied my bed" (*Volets,* 220).

The graphic scene of Maugin's agony and death, rivaled in horror only by the final scene of *La veuve Couderc* (see p. 122), is the most unbearable in Simenon's oeuvre. There, the whole of existence is summed up in an image of a man soiling himself. It calls to mind the intense despair of the fifteenth-century poet François Villon as he writes about his wasted life and reminds us that "He who dies, dies in agony. . . . His heart bursts with bile, / Then he sweats, God knows *what* sweat. . . . Death makes him tremble and pale, / Bow his head, constrict his veins / Swell his neck, soften his flesh." Villon also tells us, "There is no one to bring him relief / For he has neither child, nor brother, nor sister / Who would agree to take his place."[24] The intense suffering and solitude of the deathbed, both in Villon's verses and in Simenon's novel, serve as a metaphor for life. This vision of the human condition has led to the description of Simenon's work as a "nightmare described with unbearable artistry."[25]

The ultimate solitude of death is perhaps the only escape possible from the heartrending solitude that Simenon tried so desperately to effect through the medium of fiction. Steve Adams, the protagonist of *Le passage de la ligne,* tells of his alienation:

> I did not belong to any group. Not because I was indifferent or withdrawn, as people insinuated, but because all groups existed outside me. . . . Even as a child, as far back as I can remember, when, for example, they sat me on the doorstep of blue stone, near the water barrel, I was already dreading a moment of the day that I felt approaching with anguish, the moment when the sun would set slowly on the horizon, when you only saw a thin edge of a deeper brown above the earth, and when, suddenly, the universe seemed to stand still. . . . I do not think that it was the idea of the void that affected me so strongly but the notion of immobility, of an immobility that verged on unreality.
>
> In all groups of people with whom I have lived, either by chance or by choice, I felt sooner or later the same agonizing sensation. . . . From one second to the other without my being in any way responsible for it, there occurred a breaking off of contact. The people around me might well

> continue to move about: in my eyes they were no less frozen in place. They would move their lips and the sounds would come to me from another world. The question that arose was then and still invariably is: "What am I doing here?" (*Passage,* 44)

That Adams speaks for his creator is particularly evident when we compare his words with Simenon's direct expression of the same feelings without a fictional character as intermediary:

> I have written a great deal about solitude . . . because I understand it very well, because I experienced it for a long time . . . because I am always afraid of experiencing it again.
>
> I am not speaking of the more or less philosophical solitude of man in the face of a universe that crushes him. Nor am I speaking at present of the impossibility for people to communicate with one another.
>
> In the street, in a train, no matter where, I have always recognized the solitary. They do not walk like other people. One could say that, whether man or woman, there is no joy, no spark in them.
>
> It does not matter whether their steps take them here or there. They do not look at the passersby since they know that they can do nothing for them. I always expect them to raise their hands to their hearts in the characteristic gesture of those with heart disease. (*Homme,* 473)

Simenon uses the outsider, consigned to his role by the societal distinctions of class, religion, or place of birth, as a symbol for the existential solitude and alienation of his protagonists. In the novels set in the United States, the role of outsider is played by the newcomer to a small town. Spencer Ashby, the protagonist of *La mort de Belle,* encounters the hostility of a closely knit community when he moves from his native Vermont to teach in a prep school in his wife's hometown in Connecticut. When their young boarder is raped and murdered, Ashby, the outsider, becomes the prime suspect. His shock at their unjust suspicion makes Ashby feel guilty and he begins to suspect his own spiritual integrity. He becomes obsessed by guilty thoughts of sex and violence and, driven mad by his impotence—a form of sexual deviation common to many of Simenon's characters—Ashby ultimately commits a sadistic murder almost identical to the first. "What [Dostoyevsky] contributed above all, in my opinion," Simenon wrote, "is a new notion of the idea of guilt. Guilt is no longer the simple, clearly defined matter one finds in the penal code but becomes a personal drama that takes place in the individual's soul."[26]

In many of Simenon's novels with French settings, it is the Jew who symbolizes solitude and alienation. The foreigner in the person of the little Jewish tailor appears several times in Simenon's work, but he appears to the greatest effect in *Les fantômes du chapelier* as foil to the murderous hatter M. Labbé. When Labbé enters the café, followed by the little foreign tailor who meekly trails him there each day, no one speaks to the tailor because he is not part of the group. "He had not gone to the same schools, had not been in the same barracks. When the middle-aged card players in the café were already on intimate terms, he was living God knows where in the Near East, where people like him were transported like cattle from Armenia to Smyrna, from Smyrna to Syria, to Greece or elsewhere."[27]

M. Hire, originally Hirovitch, as he is constantly reminded (*Les fiançailles de M. Hire*), born in France of Russian-Jewish parents, becomes the prime suspect when a prostitute is robbed and murdered. He is literally hounded to death by an angry mob, while the real murderer watches. A further variation on the theme of the Jew as the incarnation of alienation can be found in *Le petit homme d'Arkhangelsk.* Jonas Milk, the protagonist of the novel, came to France as a child and grew up there, but he never forgets that he is a "foreigner, a member of another race."[28] In a recurring pattern in Simenon's work, he, the timid loner who is unsure of his masculinity, marries the town slut Gina and continues his quiet, uneventful life, punctuated only by her numerous infidelities. One day Gina disappears, taking with her several rare stamps from Milk's collection. In an instinctive attempt to protect her, Milk tells inquirers that she went to Bourges, adding details as the days pass. Little by little, the questions stop as his formerly friendly neighbors start to believe that he has killed her in a jealous rage. The authorities then decide to open an inquiry. They ask him why he had lied about his wife's going to Bourges, and why he, a Jew, had become a Catholic. As the irrelevant questions pile up, "he is no longer Monsieur Jonas, the bookseller in the square whom everybody greets cheerfully" (*Arkhangelsk,* 201). He has become a foreigner again, he is different from them, something he did not deserve,

> because he had always tried, discreetly, quietly, to live like them, with them, and to be like them. . . . He believed only a few days before that he had succeeded by dint of patience and humility. For he had been humble as well. He did not lose sight of the fact that he was a foreigner, born in far-off Archangel, whom the fortunes of war and revolution had trans-

> planted to a small town in the Berry. . . . [He] had always tried to become integrated. He did not ask the people to recognize him as one of them. He felt that was impossible. He behaved with the discretion of a guest and it was as a guest that he saw himself. (*Arkhangelsk,* 162–63)

Now Milk realizes that the others see him as a foreigner, a Jew, "a solitary, a man from the other end of the world who had come like a parasite to embed himself in the flesh of the Old Market" (*Arkhangelsk,* 211). Although a witness comes forward who saw Gina take off with her lover, Milk hangs himself because he sees that he has always been a stranger to those around him. The unexpected hostility of the neighbors, who he felt were his friends, drives him to suicide (Becker, 2490).

On first reading, *Les fiançailles de M. Hire* and *Le petit homme d'Arkhangelsk* seem to be minor variations on the same theme. Both protagonists are Jews, the Other, and, because of this, both are suspected of crimes they did not commit; both become involved with immoral, unscrupulous women; both are outsiders who watch life go on around them, their separation underscored by Milk's severe myopia: "He had wondered to himself sometimes whether on account of his short-sightedness he saw things and people differently from others. The question intrigued him. . . . Without glasses the world was to him only a more or less luminous cloud in which floated shapes so insubstantial that he could not be sure of being able to touch them. . . . His spectacles, on the other hand, revealed to him the details of objects and faces as if he had been looking at them through a magnifying glass or as if they had been engraved" (*Arkhangelsk,* 125). But there are basic differences between them that make Hire's a deserved solitude, Milk's an existential affliction. Hire is both physically and morally repellent. There is something viscous and unhealthy about him that repels the reader (Wardi, 235). "He wasn't heavy. He was greasy. His bulk was no greater than that of a normal man but you could not perceive in him either bones or flesh, nothing but soft mushy matter, so soft and mushy that it rendered his movements indeterminate."[29] Hire was once arrested on a morals charge. Now he is a confidence man who earns his livelihood by swindling innocent victims. Milk's physical appearance, on the other hand, is perfectly ordinary. He has reddish-blond hair, blue eyes and freckles, and a normal build. He is polite and unassuming and earns his living in the honorable profession of bookseller. His hobby is philately. But, nothing, and this is the desperate realization Simenon made about himself, can remove the ineradicable stigmata of the alienated. And that is why it was necessary for Simenon to debase or destroy the Jew, "[son] semblable [son] frère."[30]

"The drama is that the person finds himself alone and he feels a more and more insistent need to find a place, any place at all, among men," Simenon wrote in 1944.[31] To belong! Somewhere and to someone! That is what Simenon's protagonists seek to accomplish by various means. Some, like Joseph Lambert (*Les complices*), make vain attempts to escape solitude through eroticism. The title itself, suggesting complicity, is ironic, for it serves to bring into relief the ultimate futility of the endeavor. "It was brutal, instantaneous," are the opening words of the novel, which set the mood for the remainder of the work. "And yet," it continues, Lambert "was neither surprised nor resentful, as if he had always been expecting it," having always, like all of Simenon's protagonists, lived in the expectation of disaster.[32] Subliminally, they expect retribution for the crime of existing.

When Lambert sees in his rearview mirror that a huge bus is bearing down on him, he becomes aware that he is driving in the middle of the road. "It did not occur to him to free his hand, which Edmonde continued to press between her thighs. He would not have had time" (*Complices,* 5). The bus swerves on the wet pavement to avoid Lambert's car, leaves the road, crashes into a wall, and bursts into flames, killing the driver, two counselors, and 48 children on their way back to Paris from a summer camp. Lambert flees the holocaust almost instinctively. He thinks of stopping, but he cannot, he is driven forward by uncontrollable panic. He knows, too, that he is assured the silent complicity of Edmonde. Lambert's wordless sexual encounters with Edmonde have at times granted him momentary escape from his isolation into "a universe where all that matters is the quivering of his senses" (*Complices,* 153). These brief moments also confirm that, after a year of the most intimate relationship possible between a man and a woman, he still has no idea of what she is thinking. Failing, after the accident, to find even the fleeting response of Edmonde's body, Lambert kills himself.

In a murder that is essentially a suicide by proxy, Charles Alavoine (*Lettre à mon juge*) kills his lover when he determines that it is impossible to lose oneself in another: "The more she belonged to me, the more I felt her to be mine, the more I judged her worthy of being mine . . . the more I felt the need to consume her even more. To consume her as I, for my part, would have wanted to merge completely with her" (*Juge,* 176).

En cas de malheur tells a story similar to that of *Lettre à mon juge* of a successful professional with an authoritarian, protective wife who finds himself in sensual bondage to a young slut. Maître Gobillot, a Parisian criminal lawyer, meets Yvette when she comes to his office to have him defend her against a charge of robbery. The saying in Paris goes that "if you're innocent, take any good lawyer. If you're guilty, get in touch with Maître Gobillot" (*Malheur,* 25). Yvette is guilty. Using more unscrupulous methods in her defense than is customary even for him, Gobillot secures Yvette's acquittal. In the process, he becomes hopelessly caught by her animal nature:

> I've often slept with girls, both professionals and nonprofessionals and, when I think about it, I realize that they had certain things in common with Yvette. . . . My strongest impulse was probably a craving for pure sex . . . without any considerations of emotion or passion. Let's say sex in its raw state, the need to behave like an animal. I can't be with Yvette for an hour without feeling an urge to see her naked body, to touch her, to ask her to caress me. . . . Yvette . . . personifies for me the female, with her weaknesses, her cowardice, and also with her instinct to cling to the male and make herself his slave. (*Malheur,* 138–39)

"I cannot get along without her. . . . I suffer physically when I am away from her," he concludes (*Malheur,* 141). Gobillot's frenzied sensuality is prompted by a desire to escape and lose himself in another. As is inevitable, he is awakened from this impossible dream when Yvette is killed by her jealous young lover.

La chambre bleue reads like a cautionary tale designed to illustrate the fatal ravages of an overwhelming sexual obsession. The story is told from the point of view of the protagonist, Tony Falcone; his memories of the events alternate with his replies to an examining magistrate. The blue room of the title is the hotel room in which the two married lovers, Tony and Andrée, met secretly over a period of 11 months, their trysts described in the most detailed, sexually graphic scenes in Simenon's work. For Tony, an uncomplicated virile man who truly loves his wife, it was nothing more than a particularly intense sexual affair, but, for her, as he discovers too late, it was a much more serious matter. One night, Andrée's husband dies, presumably of natural causes since he was sickly and subject to epileptic fits. Andrée harasses Tony with urgent letters, while Tony, who loves his wife and daughter, becomes increasingly frightened of her. One day his wife asks him to pick up a few items at Andrée's grocery store. Andrée adds a jar of jam to the order, which she claims had been ordered weeks before. Tony delivers the groceries and goes to work. When he returns home that evening, he finds his wife dead, poisoned by strychnine in the jam, and he is arrested for her murder. The police then decide to exhume the body of Andrée's husband. It, too, contains poison. Convicted of murder, the lovers are condemned to life imprisonment at hard labor, the innocent Tony a victim of a miscarriage of justice, the inevitable consequence, as Simenon maintained throughout his work, of the imperfection of the French legal system and the weakness of the judicial process. As they are led away, the obsessed Andrée cries out triumphantly: "You see, Tony, we'll never be parted now!"[33]

There is no escape from solitude for Simenon's alienated protagonists. In only five novels in Simenon's vast oeuvre do the characters succeed in linking their lives to another.[34] All of the other works contain endless variations on the theme of the failure of the couple, from the sexual bondage of Alavoine and Gobillot to the devouring of the hapless Tony Falcone—his fate like that of the mate of the praying mantis—to the misalliance of the couples in a score of novels, among them *Antoine et Julie* and *Le confessionnal,* to the hatred of the elderly couple in *Le Chat,* and, finally, to the detestation leading to murder in *L'escalier de fer* and *Dimanche.* A recurring image symbolizing this failure is that of the suddenly empty home. The husband returns one day to find that his wife has abandoned him. It happens to Dave Galloway (*L'horloger d'Everton*) in Connecticut, to Jonas Milk (*Le petit homme d'Arkhangelsk*) in a small town in the Berry, to M. Monde (*La fuite de Monsieur Monde*) in Paris, to Loursat (*Les inconnus dans la maison*) in Moulins, and to Cardinaud (*Le fils Cardinaud*) in Les Sables-d'Olonne. At first, all of these men are bewildered by a seemingly inexplicable abandonment but, as they weigh the matter, they find that it was the culmination of a long misunderstanding that only their blindness had hidden from them.

When the wife of Célerin, the protagonist of *Les innocents,* is run over and killed by a bus—a form of violent death that occurs in a number of novels—he thinks back on his life and concludes that he had lived with his wife for 20 years without ever having known her. She had never spoken about herself; in truth, he had never been more than a stranger to her, a stranger who shared her bed. To find out more about his wife and their marriage, he goes to the site of the accident and there, in a neighboring hotel, he makes the shattering discovery that, for 18 of the 20 years of his marriage, when he had been the happiest man in the world, his wife had been his best friend's mistress.

Like Célerin, Jeantet (*Le veuf*) had no more of a premonition of his wife's abandonment "than travelers on a train who eat in the dining car, read, talk, doze, or watch the countryside go by a few instants before the catastrophe."[35] Only after his wife commits suicide does he see that his marriage had been a disaster, that he had stifled her with his so-called goodness. He had married a prostitute, for it was "necessary for him that she be guilty, ashamed, and miserable because he could not have endured to live with a normal wife" (*Veuf,* 183). Jeantet belongs to the group of men in Simenon's novels who cannot be part of a successful couple because they are insecure in their masculinity. Filled with doubt and self-hatred, they are able to relate only to soiled women to whom they can feel superior. The protagonist of *Le temps d'Anaïs,* like Jeantet, is impotent other than with prostitutes or with his wife, one of the nymphomaniacs in Simenon's cast of sexual deviants. He had never considered himself to be a real man sexually and tells the psychiatrist that he was pleased that his wife was what she was and that she degraded herself by sleeping with anyone. His contempt for her lessened to a certain extent the contempt he felt for himself.

In general, there is no open conflict between husband and wife in the novels. They go on with their daily lives with barely disguised hostility until the silent discord occasionally erupts into murder, as happens in *Dimanche.* After years of adapting to a marriage of convenience with a domineering woman, Emile begins an affair with a domestic at the hotel owned by his wife. After the oppression he experiences in his marriage, he is revived by the joy of sexual passion. When his wife finds out about the relationship, she subjects him to constant humiliation until he decides he must kill her. "It is claimed that a man can live a long time without eating or drinking. It is more difficult to live without one's pride and his wife had taken it away."[36] Many murders in Simenon's work, in the Maigrets as well as in the romans durs, are motivated by such wounded pride. Donald Dodd (*La main*) ultimately kills the perfect wife whose self-righteousness has humiliated him throughout their marriage. "I understood the look my wife gave me. As always, there was no reproach. Not even a silent warning. It was a special kind of look, and I had seen it over and over again through the years, probably since we had known each other. In that look lay a whole catalog of indictments. . . . Was I afraid of that look of hers? Just as, when I was a child, I had been afraid to meet my mother's eyes."[37]

While Dodd kills spontaneously when pushed beyond endurance, Emile meticulously plans his actions and waits for the propitious moment to enact a perfect crime. An even more cunning counteraction on his wife's part provides the surprise ending that is unusual in

Simenon's fiction. Berthe, with the intuition of a mother who anticipates her child's misbehavior, guesses that Emile has poisoned her lunch and forces the young woman to eat it instead. Emile sees Berthe standing over her as she eats, and her look tells Emile that he had better not intervene. "He sought for a plausible reason to leave as soon as all the customers had been served. He could find none. He lacked lucidity. Then, there was Berthe standing in the doorway. . . . 'You haven't forgotten the football match,' Berthe was saying in a natural voice. . . . Berthe was right. It was high time to leave for Cannes and to mingle with the crowd attending the football match. She would see to everything. It was better that way. When he came back, it would be all over" (*Dimanche,* 244).

Murder is also the way in which Etienne Lomel's wife, Louise (*L'escalier de fer*), intends to free herself of him in order to marry her young lover. As Lomel makes daily note of his symptoms, he realizes that he is suffering the fate of Louise's first husband, that he, too, is being poisoned. He also knows that he inadvertently shared responsibility for the murder. When he was Louise's lover, he had signed the man's death warrant by answering yes when she asked whether he would marry her if she were free. That is why he is not outraged when he sees the situation being repeated. When he discovers the identity of his wife's lover, he feels neither anger nor a desire for vengeance but decides that he must kill him in order to regain her love. He finally confronts the young man but turns the gun on himself instead, aware that Louise will always be denied him and that he must pay for his tacit consent to the murder of her first husband.

The motives for Louise's actions are comprehensible, but those of Bébé Donge can be grasped only if we see them in the light of Simenon's despair at the impossibility of human communion. One Sunday, Bébé attempts to poison her husband, François, because he has not been able to recognize the exceptional nature of her love for him. While Bébé is being held for trial, François recognizes that he erred in marrying a young girl, "bringing her into a house and then abandoning her to her solitude. Not even her own solitude! Solitude in an alien atmosphere which can seem hostile!"[38] How absurd it had been to waste the 10 best years of their lives hurting one another, living side by side without mutual understanding, he reflects. Had he been a monster not to have seen all that before or was he was merely an ordinary, fallible man? While he had misunderstood her to the point of hating her, "she had loved him to the point of total despair. And he had noticed nothing"

(*Bébé Donge,* 218). When Bébé leaves at the end of the trial to serve her five-year prison term, François is no longer the same man. He has decided to wait for her to see whether married love can indeed be a spiritual meeting of souls, although Bébé has told him that it is too late, that she had waited and hoped for too long.

Alcohol proves to be as illusory an escape from solitude as the delusion of human communion. For Alavoine (*Lettre à mon juge*), the need to find in alcohol surcease from an existential intuition of the emptiness of life is a sign of election. "I will not say that those who drink are the best, but they are at the very least those who have glimpsed something they could not attain, the lack of which pained them in the depths of their innermost being, something perhaps that my father and I stared at that evening when we were both sitting at the bottom of the haystack, our pupils reflecting the colorless sky" (*Juge,* 34).

Alcohol is also the means by which Antoine (*Antoine et Julie*) attempts to flee the loneliness and boredom of his existence. What he seeks when he drinks is "that contact, that way of looking at humanity and of feeling at one with it."[39] At times, Antoine would stretch out his hand to touch a table or a wall, "to assure himself of their stability, but that would not reassure him about himself. If the world really existed, he still had to find out what he was doing in it and what those people around him were doing who put so much seriousness, so much feeling, into their actions" (*Antoine,* 155). Antoine is never at peace with himself. When drinking he can achieve an illusion of harmony, but the rest of the time he perceives that "a man is worth nothing at all. What counts is to put on an act. . . . As for him, what difference would it make since inside it would always be the same thing. The same thing, that is, nothing" (*Antoine,* 171–72).

To escape their separateness and isolation, some characters seek to live vicariously through others; they are voyeurs who attempt to enter into the lives of those they observe. M. Hire, who is sexually impotent, hides in the darkness of his room to watch a young woman undress in the building on the other side of the street. Jonas Milk, similarly, lives through his neighbors: "The truth is that he lived intensely, in his inner self, a rich and varied life, the life of the entire Old Market, the entire neighborhood of which he knew the minutest movements. . . . Behind the shelter of his thick spectacles, which seemed to isolate him and give him an inoffensive air, was it not rather as if he had stolen the lives of the others, without their noticing it?" (*Arkhangelsk,* 125). And Kees Popinga dreams of adventure as he observes the trains go by and imagines the lives of the fortunate passengers. In *Les gens d'en face,* the Turkish consul in Soviet Batoum, isolated in a hostile environment, is spied on by a couple from the windows across the way, his every movement reflected in their eyes.

But the attempt to live vicariously proves as illusory an escape from solitude as any in Simenon's work, a failure strikingly manifest in *La fenêtre des Rouet.* Dominique Salès, the protagonist of the novel and the most desperately alienated of all of Simenon's characters, observes with intense yearning the lives of others around her as she tries to share them in order to escape from her own existence.

Dominique grew up in a milieu where everything pertaining to the body was consigned to silence, where sickness was never called by its name and words like childbirth "were never uttered to clarify the picture; everything always took place in a world in half-tones, where people only appeared washed, combed, smiling or melancholy."[40] Dominique has never lived and now, at the age of 39, she is a virgin sitting eternally at her window in the faubourg Saint-Honoré darning socks that are as unremittingly gray as her life, and watching life go on in the street below. "Everything was alive around her and there was nothing but her heart beating in a void like an alarm clock forgotten in a trunk" (*Rouet,* 181). And she wonders: "Was that what life was all about? A bit of heedless childhood, a brief adolescence, then nothingness, a tangle of worries, troubles, minor, trifling cares, and already, at the age of 40, the feeling of old age, of a joyless downward path" (*Rouet,* 175).

Dominique peers through the keyhole of the door leading to the room that she has rented to a newlywed couple and watches them make love. "When she comes close to the brown door where the key is on her side, she becomes aware that they seem to breathe as one. . . . It's strange that she has come to need them" (*Rouet,* 28). Dominique also watches the house of the Rouets across the street as she mentally supplies the dialogue for the dumb show of their lives taking place in front of windows open to the suffocating heat of summer.

The Rouets are a wealthy bourgeois family. Their sickly son married a young, vibrant, lower-class woman, a misalliance that seals his fate as surely as it does that of all those in Simenon's oeuvre who marry out of their class. One day, Dominique sees Antoinette Rouet commit a crime; she kills her husband by withholding his heart medicine. It seems somehow to Dominique that the scene taking place before her eyes avenges her for her own frustrated, repressed life. She identifies with Antoinette and her desire to live life to the full. She would have liked to say to

Antoinette: "It was life that drove you on, you needed to live . . . you did everything for that reason . . . [If necessary] you would have done even more" (*Rouet,* 119).

Now Dominique begins to live exclusively through Antoinette. She observes her constantly, she follows her, she shares her trysts as she waits outside the hotels in which Antoinette meets her lovers, she feels the other woman's pleasure and then her pain as she is ultimately rejected. As she stalks Antoinette through the streets of Paris, "she pretends to see nothing around her, and yet, like a thief, she snatches at the life that is taking place beside her. . . . Furtive, aware of her humiliation, she rubs shoulders with the crowd, which she inhales" (*Rouet,* 178).

Dominique shares the ambivalent feelings of Simenon's other characters. She is drawn by a desperate hunger for life, the "vibrant, forbidden life" (*Rouet,* 82) Antoinette represents while, at the same time, she is gripped by a fierce longing for nothingness, for death, which here assumes the guise of a poor old spinster named Augustine. In an interesting play of mirrors, Augustine watches Dominique and her newlywed tenants from her attic window across the street, just as Dominique watches the Rouets. And we know from an erotic dream Dominique has about Augustine just after the woman dies, that it is she who will win the battle raging within Dominique. And so, one day, after donning the nightgown that had been designed long before for the wedding night she had dreamed of, Dominique strews her bed with roses and takes a fatal dose of sleeping pills.

One voyeur in Simenon's oeuvre, Simenon's alter ego Louis Cuchas (*Le petit saint*), is an artist who stands in for the author; he successfully draws sustenance for his art from everything around him. He is content in his creation and unmindful of his solitude. That Simenon makes his hero an artist rather than a writer is incidental, since the process by which he transforms his experiences into art is the same as the one used by Simenon in writing. The novel takes its name from the epithet, "little saint," applied to the protagonist by his schoolmates because of his serene detachment and the "quiet and almost continuous satisfaction" that his smile reflects. "A gentle smile, without irony, without meanness, without aggressiveness, a smile that someone once compared to that of Saint Medard, whose church stood at the bottom of the street. He was happy, he watched, he went from one discovery to another, but . . . he made no effort to understand. He was content with contemplating a fly on the plaster wall or drops of water rolling down the windowpane."[41] That Louis is Simenon as a boy is evident when we compare his childhood role of voyeur with that of Simenon's avowed alter ego, the child Roger in *Pedigree.* Roger and a friend are sitting on the ground playing with bits of gravel, while his mother and her friend are seated on a bench near them chatting. Then, in "a moment that was to remain engraved forever in a certain memory," Roger, who has just knocked over his bucket of gravel,

> looks over at the bench. The picture he sees, the bit of life that offers itself to his gaze, the smell of the square, the fluidity of the air, the yellow bricks of the house on the corner—all the other bricks in the neighborhood are red or pink—Godard's empty butcher's shop on the opposite corner, the newly regrouted wall of the church youth club that blocks the end of the Rue Pasteur, all that constitutes his first conscious vision of the world, the first scene that would accompany him, just as it was then, through life.
>
> His mother will always be that woman he sees from below, still dressed in black, as of today in half-mourning brightened by the lace collar around her neck, a jabot that puffs out on her chest and is held in place by a locket, lace at her wrists, a bareheaded woman with very fair hair that curls and quivers in the March breeze. (*Pedigree* 1:153)

The world Louis observes, transformed by his vision, is the poverty-stricken but vibrant life of the working class on the rue Mouffetard in Paris at the turn of the century. Louis lives in one room with his mother and four brothers and sisters, all sired by different men. The children sleep on mattresses lined up side by side on the floor, separated by a hanging sheet from the high walnut bed occupied by their mother and her current lover (Becker, 2497–98). The children observe their mother and her lovers through a hole in the sheet and their actions are copied incestuously by the oldest brother and sister. Louis "likes the room that is divided in half by the bedsheet that hangs from a rod, he likes the smell of the mattresses lined up side by side, the portrait of his mother in a white veil and of a man with a blond mustache, the patches of wallpaper, particularly the one of the girl on a swing. He likes, above all, the warmth that the stove gives off in waves, in blasts, the way it roars at times, the glowing ashes that suddenly collapse into the drawer at the bottom" (*Saint,* 21–22). The feeling is one of warmth and security in that room in which they live "with one another as in a burrow, sheltered from the outside world, and come what may, their mother is there to protect them" (*Saint,* 118).

The mother is a warm woman, working hard for her children, getting up before dawn to push a cart across Paris to les Halles to buy the vegetables she resells from a pushcart in her neighborhood. She takes things as they come, "enjoying what is good in life, contenting herself uncomplainingly with what is less good, and ignoring the rest as if it did not exist" (*Saint,* 199).

Louis observes silently; he wants to see, smell, and touch everything about him. He develops the habit of accompanying his mother to les Halles in search of new experiences:

> There were vegetables, fruit, poultry, cases of eggs, everywhere, on the sidewalks, in the gutter, all over the storehouse, and everything was moving, was heaped in one place and transported to another.
>
> Figures were shouted out. People were writing on black pads with violet pencils. Market porters wearing big hats and carrying a side of beef on their shoulders rushed through the streets. Tubs were overflowing with guts. Women sitting on stools were plucking poultry with the rapidity of magicians.
>
> It all looked chaotic, but he would soon learn that, for all the apparent disorder, every wagon, every crate, every cauliflower, every rabbit, every man had a definite place and a precise job. (*Saint,* 99–100)

Louis goes there "in order to renew the wonder of it, to complete his set of exciting images, for example, that of the Seine. . . . He was constantly discovering images, yellow and green housefronts, signboards, nooks crowded with barrels" (*Saint,* 104). He notices that his mother is not engrossed as he is in the spectacle of the street. "She even crosses the Seine at the Pont Saint-Michel without being aware of the color of the light that day or whether there is a current in the water, and never even looks at the towers of Notre-Dame" (*Saint,* 123).

Louis's preoccupation with visual images prepares him for his metamorphosis into a great painter. The images he stores up will appear on his canvases. As he begins to paint, he is haunted by the desire to employ pure colors. "He never felt that they were limpid enough, vibrant enough. He would have liked to see them quiver. . . . What he would have liked to get down on canvas was reality itself, as he saw it, or rather as it composed itself spontaneously in his mind" (*Saint,* 168, 177). He was constantly seeking to capture "a certain sparkle . . . the quivering space between objects" (*Saint,* 218).

Years later, when asked the reasons for his success, Louis wonders, with the guilt of the voyeur: "Had he not taken something from everything and everyone? Had he not used their substance? He did not know, he mustn't know, otherwise he would be unable to carry on to the end" (*Saint,* 244).

Louis's painting is merely Simenon's fiction in another medium, the means by which the author was able for brief periods to escape from his solitude and live through others. For, as Simenon explained, "The novel is not solely an art, even less so a profession. It is above all a passion that takes hold of you completely, that enslaves you. It is a need, in a word the need perhaps to escape from yourself, to live just as you like, at least for a while, in a world of your own choosing. Who knows whether or not it is even more and above all *a means to exorcise your demons by giving them a form and casting them out into the world.* . . . The novel is not only all that, in reality, for the one who writes, it is Salvation" ("Romancier,"103).

Chapter Four
"Romans durs"—Exotic Novels

"Exotic novels" is the name given to a group of Simenon's romans durs situated in Africa, South America, Tahiti, and the Galapagos, but all of his novels, whatever their locale, delve to the heart of human experience—the easy slide into depression, or unbridled sexuality, or drugs, or alcohol; the hard, if not impossible, struggle back out. Simenon used these tropical landscapes as background in these novels, but Simenon is not a writer like Joseph Conrad or Somerset Maugham for whom the exoticism of foreign places allows for a heightened or different existence and for the illusion of liberation. On the contrary, he underlines the fact that wherever one travels, one takes oneself along, and that always limits the possibilities for transcendence. The exotic decors in Simenon's novels become, in effect, Simenon's own inner landscapes, settings for the presentation of his usual characters and themes.

Eschewing any of the exotic attractions of the tropics, Simenon chose only those elements that confirmed his assertion that "there is no such thing as exoticism. When you are *over there,* whether in Africa, Asia, or in the equatorial forest, you immediately become accustomed to the landscape and a tree is a tree, whether it is called an oak, a mango, or a coconut tree; a passerby is a passerby, white or black, dressed in cloth or simply in a few strands of dried grass. Man becomes accustomed to everything . . ."(*Etoile,* 31). According to Simenon, if you do away with picturesque elements, most tropical adventures assume a tragic aspect, "a day-to-day tragedy, heavy as the sky, thick as the forest, a nightmarish tragedy, an oppression, the emptiness of the mind and the soul before a landscape that is always the same, that remains forever alien and where, nonetheless, you must die, knowing that there is in France, a village, a city in which. . . ."(*Etoile,* 68).

But this ubiquitous "everyday tragedy," this "emptiness of the mind and the soul" that he discerns in the tropics, reflects Simenon's weltanschauung and exists to the same degree within all of the characters in all of his works. Just as Baudelaire's "Tableaux parisiens" presented only the horrors and misery of Paris, with death stalking the unwary walker at every turn, so also do Simenon's tropics reflect his personal vision that ignores all of the splendor of the tropics and sets forth only the dismal, hostile aspects. Mythical exotic paradises become, in Simenon's oeuvre, morasses of unrelenting rain and intolerable heat, decay, deterioration, tropical diseases, filth, cannibalism, poisonous snakes, and myriads of "swarming insects, strange flies, flying scorpions, hairy spiders."[1] In *L'heure du Nègre,* a series of articles published after his return from Africa, Simenon wrote:

> . . . nature is sad. The African sun is a trap. It is gray, as implacable as a stormy sky. The virgin forest is also gray, and gray, too, drab in any case, in the light over there, are the most vivid flowers of the equatorial forest. . . . the sadness of all of Africa, of the trees, rivers, animals, the sadness even emerges from the sight of the monstrous continent reproduced on a map. . . . They speak about the lush vegetation? Pardon! What is lush, what overruns everything is the creepers, the parasites of all sorts that form a sinister and impenetrable mass.[2]

A veritable inventory of tropical horrors can be found in one of the articles of *La mauvaise étoile* titled "The Man Who Fought Rats or the Most Banal of Stories," in which Simenon describes the conditions leading to the tragic death—either by suicide or murder—of a young engineer:

> For hours and for days on end, the rain falls in tepid sheets, inundates the landscape, and, as soon as the lemon-colored sun appears behind the solid curtain of clouds, steam rises from the ground while human lungs dilate in vain and breathing is difficult.
>
> It is evening. Small streams of water have entered the hut and mildew eats into the boots, covers everything made of leather. The papers spread out on the desk are soft, like wet cloths. . . . The man, half naked because of the heat that makes his skin glisten with sweat, writes as he pants, stopping after each sentence. . . ."You must act quickly, I beg of you. Let D . . . bring me a large quantity of antiscorbutic syrup without delay and an even larger quantity of parts. . . . Bed bugs, rats, stifling heat, sleepless night. Here, the rats are winning. It is a real scalp dance. I have just killed two, but there are one hundred of them and I dare not extinguish the light. . . ." (*Etoile,* 34–35)

This young engineer is one of those whom Simenon names "les ratés de l'aventure" (adventure's failures). They were men "who were greedy for a broader, freer, more beautiful life and who did not hesitate to leave everything to court adventure. . . . men who left full of life, of vigor, of hope, and of plans, whom the tropics reduced to such a state that. . . ."

(*Etoile,* 14). Still, while the unmerciful rain, heat, insects, and diseases of the tropics destroy them quickly and relentlessly, Simenon's "adventure's failures" are, in reality, not different from his other protagonists. Similar lives are played out in French villages and cities, where men who have never left home sink into alcoholism, madness, and suicide—only the catalyst is different. In more than a third of all of Simenon's novels one finds suicides; madmen, alcoholics, and tramps are ubiquitous. Like virtually all of the characters in the author's universe, they are distinguished by an absence of will. They do not direct their own lives. Instead, they are carried along by forces stronger than themselves; they watch helplessly as they are crushed beneath the weight of pressures too heavy to bear.

When Joseph Timar, the protagonist of *Le coup de lune,* arrives in Gabon, determined to make his fortune in the colonies, he appears to be a likely candidate for success. But his basic character flaws become evident almost immediately after he discovers that the company that hired him is on the verge of bankruptcy, that the job is a 10-day's boat journey away in the heart of the forest, and that, even were he to find a way to get there, his actions would be futile since the post is still occupied by a demented old man who threatens to greet his replacement with a shot to the head. "Then, it was no longer the anguish of homesickness that gripped his heart, it was the anguish of uselessness. Useless to be there! Useless to struggle against the sun that penetrated all his pores! Useless to swallow each evening that quinine that nauseated him! Useless to live and to die, to be buried in a makeshift cemetery by half-naked Negroes" (*Lune,* 67). Incapable of seeking a solution to his problems, Timar retreats into alcohol, remaining "seated at times for hours in the same chair, staring straight ahead of him, without thinking!" (*Lune,* 88). In his drunken lethargy, he becomes a pawn in the hands of Adèle, the proprietress of his hotel. His submission to a dominant, manipulative, murderous female results not from his presence in the tropics; it occurs similarly among weak-willed men throughout Simenon's work.

Adèle convinces Timar to use his family's connections to obtain a lumbering concession, for which she will supply the capital. His association with Adèle, whose shooting of a native has caused an uproar in the colony, has cut the young man off from the colonial authorities. Incapable of independent action and in sexual thrall to Adèle, he follows her into the interior to the concession. There, heat, drink, fever, and his own lack of will destroy him completely. After denouncing Adèle as the murderer at a trial that had been rigged to frame a poor native, Timar is shipped back to

France, half-mad, muttering: "But there's no such place as Africa!" (*Lune,* 183). The Africa to which he refers—the mythical mysterious dark continent of colonial recruitment posters and romantic travel literature, "the so-called mysterious Africa"[3]—*that* Africa does not exist.

There are others, again like many of their counterparts in France, who become alcoholics and tramps but with a difference. Simenon pointed out in *La mauvaise étoile* that, compared with the lot of "adventure's failures," the gentle fate of the failures in France seems enviable: "They eat. They live. They have a family, or in-laws, or relatives, or children. Some become embittered. Most of them drink. The days pass all the same, bringing with them their hopes and small pleasures" (*Etoile,* 11). The fate of Joseph Dupuche in Panama (*Quartier Nègre*) provides a striking illustration of this difference.

When Dupuche, a young, provincial French engineer, arrives in Panama with his bride of two weeks, he, like Timar in Africa, discovers that the company that hired him in Paris has gone bankrupt and that his letters of credit are worthless. Alone and penniless, he and his wife Germaine turn to the white community, which is composed in large part of ex-convicts and shady entrepreneurs. She is hired as cashier and given a room in the French-owned hotel and he, unable to find employment, is lodged in the native quarter. Germaine survives and prospers, but is unable to save her husband, who is fated to fail. "He had something against Germaine without knowing precisely what. On the other hand, yes he did! Until their marriage, above all when they were engaged and he was studying in Paris, she looked upon him as the strongest, as the most intelligent person. But no sooner were they aboard, than she began to say: 'Don't do this . . . Say hello to the captain. . . . You are wrong to. . . . ' "[4] Now Germaine sees that he is weak and humiliates him when she orders him to refrain from visiting her when he has been drinking. Dupuche then becomes involved with a young native girl and, like so many of his counterparts in France, finds that he prefers an instinctive, earthy woman who poses no threat to his masculinity. Like the mildly retarded servant Ada in *Dimanche* (see p. 84), his lover is both "his pet dog and his slave at the same time. She did not judge him, did not try to understand him or guess what he was thinking. She had adopted him as a master, just as a stray dog, for no apparent reason, attaches itself to the heels of a passer-by" (*Dimanche,* 104). Driven by weakness, insecurity, and inadequacy, an inordinately large number of Simenon's protagonists are able to relate only to stupid or promiscuous women to whom they can feel superior.

Dupuche becomes addicted to the mind-numbing native alcoholic drink, "chichà," a drink prepared by Indian women who chew corn for hours and spit it, mixed with their saliva, into a receptacle of baked clay (*Quartier Nègre,* 88). His alcoholism, nonetheless, was inevitable. He drinks because he has always been ill at ease in life; even in France he always felt out of place, he never belonged. Alcohol provides him with an escape from loneliness—permitting him to live "in himself! . . . He was sufficient unto himself . . ." (*Quartier Nègre,* 194).

As Dupuche sinks lower and lower, he ceases to feel any humiliation. In a perpetual alcoholic stupor, he becomes indifferent to everything, scorning all social life and all socially acceptable behavior. He dies 10 years later of acute blackwater fever "after having realized his ambition: to live in a hut at the water's edge behind the railroad, among the rank weeds and the refuse" (*Quartier Nègre,* 207). It seems paradoxical to regard Dupuche's degradation as the realization of a lifelong ambition, unless we consider the fact that Simenon admires what he sees as the tramp's strength of character that permits him to live as he chooses, responsible only to himself (see p. 18).

Another exemplary destiny of "adventure's failures" is that of Oscar Donadieu, who dies a suicide in *Touriste de bananes.* "Banana tourist," Simenon explained, is the contemptuous epithet applied to those of all classes and all countries who go to the tropics, "the Adams of Chicago and the Eves of Manchester and Oslo in the new earthly paradises" (*Etoile,* 56):

> One fine day when they were disgusted with their mediocrity, or frightened by impending destitution, someone told them: "In the islands, you can still live as if it were heaven on earth, without money, without clothes, without worrying about tomorrow . . ."
>
> They sold everything to pay their passage. When they debarked, the prudent authorities, who had often been burned before, required them to deposit enough money for their return fare. . . .
>
> The next day, every good banana tourist has already bought a paréo and a straw hat. Half-naked . . . he strides off toward the endless beaches.
>
> He is evidently a bit astonished to see that the natives are wearing detachable collars and are riding bicycles and he is indignant when buses full of Kanaka Indians pass him on the road. (*Etoile,* 57)

The suicide of Oscar Donadieu, however, was as inexorably preordained by his nature as was the madness of Timar and the alcoholic undoing of Dupuche. His naive search for innocence led him to Tahiti, but the "noble savage" does not exist. Overwhelmed by the sordidness and corruption he discovers there, Oscar kills himself after spending the night with Tamatéa, a Tahitian prostitute. The hysterical shrieks of Tamatéa, who has awakened in a pool of blood, convey the horror of Simenon's tropical hell, with the ever-present sleazy bar-hotel run by an escaped convict, the colonial club where the colonists drink themselves into daily stupors, the intense heat, tropical fevers, deadly insects, and rats (Becker, 2500).

The fate of the protagonist Ferdinand Graux in the novel *Le blanc à lunettes* suggests that the tropics are not necessarily an implacable enemy and that inner strength independent of external influences—as illustrated in France by Louis Cuchas (*Le petit saint,* see pp. 88–91)—can overcome the ill fortune meted out to those who have succumbed to their fate. Still, Simenon is unable to abandon his archetypal divided and homicidal couple; in this novel they play secondary roles. The husband, Georges Bodet, driven mad by heat, drink, and failure, fires at his wife and kills himself. Yet their fate was sealed even before their arrival in Africa. On board ship crossing the Mediterranean, Georges Bodet constantly drank himself into a stupor. His furious impatience with his wife's vulgarity, her piercing voice, her nagging, and her repeated shrill enjoinders to stop his excessive drinking presage the tragic denouement of their tropical adventure.

Graux, a French coffee planter in the Belgian Congo, possesses the force of character and basic equilibrium prerequisite for success, a rare exception in all of Simenon's work and most particularly in his exotic novels. As the novel opens, Graux is returning from home leave. When he arrives at his plantation, he learns that a private plane carrying a young English noblewoman, Lady Mackinson, and the pilot, Captain Philps, made a forced landing on his property. The couple belong to a parasitic social class seen frequently in the Maigrets, who travel from one grand hotel to another in an effort to escape their boredom through drugs, alcohol, and sexual promiscuity. Lady Mackinson's sexual freedom is misunderstood by Graux, who falls desperately in love with her after a night together. She is unaffected by their encounter and leaves without hesitation to rejoin her husband and children in Constantinople. Enslaved by sexual obsession, Graux follows her.

During Graux's absence, his fiancée, Emmeline, alarmed by the tone of his letters, flies to the Congo and takes over the management of the plantation as she awaits his return. And he does return; he is able to overcome his sexual obsession. "Did it make any sense to attach so much importance to what was nothing more than a chance encounter? And to change one's ideas completely! To lose one's head over it! To have thoughts of which he, himself, was ashamed. . . . For he had gone so far as to think that his whole life had just changed! For what? For an hour's sweaty embrace! For a gesture without beauty!"[5] In the journal he keeps of his fugue, Graux writes: "I wonder what would happen if I didn't possess an instinctive need for equilibrium. . . . What pushed me to come to Istanbul whatever the cost? I thought I was irresistibly driven toward catastrophe of one sort of another. . . . I even began to hallucinate, to think of mass murder. . . . I even thought myself capable of living forever in her wake. . . . Romanticism" (*Blanc,* 209–10).

"Life is a serious matter" (*Blanc,* 212) for Graux and Emmeline. Unlike the naive, so-called "touristes de bananes," they are pursuing a realistic goal. Seeking neither a mythical tropical paradise, nor an escape from intolerable pressures in France, nor a great fortune, they are like those who cultivate the land everywhere in the world by dint of patience and hard work. An atypical character in Simenon's oeuvre, Graux is patterned on the only planter who did not fail among all those whom Simenon claims to have met during his travels: "In the heart of the Congo, I have another friend who left one day with a small inheritance and who set up a model plantation three hundred kilometers from any village. He lives there, the only white among three or four hundred blacks. Elephants replace tractors there. He produces a substantial amount of coffee. He built an infirmary and takes care of his men and delivers the women's babies. . . . Only, as he told me the evening we dined together on his veranda, he just makes ends meet and he will have to save for five or six years to pay for a trip to Europe" (*Etoile,* 145–46).

Other than this exception, all others conform to Simenon's pessimistic view of people and of their chances for success or happiness. An excellent illustration of this is Simenon's choice of protagonists in the novel *Ceux de la soif,* which takes place on the island of Floreana in the Galapagos islands off the coast of Ecuador. In this novel, a bourgeois expatriate couple, much like Graux and Emmeline, work hard and succeed. But Simenon dismisses them as unworthy of note. He describes them as very ordinary people "who were born to get along somehow on the banks of the Rhine and to drink hot chocolate on Sundays in *Conditorei.*"[6] The real prototypes of this couple, Margret and Heinz Wittmer (Herrmanns in the novel), whom Simenon did meet in the Galapagos, are discounted because they are not his stereotypical failures. The Wittmers, in truth, built a home for themselves and for their children on a remote island, struggling against an often hostile nature and in the face of insuperable odds. Their success, however, contradicts Simenon's proposition that "every enterprise of this type is doomed to failure" (*Soif,* 174). "A few men tried to live in the archipelago (Galapagos)," he wrote elsewhere, "but met there implacable enemies, insuperable solitude, and uncompromising tropical nature" (*Drame,* 27).

It is interesting to note the way in which Simenon combines fact and fiction in *Ceux de la soif*—transforming real-life experiences in order to support his own biases—by comparing it with seven newspaper articles he wrote in 1935 for *Paris-Soir,* titled *Le drame mystérieux des îles Galapagos,* and Margret Wittmer's autobiographical work *Floreana.*[7] All three tell basically the same story. In 1932, Margret Wittmer, her husband Heinz, and her 12-year-old stepson Harry migrated to Floreana in the hope that the climate would be salubrious for the tubercular boy. Two other Germans had been living there for three years, Dr. Karl Friedrich Ritter (Müller in the novel) and his disciple Frau Dore Strauch (Rita).[8] Dr. Ritter, a dental surgeon, suddenly left Berlin in 1929 to live in accordance with a new "nature philosophy" on Floreana, away from the world that he despised. A vegetarian, Ritter lived entirely on what he grew himself; he practiced nudism and intended to prove that one could reach the age of 140 by living according to the laws of nature.

A few months after the Wittmers' arrival on Floreana, there appeared on the island a small slim woman of about 40 riding on a donkey, accompanied by two men, both of whom were her lovers. The woman introduced herself as the Baroness Wagner-Philipson (la comtesse von Kleber), the young man as Herr Lorenz (Kraus), and the other man as her husband, a German Robert Philipson. In the novel, Philipson becomes Nic Arenson, the unsavory, corrupt stereotypical Jew found all too frequently throughout Simenon's oeuvre.

The baroness informs them that she intends to build a hotel on Floreana for American millionaires, to be called Hacienda Paradiso (l'Hôtel du Retour à la Nature in Simenon's novel). It becomes evident from the outset that the woman is mad. Her actions, as described in all three accounts of the drama, become increasingly more bizarre, provoking Ritter, who despises her, to write to the governor demanding that she be removed at once from the island on the grounds that she is clearly insane.

Millionaires do not come to her so-called "hotel," and her supplies begin to dwindle. The baroness is particularly disturbed by a lack of cigarettes and alcohol and takes out her frustration on Lorenz, who fears for his life and seeks refuge in the Wittmers' home. The baroness leaves a message for Lorenz that she and Philipson are leaving for Tahiti with friends who are due to arrive the next day. Lorenz, however, deems it to be a trap to lure him back to the Hotel Paradiso, perhaps to be murdered. He disappears for two days; then returns, stating that there is no trace of the baroness and Philipson anywhere on the island. While all agree that there had been no boat, Ritter and Lorenz seem quite sure the baroness will never return, leading Wittmer to conclude in her memoirs that they had disposed of the couple. Both had good cause for murder; Ritter, because she had destroyed his tropical paradise, and Lorenz, because she had beaten, degraded, and robbed him. Lorenz also knew all the unsavory details about her past as well as her mad actions on Floreana. Certain that she would not permit a potential blackmailer to leave the island, he might well have been tempted to strike first.

In his articles, Simenon proposes several different solutions to the mystery of the disappearance of the baroness and Philipson but opts in the novel for his customary solution, suicide. For the baroness and Philipson it would have been, he proposes, "the only way to retain their prestige and to awaken some admiration in people" (*Soif,* 199). Wittmer's explanation seems more plausible.

Assigning minor roles to the Wittmers (the Herrmanns in his novel), Simenon focuses instead on other actors in the real-life adventure on which he based his novel, since theirs was the typical fate of all of "adventure's failures." Thus, *Ceux de la soif* becomes "the barely fictionalized adventure of the baroness de Wagner and of Dr. Ritter" (Assouline, 259), both of them exemplary failures. Doctor Ritter is as destined to fail as are all those who "leave to flee civilization under the illusion that there is a place where they can live without worrying about other men and their needs, their laws and their exigencies. . . . [Ritter] thought he was a wise man, and hoped to live naked in a garden without doing anything but dream about his philosophic ideas." Also predetermined is the downfall of la baroness de Wagner, one of the "true adventurers who leave home with the intention of making a fortune in a few years." In the Galapagos, she wanted to "set up a hotel for billionaires. Of course she failed!" Simenon concludes (*Etoile,* 143–44).

In *Ceux de la soif,* the death of Müller (Ritter in real life) from apoplexy seems to be connected in some way to the terrible drought that has taken hold on Floreana, almost as if it were nature's revenge for the presumption of those who sought to colonize the island. Shortly before his death, he writes in his diary: "This proves what I have always maintained, which is that what are called the enchanted islands are not a place for colonization or for any other enterprise. There nature defends itself against men's arrogance. Yesterday, I found a dead bull against the garden fence and, this morning, I shared my pail of water between two donkeys who no longer had enough strength to stand up. If Heaven does not take pity on those creatures, they will all die. . . . And undoubtedly that is the way it should be" (*Soif,* 200).

The true face of even the most exciting of tropical adventures is almost always tragic, Simenon wrote, but that is true of his entire oeuvre. "I have no imagination. I am incapable of adding anything at all to anyone. I take people as I see them," he added (*Drame,* 11). And, indeed, he did take people as he saw them, and what he saw everywhere were victims, typified by an absence of will, powerless as they are shunted about by the vicissitudes of life. His characters are doomed in all surroundings; their ruin is merely accelerated in the tropics. He seems oblivious of those whose success contradicted his premise, as he was to virtually all of the beauty of the tropics.

Chapter Five

The Gift of Narration

Simenon has the "gift of narration, the rarest of all gifts in the twentieth century," wrote the American novelist Thornton Wilder (quoted in Marnham, 274). But Simenon is more than a brilliant storyteller; he is also a poet whose images speak to all of the senses. Unlike the traditional bourgeois novelists, notably Balzac to whom he is often compared, Simenon does not attempt a mimetic reproduction of life. Instead, he seeks to reconstitute reality by the use of suggestive details that stimulate the reader to supplement them with his own sensory memories. He does not copy reality, he transforms it. As Simenon explained in the preface to *Pedigree,* "above all, I took the liberty to recreate [the characters] from heterogeneous materials, staying closer to poetic truth than to reality pure and simple" (*Pedigree* 1:6–7).

Simenon described his method of writing a novel as an intuitive approach impossible to replicate. The creative process would be set in motion one day when he felt great tension and realized that he had to begin writing in order to vent his anxiety: "One day I become peevish, dissatisfied with myself . . . then I am not mistaken, I *need* to write" (Parinaud, 414). At this point, he would rid himself of all social and family responsibilities for 10 days and would go off alone, seeking to put himself in what he called a "state of grace," emptying himself "of all preoccupations that personally affect [him], the man called Simenon, so as to become a sort of sponge that can absorb other people's personalities, live through other people's memories, and finally bring them out again—breathe them out—in the form of literature."[1]

While in this "state of grace," he would be receptive to some sensory impression that would recall an atmosphere from his past. A particular sound, an odor, would plunge him into the past, evoking certain memories:

> The day is ending. . . . It is the best time of day. . . . The contours of things become blurred, an ordinary street corner, the dark entrance to a house, a reflection on a wet pavement, everything easily takes on a mysterious aspect. That reminds me of ten, fifty small cities in which I roamed in the same way, and then it happens, by degrees memories come crowding back and move me. A certain café in Dunkerque, one autumn

> evening, with its fishermen who looked as if they were sculpted in their slickers glistening with salt water. . . . There was sawdust on the floor and the men had at their feet the few fish they had kept for their evening meal. . . . A detail that still comes back to me: the cuckoo clock. . . . It made me jump at exactly six o'clock . . . the smell of spirits, of the alcohol which they call there "fil en six." Didn't these men hail from a boat named the Marie-Jeanne? . . . It would be good to live among them for a few days. ("Romancier," 100–101)

The sights, sounds, and smells of the fisherman's café would later provide the setting for one of the early Maigrets, *Au Rendez-vous des Terre-Neuvas.*

After the setting, Simenon created the protagonist, generally a composite of many people with whom he had come into contact. He then gave him a name, a family, and a house, and he did this by consulting the more than 150 telephone books for all countries that he kept in his study. After this, he would write the name he chose on a yellow envelope—the rites Simenon followed were as rigid as those observed by his protagonists—and added to the name the protagonist's telephone number, his address, his father's age if alive, his mother's age, his children, wife, friends, and so forth. Often he would sketch a rough plan of the character's house, for he wanted to know whether he opened the door to the left or the right when he got home.[2] Finally, he would give a complete identity to each of the secondary characters, although he infrequently made use of this material.

The next stage in the genesis of a novel was crucial. "I have such a man, such a woman, in such surroundings. What can happen to oblige them to go to their limit? That's the question. It will sometimes be a very simple incident, but it will be something that will change their lives."[3] The incident, or catalyst, triggering this reaction, stated Simenon, is the only contrived part of the novel, the rest follows as inexorably as the workings of destiny in Greek tragedy.

In fact, for Simenon, the modern novel is the tragedy of our day and, like those of ancient Greece, poses the basic problem of man's destiny. Simenon has called his novels "romans-tragédie" (tragedy-novels), and in them he has adopted many of the rules that governed the classical tragedies. Like them, his novels start at the moment of crisis and lead rapidly and inexorably to an often tragic conclusion (Becker, 2500). Destiny, envisioned in classical theater in the form of the irresistible power of the gods, becomes in Simenon's work inescapable psychological determinism. The first incident in the novel sets off an inner fatality;

the protagonist becomes aware of his true nature and acts accordingly thereafter. The events in his past, which he examines ad infinitum, are transformed retrospectively into destiny.

There are no long introductions or chronological expositions in Simenon's novels; the past is evoked rapidly in a series of flashbacks. In first-person narration, these flashbacks can be in the form of personal memories or based on what the character has heard about his birth and childhood. Information about past events can also be provided by a secondary character who narrates them directly in conversations with the protagonist, as in *Le destin des Malou,* or who includes it in a letter, as in *Le fils.* In both of these novels, a son learns about his family by someone who remembers events he, himself, could not have witnessed. In third-person narration, the past is called up by the use of free indirect style. By combining the words of the narrator-author and the thoughts or words of the character, free indirect style has the effect of attributing to the protagonist what is actually said in the third person.

There are few characters and no subplots in Simenon's novels, action is limited, and attention is focused on the eternal drama of human existence. What Simenon attempted to write was the quintessential or "pure" novel, reduced to what he considered to be its basic elements, "man and his eternal drama," containing nothing that could be depicted through other media.

All of Simenon's novels, with the exception of a few long works—*Pedigree, Long cours, Le testament Donadieu, L'aîné des Ferchaux*—are crisis novels that focus on a character at a turning point in his life. There are minor differences among them. In a few, complications of character and situation create a situation that culminates in a climactic moment—Julie's death in *Antoine et Julie,* Mahé's suicide in *Le cercle des Mahé,* and the widow's murder in *La veuve Couderc*—that is followed by a tying up of the threads of the narrative. But most of the romans durs are novels in which the usually violent climactic event takes place at the beginning, and the remainder of the novel traces the actions and reactions of the character as his familiar world disintegrates around him. All of the novels contain from 9 to 12 chapters that rarely go beyond 250 pages, usually fewer. Simenon believed that in order to be effective the novel must be short enough to be read in one sitting. The intense, concentrated crisis novel offers the same advantages as a play or a film that is seen as a whole so that there is no break in tension. The style, whether dialogue or narrative, is characteristically simple and sober. The vocabulary is limited; there are a few common, ordinary verbs, and no adverbs.

The nouns stand for familiar objects, well-known concepts, or common feelings. There are no long descriptions. "I try to communicate to the reader the type of vibration I feel when I write, to communicate it to him by using the simplest words, by the most ordinary means" (Parinaud, 397).

Simenon's novels remain in the tradition of the social, or bourgeois, novel that seeks to transmit a believable image of society by linear chronology, description—or, as in Simenon's case, evocation—of the ambience, believability of the characters, and division of the narrative into the standard three, or in Simenon's case four, parts—exposition, crisis, action, denouement.

In *La mort d'Auguste,* we find these elements of the bourgeois novel combined with Simenon's impressionistic evocation of atmosphere. The novel portrays a segment of Simenon's Paris that has all but disappeared, the restaurant that brings together provincial and city life. A short exposition introduces the reader to the milieu at the same time as it sets out the elements of the drama. Auguste Mature, who founded the restaurant in 1913 when he was 26 years old, named it l'Auvergnat after his native Auvergne. It is on a shabby side street in the neighborhood of what was formerly the Paris central market, les Halles. Although it has flourished since the Second World War, its external appearance has not altered considerably. It is distinguished from the other restaurants in the area by the large hams and salamis that hang in the windows and the piles of large loaves of bread, which Auguste still receives from his native province. By the use of a few ordinary everyday words, rather than a long, detailed description, Simenon sets forth the restaurant exterior.

The interior, however, has changed; it has been enlarged and its décor reflects the success of the establishment. Three Utrillos, which August had obtained years before from a friend who was unable to repay a loan, hang on the wall. The paintings evoke the years of Auguste's youth, when starving artists bartered works that were to become priceless for a meal. That the paintings are specified as Utrillos is a seemingly gratuitous detail, but it is one that imparts life to the description and makes it unforgettable.

The novel opens on a night in 1966 when a young, newly married couple enters the restaurant, deceived by its external simplicity. They are observed with disinterest by Antoine, Auguste's middle son, who has been his partner since 1945, and Antoine's wife Fernande, the cashier. Antoine doesn't bother to leave the back room for such unimportant clients but has one of the waiters seat them at a bad table in the middle of the restaurant. In this brief opening scene, Simenon uses a few verbal strokes to convey the cold, calculating snobbery of certain restaurateurs. He avoids psychological explanations to allow the character to reveal himself by his gestures, his attitudes, and his actions. The reader's immediate dislike for Antoine and Fernande is a reaction intended by Simenon, who explained that all such effects are produced by the order of presentation and the movement of the sentence. "I have always tried," he explained, "to perfect a style that conveyed movement, that was all movement. Suppose that someone enters this room, takes off his hat, his gloves, opens his mouth to say something. According to the order in which you describe these gestures, you are going to have a different picture of the character. If he takes off his hat first and his gloves next, you do not have the same image of him as if he had done the reverse. The order of words in a sentence is of capital importance, of greater importance, in my opinion, than a refined syntax"(Parinaud, 395).

Soon after the arrival of the young couple, the British ambassador arrives with a party of eight, and old Auguste strolls from table to table, chatting with all regardless of social position, as he has always done since he and his restaurant were young. Suddenly, as he is telling the young couple the story of his success, Auguste collapses at their table, dragging to the floor with him, not just any tablecloth, but a distinctive red-and-white checked tablecloth to which he is clinging. He is carried upstairs to his bed in the apartment he occupies with his senile wife on the floor above the restaurant. Although his wife had ceased to recognize him, Auguste, who still loved her, continued to share with her the bed they bought when they were married. "He had not spent a night away from her ever since they had been married, and even in recent times, when she looked at him as if he were a stranger or pet dog, he would often sit down in front of her in the hope that they might pick up the thread of God knows what conversation."[4] Here, there is another seemingly extraneous detail, the senile wife who disappears immediately from the narrative, but without her, the reader would not have been present in the room to which the dying man is carried.

Auguste dies during the night, and all the rest of the novel is the progressive unfolding of the effects of this critical incident. His death prompts a search for his missing will, a search that is merely the means to explore the characters of his three sons. There is no dramatic action in *La mort d'Auguste,* because here, as in all of Simenon's novels, the interest is centered on inner states of being and tensions. The reader learns about the brothers gradually, as one would in life. Ferdinand, the oldest, is a lawyer who has always been ashamed of the restaurant but is now anxious to find out how much of his father's estate he can expect to inherit. He had always been pleased that Antoine had stayed with their parents and relieved him of the responsibility. But, now that his father has died, he wants to make sure that Antoine does not behave as if he were specially privileged. He begins to think about what he would do if he had the money to retire. He had always thought his life was satisfactory, even enviable, but he suddenly realizes that it is empty, that he has no passions or hobbies. At the age of 53, he is suddenly confronted with the emptiness of his life.

Bernard, the youngest son, fat and spoiled and always short of money, is the black sheep of the family. His "irresolute face revealed the child of long ago, the young man who was at ease nowhere, the maturing man who had not managed to find his place in the world" (*Auguste,* 125–26). Antoine, the third son through whose consciousness much of the novel is filtered, had let himself be persuaded to join his father when he returned at the end of the war from a German prison camp. It was a small restaurant then, his mother did the cooking and there was one waiter. Antoine and his father had drawn up a written agreement: "The moment before they were still a father and son standing next to each other and watching the traffic in the street. But, the moment Antoine gave his answer, the relationship between the two men changed. As naturally as could be, they became partners, accomplices of a sort, and the difference in age ceased to exist" (*Auguste,* 80–81).

As the search for Auguste's missing fortune goes on, Antoine discovers not only the character defects of his brothers but also their resentment of him; the attitude, tone, and look on Bernard's face were expressions, "not of a momentary bitterness, but of a hatred that had matured over the years" (*Auguste,* 126). The search for the will is difficult because nothing is known about Auguste's affairs; he had brought with him from the provinces the peasant's cunning and reticence in money matters. Antoine discovers ultimately that Auguste had had a "business adviser," a man in whom he had complete confidence because he was also from the Auvergne. Auguste's trust had been misplaced; the adviser had died in prison where he had been sent for fraud. In Auguste's wallet, they find a few objects that are, in a sense, keys to his character—a safe deposit key, a prescription for reading glasses, which his pride had prevented him from buying, photos of his three sons and of his wife at the age of 16, the way he saw her until his death.

The three brothers go to the safe deposit box and find that all the stocks in it are worthless. Because Auguste had imagined he would be leaving a fortune to his sons, he had never spoken to them about money. He had wanted to surprise them. When he discovered the truth, he did not lodge a complaint against the dishonest adviser because to have done so would have been to admit that he was naive and to let his sons know that he was not leaving them the inheritance they anticipated. "He had worked all his life, ever since the age of 12, to accumulate a fortune, counting every penny, and all that remained of it was the restaurant, which was really run by Antoine. . . . He had lived for months with a sense of shame, knowing that when he was gone he would leave behind him bitterness instead of regret. Antoine had the feeling that he had never understood his father so well, his peasant character, his humbleness and pride" (*Auguste,* 242–43).

Antoine permits his brothers to divide up the cash they found in the box, the last payment he had made to his father. He leaves them together in the restaurant because "he had no desire to be present when the money was divided amidst the glasses on the table, beneath the eyes of the indifferent waiter" (*Auguste,* 244). The initial dislike that the reader felt for Antoine has given way in the course of the novel to sympathy, even admiration. This is in accord with Simenon's technique, which attempts to reproduce the rhythm of life in which you meet a person, react to his social personality, and then learn as you penetrate beneath the surface what the person is really like. The novel also conforms to Simenon's description of the modern novel in which there is "never a story in the traditional sense of the word but merely the presentation of a moment of varying duration in the life of a man. It doesn't matter whether the events in the novel are dramatic or mundane, since the only thing that does matter is man himself, man and his relationship with the world, that is to say with life."[5]

While the story in most of Simenon's novels is secondary to the characters and serves only insofar as it helps the reader to understand them, many of the works, particularly those set in exotic locales or on ships, are also exciting tales of adventure and suspense, for Simenon is a remarkable storyteller. *Le passager du "Polarlys"* is a story of drug addiction and murder, told from the point of view of the ship's captain as he investigates a murder on board ship during a violent storm. *Les Pitard,* another seafaring adventure, tells of shipwreck and rescue at sea, of violence and suicide. On the cargo and passenger vessel, the "Aramis"(*Le passager clandestin*), en route to Tahiti from Panama, the stowaway is a young woman and the passengers are a card shark and an ex-convict, all three venal and avaricious. "L'Aquitaine," a ship returning to France from French Equatorial Africa (*45° à l'ombre*), seems to be subject to the evil eye, a malady that "attacks boats on all the seas of the world, and the causes of which belong to the great unknown domain called Chance. . . . Even if the start of the trip seems favorable, the signs of the evil eye cannot escape the sailor's eye. Suddenly, without reason, a part of the rigging breaks like a violin string. . . . Or the cabin boy cuts open his thumb. . . . It's not yet the evil eye. The evil eye requires a series. But it is rare for new damage not to follow that night or the next day. From then on, everything goes from bad to worse and the men, with clenched jaws, have only to count the blows."[6] To a series of mechanical difficulties on the "Aquitaine" is added a yellow-fever epidemic that breaks out in the hold, a fact that is kept from the first-class passengers who are the typical complement of any "ship of fools."

The first part of the unusually long novel *Long cours* also takes place on a ship, this one carrying contraband arms to revolutionaries in Ecuador. The second part takes place at a gold mine in Colombia, and the third in Papeete. The novel incorporates many of the stories of murder, suicide, madness, and adventure found in *La mauvaise étoile* (see chapter 4). The shipwreck of the "Télémaque" off the coast of Rio de Janeiro in 1906 provides the background for a story of sibling rivalry between twin brothers, Pierre and Charles Canut (*Les rescapés du "Télémaque"*), sons of a sailor who died in the wreck, victim of cannibalism that permitted the others to survive. The second part of *L'aîné des Ferchaux* deals with murder in the tropics and traffic in shrunken human heads, and *Les gens d'en face* is a chilling portrayal of Soviet secret police activities, terror, and murder in Batum in the era of Stalin.

The story "Sous peine de mort" is pure storytelling at its best in which the events are more important than the characters. It opens on a note of suspense as Oscar Labro, the protagonist, receives another in the series of postcards he has been receiving for several months, each postmarked closer and closer to Labro's island of Porquerolles and all containing the message: "We'll finally meet, you scum. On pain of death, do you remember? Your old Jules."[7] Finally, on the one hundred sixty-ninth day after receipt of the first letter, Jules arrives. As he debarks, it is apparent that he has a wooden leg. When the people on the dock look at the two men as they confront one another, they feel instinctively that they have a score to settle.

As the story continues, the reader learns that Labro was sent to Gabon by his employer when he was 22 years old, to the hottest and most unhealthful part of the jungle to arrange for the collecting of palm oil. For three days he battled the mosquitoes in the unbearably hot Umbolé swamp. All about him were "canals, rivers of muddy water where large bubbles burst continually on the surface, where animals of all sorts swarmed. . . . You could travel for days without seeing a hut, a human being, and then it happened that he saw a dugout canoe between the roots of a mangrove tree and on this canoe there was a sign: 'It is forbidden to swipe this craft on pain of death.' " (*Peine,* 117). The sign gave Labro an idea. His misery prompted him to steal the canoe, to write an obscenity on the sign and to put his name to it.

Jules, the putative owner of that canoe, discovered Labro's whereabouts when he read the announcement of his daughter's wedding in the newspaper, and had come to carry out his threat. Day after day, Jules and Labro go fishing together as Jules tortures him with uncertainty about the day he has chosen for Labro's death. Each day, Jules has a new idea and confides in Labro, as one confides in a close friend, the various types of death he has envisioned for him. Jules sadistically plays on Labro's fears until he finally goes too far by asking Labro for suggestions on how to commit the perfect crime, thus giving him the idea of getting rid of his tormentor in the same way. One day, after a brief struggle in the boat, they overturn, and Labro drowns Jules by knocking him unconscious.

Everyone in the tightly knit island community is pleased to be rid of the intruder, particularly the police, who reveal that the man was not who he pretended to be, but a petty thief named Marelier who was sought by the police in five countries. He had never been to Gabon, he had lost his leg in a prison break, he had never owned a canoe, he didn't even know how to swim; Oscar had killed for nothing. He had killed a "poor fellow who undoubtedly meant him no harm, a common thief who sought only, by threatening him from time to time, to sponge on him and to spend peaceful days in Porquerolles" (*Peine,* 140).

But, narrative gifts are not sufficient in and of themselves to account for the brilliance of Simenon's oeuvre. The essential element, one that has been constantly analyzed and proven virtually impossible to pin down—as filmmakers have discovered (see chapter 6)—is the spellbinding atmosphere he creates. Simenon remarked that what critics call his atmosphere is nothing more than the impressionism of the painter adapted to literature. It is the depiction of scene, emotion, or character by the use of detail that is intended to achieve a vividness, colorfulness, or effectiveness more by evoking subjective and sensory impressions than by recreating or representing objective reality. The selection of typical details and characteristic objects permits the reader to reconstitute the whole from the detail provided. The function of familiar, evocative images is to sum up in a few strokes a complete decor, an ambiance—a couple embracing one another in the shadows (*Lettre à mon juge, Le voyageur de la Toussaint*), or a young woman on the bridge of a barge nursing an infant (*L'écluse no. 1, Un crime en Hollande*).

Like the impressionists, Simenon tries to give weight to his impressions:

> A commercial painter paints flat; you can put your finger through. But a painter—for example, an apple by Cezanne has weight. With just three strokes. I tried to give to my words just the weight that a stroke of Cezanne's gave to an apple. That is why most of the time I use concrete words. I try to avoid abstract words. Or poetical words, you know, like *crépuscule* [twilight], for example. You don't feel them. Whereas the word *pluie* [rain] is material, you lose all the materiality of the rain if you speak of *ondée* [heavy shower]. I try to use only material words and, even to express ideas, I force myself to do so with concrete rather than abstract words. (Parinaud, 395)

His goal, he stated elsewhere, is "to bring a tree to life at the far end of the garden despite the drama that is unfolding in that garden . . . To give to the leaves of that tree their weight, their presence . . . I think that I have just found the word: their presence. The presence of a piece of paper, of a patch of sky, of some object or other, of those objects that assume mysterious importance during the most pathetic moments of our lives" ("Romancier," 96–97).

Using only concrete words, Simenon conveys the atmosphere of the city of Liège during the German occupation in World War I:

> But the story of the occupation can't be told any more than the story of the inflation. It is not made up of facts: it is an atmosphere, a state of being, a barracks smell in the streets, the moving blob of unfamiliar uniforms, it is marks that replace francs in your pockets, and the preoccupation with eating that replaces all others, it is new words, unfamiliar music, and mobile soup kitchens along the sidewalks; it is the habit the eye falls into of looking for the new handbill on the board that tells the hour after which it is forbidden to circulate in the streets or that announces a new consignment of sugar at the food supply center, or else the necessity for all men over 18 years of age to present themselves to the

> Kommandatur, unless the handbill is red and lists the names of recently executed civilians. (*Trois crimes,* 11–12)

Simenon suggests rather than describes; we never have before us anything but fragments of landscapes, outlines of scenery. With only a few brush strokes, he gives us the feeling of a rural scene, a town, a village, a stormy sea. He excels in conveying a few decisive sensory impressions that evoke an atmosphere more vividly than any long itemized description. A spot of sunlight on his desk reminds the bourgemestre of Furnes of the jetty at Ostend with its sand "the color of blond tobacco, the changing sea that always remains pale, the parasols, the light dresses on the benches, on the rented chairs, the children running, the large red rubber balls that hit you in the legs" (*Bourgmestre,* 226).

Smells and sounds play as important a role in fashioning Simenon's atmosphere as do shapes and colors. In an article titled, "Georges Simenon, 'romancier-nez,' " Ralph Messac remarks that "it was by opening his pages to olfactory memories that Simenon was able to recreate an atmosphere. Fog and mist may serve very well to situate a novel, but would you have the fish market in La Rochelle if you didn't put in some odors, would you have a café without the smell of Gauloise cigarettes, a shady hotel without the rancid odor of cheap soap, of mildew and of foul kitchen smells, not to mention a pinch of light tobacco ashes?"[8] By stimulating the reader's sensory memories, Simenon is able to evoke familiar places and scenes and integrate them into a distinctive atmosphere.

Olfactory and visual images predominate in Simenon's evocation of the wonders of "December with Saint Nicholas's day, then Christmas, then the New Year . . . a month heavy with mystery, of sweet, somewhat troubling impressions that follow one another in a breathless rhythm" (Pedigree 2:93):

> The breath of the city is laden with smells that are characteristic of the days that precede the Feast of Saint Nicholas. Although it is not yet snowing, invisible specks of ice float in space like dust and pile up in the luminous halos of the shop windows.
>
> Everyone is out of doors. All the women run, dragging behind them children who would like to stop longer in front of the displays. . . . The confectioners' shops, the pastry shops, the grocery stores are swarming with people. . . . Two smells dominate the others, so characteristic that no child could mistake them, the sweet, fragrant odor of gingerbread and that of chocolate figurines, which is not the same smell as that of choco-

late bars. From top to bottom, the store windows are piled with honey cakes, some of them stuffed with multicolored, preserved fruits. Life-size gingerbread figures of Saint Nicholas stand with cotton wool bears, surrounded by sheep, donkeys, barnyard animals, all brownish colored or the color of whole wheat bread, sugared, perfumed, edible. It makes your head swim. . . . The students are feverish. Night falls and the snowflakes become thicker, slower. . . . They open their mouths, put out their tongues, they try to catch a snowflake, which has a faint taste of dust. They affirm with conviction: "It is good." And it is good, in fact, the first cold spell, the first snowfall, a world that has lost its daily appearance, roofs that are blurred against the dull sky, lights that scarcely illuminate any longer and passersby who float in space. Even the streetcar becomes a mysterious vessel, with windows for portholes. (Pedigree 2:91, 92, 95)

Simenon often establishes relationships between olfactory and visual images. Maigret, tracking a criminal, saw the dawn break: "He saw the first anglers settle themselves on the banks of the river from which a fine mist was rising; he saw the first barges bottled up at the locks and the smoke that was beginning to rise from the houses in a sky the color of mother of pearl. . . . It was amusing after the night he had just spent to walk in the grass that was wet with dew, to smell the odors of the earth, that of the logs that were burning in the fireplace, to see the maid, who had not yet done her hair, come and go in the kitchen."[9] On an evening on the island of Porquerolles, "the air had a curious odor at that time. The sea also. The sea above all. And the universe was of an extraordinary color. Everything was light, almost pale, but of a luminous paleness. Pale blue. Pale green. Even the bright colors of the boats had an astonishing lightness. Everything was wrapped in a light vapor."[10]

Sensory images are not only juxtaposed, but, by a process of synesthesia, are often perceived as a sensation or image of a sense other than the one being stimulated. Maigret, like Maugin in *Les anneaux de Bicêtre* (see p. 73), transforms the sound of church bells into a visual image:

Here, something unexpected was taking place with the bells. They were real church bells, however, but faint and thin like those of chapels or of convents. You were bound to believe that the quality, the density of the air was not the same here as elsewhere. You clearly heard the hammer strike the bronze, which gave forth a small, nondescript note, but it was then that the phenomenon began: a first ring took shape against the pale sky which was still cool, stretched out, hesitating like a smoke ring, became a perfect circle from which other circles magically came forth. The circles, ever larger and ever purer, passed beyond the square, the

> houses, stretched out above the port and far off over the sea where little boats were rocking. You felt them above the hills and the rocks and they still had not ceased to be perceptible when the hammer struck the metal once again and other sonorous circles came forth, to recreate themselves, then still others that you listened to with the same innocent amazement as when you watch fireworks.[11]

Simenon's images speak to all senses. A critic has pointed out that the sense of touch is so pervasive that Simenon even invented a new word, or rather transformed an adjective *mouillé* (wet, damp, moist) into the more concrete noun *le mouillé* to signify something indefinable and omnipresent in his work. It is neither rain, nor fog, but something more tenacious, so that you have a face "caked with mouillé," a "night of mouillé," a boat floundering "somewhere in the mouillé."[12]

From the very beginning, Simenon was interested in the influence of ambience on temperament, the way in which weather determines mood. "I understood, using my own life as an example, that on a stormy day, for example, a discussion that could have been without importance, heaven knows, quickly goes tragically wrong."[13] The beauty of the spring day on which *Maigret et les vieillards* opens makes Maigret feel both light-hearted and melancholy, preparing for the ambivalent mood of the novel.

> It was one of those exceptional months of May such as one experiences only two or three times in a lifetime and which have the brightness, taste, and smell of childhood memories. Maigret called it a hymnal month of May because it reminded him both of his First Communion and of his first spring in Paris, when everything was new and wonderful for him. In the street, on the bus, in his office, he would stop short, struck by a sound in the distance, by a puff of warm air, by the bright spot of a dress that took him back 20 or 30 years.[14]

The rainy season in Tahiti weighs down on Oscar Donadieu *(Touriste de bananes)* as he finds himself in the "realm of water, water that fell in large vertical drops and, because they were warm, these drops seemed more liquid than others. . . . The rain kept falling. . . . The walls oozed water . . . this rainy season that was lasting longer than usual! Why? To discourage him? To show him the vanity of his hopes?" (*Touriste,* 29, 30, 37). He is lifted from his depression when the rain stops and the sun transforms the early morning landscape: "It was an entire universe, a more extraordinary world than he had dreamed of, a pink and blue, green and golden universe, with shades that had no name, like those you see on certain pieces of mother-of-pearl. . . . In the foreground, the large royal poincianas formed a dark green setting and the road was red, a sumptuous red of crushed brick. . . . There were not only colors, there were sounds, voices, a new life, both young and languorous at the same time" *(Touriste, 59)*.

Weather plays a key role in the creation of Simenon's atmosphere. In Northern Europe, it rains continually. "When she had taken the train in Brussels, it was six o'clock in the morning and the darkness was heavy with icy rain. The third class compartment was also wet, the floor wet beneath the muddy shoes, the partitions wet with a viscous mist, the windows wet both on the inside and on the outside. People in wet clothing dozed. . . . In the waiting rooms, the umbrellas shed rivulets of running water which smelled of sodden silk."[15]

On the Côte d'Azur and the island of Porquerolles, "the sun weighs down. Everything requires an effort, an effort to adapt, to understand. . . . The air is thick and heavy. The ground, trees, walls steam, emitting waves of heat" (*Mahé*, 15, 18). In La Rochelle, the climate is changeable as in all temperate regions. The cold, damp days of late fall and winter after the arrival of Gilles Mauvoisin in La Rochelle—"This cocoon-like weather. . . . This white and gray world in which the sounds, particularly the boat sirens become shriller, even heartrending"[16]—give way to the splendid days of spring. *Le clan des Ostendais* begins on a Sunday morning in May 1940, when refugees fleeing the Germans were pouring into La Rochelle. It was "a bright, absolutely calm morning. A smooth sea beneath a sky of iridescent blue. The world, by its tints, resembled the interior of a seashell." It was a particularly beautiful spring. "The weather had never been as radiant for weeks on end. There was not a cloud in the sky, not a ripple on the sea, and the thick, glossy grass in the meadows was immobile in the sunshine."[17]

In the American novels, Simenon evokes the parched Arizona desert and the "luminous mist that rose from the desert of sand . . . the ever-changing colors on the mountains that seemed, far off, to close in the world on all sides."[18] Or else, in *Le fond de la bouteille*, the swollen Santa Cruz river during the rainy season when it was "high, already higher than during the night. It formed a dark yellow mass, flowing slimy and thick, heaving in places, breathing like a beast, carrying along tree trunks, empty cans, all kinds of filth . . ." *(Bouteille*, 28–29). The fateful first chapter of *La main* takes place during a blizzard in Connecticut when "the snow sketched almost horizontal stripes in the beam of the headlights," when it was necessary to follow the "black line of the trees because one could no longer see the edges of the road" (*Main*, 22). *Les frères Rico* provides an unforgettable impression of the sea at sunrise in Miami: "The sea was calm. All he heard was one small wave, the one that, forming not far offshore in a barely perceptible undulation, rolled onto the sand, in a sparkling curl and churned up thousands of shells."[19]

Above all, in 106 of the 193 novels signed Simenon, both Maigrets and romans durs, it is Paris in all seasons. The cold November rain falls "from a sky of low, unbroken gray, one of those steady showers that seem wetter and somehow more perfidious, especially the first thing in the morning, than ordinary rain."[20] On a cold, wet, and dismal day in early March at 11 in the morning, "the offices were still bathed in a melancholy half-light, reminding one of an execution at dawn. At noon, the lights were still on and at three o'clock dusk had fallen again. Water was everywhere, the floor had puddles. People were incapable of saying three consecutive words without blowing their noses. All the newspapers printed photographs of suburbanites going home in rowboats through streets that had become rivers" (*Echec,* 9–10). On a day in August, Maigret glances out of his window

> at the motionless leaves on the trees on the Quai des Orfèvres, and at the Seine, which was flat and smooth as silk. . . . Every day toward early evening, for almost a week now, a brief but violent storm, accompanied by lashing rain, had sent the people in the streets scurrying in for shelter in doorways. These storms dissipated the intense heat of the day, and the cooler evenings that followed were a welcome relief. Paris was empty. Even the street noises were different, with intervals almost of silence. . . . On the streets at this time of year, it was almost a shock to hear someone speaking French.[21]

It is Simenon's ability to convey every mood and every aspect of Paris and of France, of Northern Europe, Africa, Tahiti, South America, the Galapagos during the first half of the twentieth century that led George Steiner to remark, in *Language and Silence,* that "Simenon may be among the last to have taken an entire culture for his verbal canvas."[22]

Chapter Six

Novel into Film

Simenon's novels have been adapted for the screen more often than those of any other writer (see filmography). Since the early years of the talkies, almost 60 feature films based on Simenon's novels, 8 of them in English, have been made for theatrical distribution, and scores of films have been produced expressly for television. In addition, there have been television series in many languages drawn from the Maigrets. While some of the novels have become successful films, filmmakers almost invariably have been unable to capture on screen the essence of Simenon's genius, the distinctive atmosphere that results from his blending of impressionistic notations of subtle psychological states, sensory impressions, and minute details of everyday life that lend veracity to what are often trivial or contrived plots.

"The reason I never see films or television programs based on my novels," wrote Simenon, "is easy to understand. . . . When I write a novel, I see my characters and know them down to the most intimate details, including those I do not describe. . . . How could a director or an actor convey an image that exists only within me? Not by means of my descriptions, which are always brief, since I want to give the reader the opportunity to give full play to his own imagination" (*Intimes*, 422). Cinema, however, leaves no room for the spectator's collaboration sought by Simenon; everything is set forth before him. What was suggestive and intuitive now becomes concrete. Olfactory, tactile, and gustatory sensations can no longer contribute to the overall ambience. Simenon's universe functions rather in the manner of a dream world, an association of images triggered by a few stimuli. These images are filtered through the consciousness of the protagonist and expressed by means of free indirect style, which, combining the words of the narrator-author and the thoughts and words of the character, has the effect of attributing what is actually said in the third person to the protagonist.

Another reason for the lack of success of filmmakers in translating Simenon's novels to the screen is that cinema requires action, and there is little external action in his novels. Even the least action-oriented film is dependent on discernible movement, but Simenon is a novelist of feelings, and the essential in his work takes place within the protagonist. Film characters, on the other hand, have no perceivable inner life, all their thoughts must be conveyed through action and dialogue, but no action or dialogue can communicate the painstaking search of Simenon's characters for self-knowledge. Everything in a Simenon novel comes from within the protagonist and even he is unable to verbalize what is transpiring within him. "He knew what he was trying to say. There was no word for what he had in mind," a leitmotif in Simenon's oeuvre, is the protagonist's admission that it is impossible to explain oneself to another.[1] For all of these reasons, the director of a Simenon film must choose between a faithful adaptation of the novel at the risk of boring the spectator with an essentially static production *(Trois chambres à Manhattan)*, or a film that has very little to do with the novel but that will prove more interesting to the spectator (*Le fruit défendu* [Forbidden fruit] from *Lettre à mon juge*)—two very different variations on the same theme.[2]

The point of view of the novel *Trois chambres à Manhattan* is that of the protagonist, François Combe, a successful actor who has fled Paris to escape the scandal caused by his wife's affair with a very young man. He has been at loose ends in New York for six months, isolated in an anglophone milieu. His chance meeting with Kay, a lonely, world-weary French woman, is followed by an aimless, rambling nocturnal walk through deserted streets, culminating at dawn in passionate coupling in a small hotel room. Combe judges her with cold lucidity: "She's the three-o'clock-in-the-morning type of woman, the one who cannot make up her mind to go to bed, who needs to keep up her state of excitement, to drink, to smoke, to speak, to finally fall into a man's arms when her nerves are frayed out."[3] But then he becomes aware that Kay is indispensable to him and he is resigned to stop struggling against his love no matter what he may learn about her former life. He understands that the past does not matter, since they are starting afresh. "To begin a life from scratch. Two lives. Two lives from scratch" (*Chambres,* 53). Combe expects not only a definitive obliteration of the past by their love but also a passport to a new life. It seems to him that he has gone full circle to arrive there. Combe, like Simenon's other characters, is unable to express his feelings. He and Kay have only to look at one another for him to have an almost "sacrilegious feeling of being present at the birth of happiness" (*Chambres,* 244). They do not embrace but stand quietly cheek-to-cheek for a long time.

While the story of redemption through love is moving on the printed page, the wandering of two lost souls through the streets of New York, as shown in the film, which is only occasionally interrupted by pauses in a series of impersonal rented rooms, makes for a tedious film. The film does not convey the overwhelming physical passion of the novel; the sexual relationship depicted seems more a way to fill time. The addition of several scenes and characters, including Combe's humiliating rejection by his wife in Paris in the opening scene and Kay's encounter with her former husband as she visits her sick daughter in Mexico, is insufficient to sustain the viewer's interest.

Le fruit défendu, the film version of *Lettre à mon juge,* by betraying Simenon's novel in every respect, becomes a more interesting film than *Trois chambres à Manhattan.* The novel, as its title suggests, is a letter to the judge who presided at his trial, from Dr. Alavoine, a convicted murderer. The opening words of the novel—"I would like to have a man, a single man, understand me. And I would like that man to be you" (*Juge,* 7)—express the writer's desperate need to share with another human being his struggle with the inner demons that he has never managed to vanquish, demons that drove him to murder and, as we learn in the epilogue, to suicide. Alavoine tells the story of his life and the inexorable forces that led him to murder the only woman he ever loved. He was a successful doctor in the Vendée who was dominated and controlled by his mother and wife. One night, on his way back from the hospital of a neighboring city, he meets a young woman named Martine at the station. They spend the night together, and Alavoine feels that this is the only time he has ever experienced true passion.

Alavoine then introduces Martine into his home. "Did I even know where we were going? There was only one thing I knew, it was that I could no longer do without her and that I felt physical pain as violent as that felt by the sickest of my patients as soon as she was no longer near me, as soon as I did not see her, as soon as I did not hear her" (*Juge,* 106). Alavoine notes further: "If you were to ask me how one recognizes love, if I had to diagnose love, I would say: 'First the need for a presence . . . a need as necessary, as absolute, and as vital as a physical need' " (*Juge,* 144).

When the situation at home becomes unbearable, Alavoine leaves his mother, wife, and children and goes to live in Paris with Martine to be with her continually. There he has the exhilarating sensation of starting life anew. He will deliver Martine from her former life, a frequent theme in Simenon's oeuvre, but Martine's sordid past refuses to be buried. Alavoine believed that his love wiped out her past. Yet, despite her efforts, despite her love, Martine could not rid herself of the other, "she was the other and she knew it" (*Juge,* 171). Alavoine finally murders Martine to exorcise the part of her that was standing between them. "I had to kill the other once and for all so that my Martine could live at last. I killed the other, fully conscious of what I was doing. . . . I killed her so that she might live and our eyes continue to embrace to the very end" (*Juge,* 186). Alavoine's final words, penned just before he kills himself to rejoin his love, are: "We have gone as far as possible. We have done everything possible. We wanted the totality of love" (*Juge,* 187). Questions remain, as they do at the end of all of Simenon's novels. Did Alavoine break through the barrier of incomprehension by his letter? Did the judge empathize with him? We can assume that both questions can be answered in the negative, because all of Simenon's characters remain immured in their solitude. Simenon presents but never concludes; his endings, faithful to reality, remain uncertain. The cinema, however, cannot content itself with ambiguity—that is why every film based on Simenon's novels arrives at a more or less satisfactory conclusion for the viewer.

The film *Le fruit défendu* ignores Simenon's basic concept of physical passion as a devastating illness and tells the banal story of a respectable doctor torn between duty and temptation, as personified by his cold, efficient wife and his passionate, sluttish mistress. While the screenplay totally distorts Simenon's novel, *Le fruit défendu* works better on the screen than *Trois chambres à Manhattan,* perhaps in part because it satisfies the moral requirements of the movie audience, while the novel expresses Simenon's distinctly personal views of sex, jealousy, and morality. The film opens with a dinner in honor of the doctor's forty-fifth birthday in the course of which he is called out to deliver a baby. The remainder of the film is made up of flashbacks that tell the story of his marriage, his meeting with a young woman with a sordid past, their affair, his wife's discovery of their liaison, and his decision to abandon his family and leave for Paris with his lover. The film ends as he returns to the remains of the birthday dinner after having spent the night delivering a baby. His wife is waiting for him. She confesses that she did not love him sufficiently and they go up to bed together in a final fade out. Such happy endings take place in the never-never land of films, not in Simenon's dismal domain.

The formulaic plot of the film has little more to do with the novel than the basic triangle, but it is difficult to imagine how a film could find a visual vocabulary to convey a text written from within the mind of a murderer, a man devoured by insane jealousy who construes his murder as an act of love. It would be impossible to guess from the film that the novel was the story of an obsession, one without hope, which could end only in death.

Two films made at about the same time, *La veuve Couderc* from the novel of the same name in 1971, directed by Pierre Granier-Deferre, and *L'horloger de Saint-Paul* from the novel *L'horloger d'Everton* in 1974, directed by Bertrand Tavernier, demonstrate how the essence of Simenon's work must be modified substantially to meet the expectations of filmgoers. The acts of violence at the heart of the novels are portrayed in both films as responses to external social and political pressures, while in the novels they are consequences of unbearable internal stress.

The novel *La veuve Couderc* builds up inexorably to just such an existential murder. Freed after five years in prison, Jean Passerat-Monnoyeur is hired as a farm hand by the widow Couderc. On her farm, he lives some of the happiest hours of his life, "uncovenanted hours, hours he had not reckoned on, and his head was full of light, his nostrils drunk with summer scents, his limbs heavy with peace."[4] But, for Simenon, the past is inescapable; it weighs heavily on the present and determines the relentless march toward the future. "At the age of 18," Simenon maintains, "a human being has absorbed impressions, sensations, images, involuntary observations that have formed him little by little. He will live henceforth on what he has acquired. This is the material that he will use during the rest of his life" (*Balzac,* 219). Simenon skillfully integrates all of these formative elements into his novels, but their psychological impact cannot be captured on film.

Jean's past is revealed as the author moves back and forth from Jean's point of view to that of an omniscient overview. Jean was the neglected motherless son of a wealthy, promiscuous man. Deprived of discipline as well as of love, he led a dissolute life. One day, he robbed and murdered a man. Before he committed the murder, he told himself to stop. And "if he had not done so, was it not precisely because he wanted to be done with it all? Was it not because he was sick at heart, because he had had enough?" (*Couderc,* 105). His crime was motivated by disgust with life and a desire for death. Murder as suicide turned outward is a constant theme in Simenon's work.

Jean becomes the lover both of the widow and of her niece, of whom she is intensely jealous, and he realizes that all he did to withdraw from life's pressures was in vain. "It would start all over again—real life, complications, and, as always, he would be the one to bear the brunt of fate.

He was sure of it. . . . He was dreadfully tired. Not only because of the past, or the present, but because of all the complications he could foresee" (*Couderc,* 182). He had just thrown away the innocent peace he had known only twice in his life, once when he was ill and had ceased to think about school, and again there on the farm, before complications set in. He knew that he would never again find such peace. "Always that vague sensation of disquiet, even of anguish. He looked around him as if wondering from which quarter the blow would fall on him" (*Couderc,* 184).

The widow begs him not to see her niece. When she falls at his feet in supplication, he can bear it no longer. He takes a hammer and, in one of the few—but certainly the most gruesome—scenes of violence in Simenon's novels, and, in effect, the only action scene in the novel, kills her with several hammer blows to the head. "What good would it be?" he wonders. "It would only start all over again! And then again, and again! He had had enough" (*Couderc,* 212). His final words, as the police come to arrest him, "I'm tired. . . . I'm so tired," (*Courderc,* 215) express his infinite weariness, his realization that not only is there nothing more in the world for him but there is also nothing to justify life.

In the film, Jean is no longer the alienated young man of the novel who is tormented by the memory of the sordid murder for which he served five years in prison and who is haunted by a phrase that has run through his head since the time of his trial, "Every man condemned to death will have his head cut off" (*Couderc,* 119 et passim). He is now a debonair young man, with no discernible past; we learn only seconds before the film's final fade out that he was the son of an eminent physicist and that he had killed two important (we may assume political) figures because, as he had declared at his trial, he was "fed up with them." He has not served his term, but has escaped from prison. He is a dynamic figure, a rebel at war with a corrupt society that is increasingly menaced by the rise of fascism, signs of which are evident throughout the film—the widow's brother-in-law reads the reactionary *Action Française,* large letters on the side of the church indicate that "God's house is not for Jews," the fascist vigilantes, the Croix-de-feu, offer their services to the police to help root out "yougos" and "jews."

While in the denouement of the novel Jean loses his battle against his inner demons, in the film he is the victim of society, a cinematographic rather than an introspective conflict. Jean is denounced to the authorities by the widow's in-laws and the farmhouse is surrounded by scores of mounted police and sharpshooters. The widow refuses to leave Jean and is shot to death, her death marked by splatters of blood on the wall behind her, her face unscathed, as a fire spreads through the house. Jean, who has fled the house in an effort to divert the attention of the police, is riddled with bullets, his graceful body flies up slowly into the air from the force of the impact before he falls to the ground, his handsome face undamaged and untroubled in death.

The film, from the opening scene in the bus to the violent shoot-out at the end, is visually stimulating. It tells a rather pedestrian story of a rebel against society who finds refuge on a farm, where he is caught between a valiant older woman and her sensual young niece, again the basic triangle of movie plots. As he works alongside the older woman on the farm, sharing all of her chores in the idyllic countryside of a city dweller's imagination, he realizes that he returns her love, and they die at the end in a spectacular liebestot. As a film, *La veuve Couderc* is engrossing and scenically beautiful, but it is a film whose mood is very far removed from the weltschmerz at the heart of Simenon's work.

The film version of *L'horloger d'Everton,* titled *L'horloger de Saint-Paul,* similarly transforms a contemptible crime into a politically justified murder, a concept foreign to Simenon's work in general, this novel in particular. The novel opens with one of the slow, compelling evocations of atmosphere at which Simenon excels, here a feeling of order, quiet, and tranquillity, an appropriate ambience for a work concerned with the intangibles of the soul. The local color here, as in all of Simenon's novels, is reduced to a minimum. With just a few strokes, Simenon recreates small-town America of the fifties—Main Street with its row of small businesses and a movie theater, and the side streets with their small private homes, a car in each driveway—a view of basic calm, order, and innocence that will stand in sharp contrast to the events to come. The life of the protagonist Dave Galloway, the watchmaker of Everton, is in harmony with these peaceful surroundings.

One Saturday evening in May, Galloway follows his usual Saturday routine as he closes his store and goes to spend the evening at the home of a friend. "Would he have spent that evening differently, or would he have tried to enjoy it more, if he had foreseen that it was his last evening as a happy man?" the narrator asks. "To this question and many others, including that of whether he had ever been really happy, he would later have to try to find an answer" (*Horloger,* 7). Notes of foreboding like the above, similar warnings of impending tragedy, occur at the beginning of many of Simenon's novels. The reason for such warnings, Richter states, is that the protagonist is inadequate for the tragic role he must play. The seriousness of destiny does not correspond to the insignificance of the individual whom it destroys. Thus, Simenon's hero is at a loss when tragedy strikes; he is on unfamiliar ground and does not know what to do. He is disoriented by tragedy because he is unable to recognize it when it appears, and it is his blindness as he stumbles into misfortune that these first pages describe (Richter, 75).

When Galloway leaves his friend and returns home at midnight, he discovers that his son, Ben, has run off with a 15-year-old girl, abandoning him just as his wife did years before when Ben was an infant. Since then, Galloway's only thought has been for his son's happiness. Now he realizes that his belief in the close relationship between them had been an illusion, since his son had kept such a major decision from him. His anguish grows as he learns that Ben robbed and killed a man as he fled, and his first reaction is an instinctive desire to protect his son. "Ben was himself; he was ready to stand judgment in his stead and to accept the punishment" (*Horloger,* 137).

When Ben refuses to see his father after he is arrested, the police inspector tells Galloway sympathetically that parents, without exception, are the last to know their children. And when he ultimately sees his son, Galloway understands what the policeman had been trying to tell him. "It was as though 16 years of shared life and daily intimacy had suddenly ceased to exist. There had been no glint in his son's eyes, no emotion on his face. Nothing but a knitting of his brows, as when one sees something unpleasant in one's way" (*Horloger,* 191).

Ben is sentenced to life imprisonment, and Dave returns to his home, where he attempts to understand why his apparently ordinary son became a thief and a murderer. He has a frame made for three pictures: one of his father at 38, one of himself at 22, and one of Ben at 16. "It seemed to him that those three photographs contained the explanation of everything that had happened, but he realized that he, alone, could understand. . . . Didn't the gaze of the three men reveal a shared secret life, a life, rather, that had been made to recoil upon itself? A look of timidity, almost a look of resignation, while the identical drawing in of the lips hinted at suppressed revolt. Some people are able to prevent their revolt from coming to the surface for their entire life, but with others it breaks out" (*Horloger,* 238). Galloway's father, who had bowed his head all his life, had once stayed out all night—an act that might pass for revolt—and had been made to pay for it by his wife until his death. His own revolt had been to marry the town tramp, while Ben, at 16, had carried his revolt to an extreme. All three had imagined that they were going to set themselves free, and each had had to pay for his act.

When Galloway discovers that Ben is to be a father, he hopes that his grandson will be free of the Galloway heredity. "Often, in his apartment, in his shop, and even in the street, Dave talked in a low voice to his father and to his son, who went with him everywhere. Soon, he would talk to his grandson as well, to reveal to him the secret in men" (*Horloger,* 246). Simenon does not, or like his protagonists is unable to, communicate what this secret is. Is it the primacy of heredity because of the unbreakable links it forges?[5] Or is it the fact that men are terribly alone, terribly wicked, but terribly pitiful because they are unhappy, and it is better to try to understand and to love them than to judge them?[6]

Simenon never writes about the external realities of the world, but the outside world of action and conflict of necessity supplants the novel's inner drama in the film *L'horloger de Saint-Paul.* The director Bertrand Tavernier said that most of his film is tangential to the novel—very little of the original dialogue remains and about 80 percent of the scenes were created expressly for the film. What does remain is the heartrending discovery by a father that his son has killed a man.[7]

Unlike the deceptively serene opening of the novel, the first scene of the film, its locale moved to France, shows a train hurtling noisily through the darkness toward Lyon, while a little girl at the window of one of the cars of the train sees an automobile in flames; it continues to burn during the opening credits. Similar visual and auditory assaults on the senses punctuate the film. The camera then moves to a noisy restaurant where the watchmaker, Michel Descombes, unlike the solitary Galloway, is dining with four friends who loudly discuss politics, a whores' strike, capital punishment, and the French voters' fear of the left. Descombes leaves the restaurant with his friends and, surrounded by the blaring sounds of the city, walks home to his apartment in a building that resounds with the din of late-night revelers. The noise that runs through the film symbolizes the increasing impingement of the outer world on the consciousness of the watchmaker and indicates the important influence of external events on his psyche—so different from the novel, which is an accumulation of silences cocooning the watchmaker's inner drama. The next morning, and here the film is faithful to the novel, Descombes learns that his son has killed a man—it was the murdered man's car that was seen burning in the opening scene—and that he has disappeared together with his lover, Liliane Torrini. But this murder is very different from Ben Galloway's heinous crime; Bernard Descombes has committed a political murder. The man he killed was not an innocent holdup victim, mourned by his family, but a despicable fascistic company spy, who molested Liliane and all of the other young women working under him in the factory. Bernard's crime then becomes heroic rather than despicable; it is one that the spectator can understand and tacitly approve, even while intellectually deploring vigilante justice. "I killed him because he was filth," Bernard remarks, and the viewer can both empathize with him, and commend his father's proud assertion that he stands firmly behind his son. He, too, he later tells his son, rebelled against the injustice of power during the war when he refused his general's order to return to a burning building to retrieve his violin. The solidarity of father and son against the repressive forces of society can be easily conveyed on the screen, but it is a concept that has nothing to do with the vagueness of the musings of Simenon's fictional hero as he seeks to find some justification for his son's crime. These incomprehensible, inexplicable pulsations of the subconscious that are within Galloway, those complex inner movements that underlie the most ordinary human interchanges in Simenon's oeuvre, resemble what Nathalie Sarraute called "tropisms"; they are what is felt fleetingly and are impossible to verbalize.[8]

Despite certain concessions to the exigencies of cinema, the transposition of *Le chat* into film remains one of the most faithful to Simenon's soul-searching fiction.[9] The novel, which was inspired by the second marriage of Simenon's mother (see pp. 10–11), opens in medias res. An old married couple (Emile Bouin is 73, his wife Marguerite 71) are sitting together in their living room silently spying on one another while the house shakes from the impact of the steel jaws of the crane crashing against the ground at the demolition site on the other side of the street. "They had been observing each other that way for years, slyly, constantly refining their game with new subtleties."[10] After a while, Emile writes a note on a piece of paper, folds it, places it between thumb and middle finger and flicks it onto his wife's lap. On the paper is written in block letters, THE CAT. Without a word, Marguerite walks over to a stuffed parrot in a cage, her lips move soundlessly—THE PARROT, she replies silently. Notes are their only means of communication; they stopped speaking to each other four years before. Every action they perform is calculated to offend or annoy. Emile cooks himself hearty dishes, frying the onions he knows disgust her, while Marguerite retaliates by eating tiny meals to show how refined she is. Their food is kept in two separate locked cupboards.

The events that led up to this strange situation are presented in flashbacks from Emile's point of view. Emile is a retired mason, Marguerite is the daughter of a previously wealthy bourgeois family who once owned the buildings that are being demolished around them. They met by chance, a lonely widow and widower, both of whom had lost compatible spouses from their own class. They married when he was 65 years old, she 63, a couple as ill-matched as any in Simenon's work. After their marriage, he had crossed the street to live in her house, accompanied by his cat, an alley cat named Joseph. The memories of their dead spouses intensify their incompatibility, but their relationship is irretrievably destroyed when his cat is poisoned, probably by Marguerite. But Simenon only suggests that Marguerite may be guilty by having Emile notice that a can of rat poison has been slightly displaced on its shelf in the basement. Emile grabs the dead cat and, in a brutal scene that the director eliminated in the film as he did the bludgeoning to death of widow Couderc, both considered too gruesome for the film audience, rushes upstairs, grabs Marguerite by the hair and keeps rubbing the dead cat's fur against her face. Emile then takes his revenge. In a horrifying scene, he pulls out the parrot's feathers one by one, just as Henriette Simenon's second husband had killed a parrot her beloved son Christian had sent her from the Congo (Assouline, 540). Both the parrot and the scene are absent from the film, the wife's loss in the film becomes the loss of a career.

Then their relationship becomes a war of attrition—each intent on surviving the other—punctuated by the deafening noises of the demolition crews. Both try in different ways to escape from this intolerable situation but realize intuitively that in some way the relationship is necessary. They hate one another, but neither can live without the other. Their life is given a purpose and a focus by hate. "Neither of them had the right to disarm. The game had become their life. It was as natural and necessary for them to send venomous notes to each other as for others to exchange pleasant words or kisses" (*Chat,* 178).

One day, Emile finds his wife lying dead. He loses consciousness and awakens in the hospital where a doctor informs him that he will live but that his convalescence will be long. He has won the battle for survival, but his is a Pyrrhic victory—with her death he has lost his raison d'être. "There was no longer anything," the novel concludes (*Chat,* 189).

The film generally follows the outlines of Simenon's novel, but in the film the couple has been married for 25 years. They were married when they were young and it was the first marriage for both of them. In the opening scene, an ambulance races to a hospital through a desolate urban landscape containing the shells of buildings that are in various stages of demolition to make way for new apartment buildings. A nurse appears at the entry desk to the operating unit and asks how to spell the name Bouin. "It's spelled just as it sounds," is the reply. The camera then fades in to a scene in which the Bouins, now named Julien and Clémence, follow one another into different food stores, return home separately, open their locked cupboards, and prepare their lunches, he, his odorous fried onions, she, her delicate salad, to the deafening demolition noises outside. The external noises in the novel are reproduced in the film, accompanied by recurring visual images of a wrecking ball crashing into a building. Unlike the cacophony of city sounds in *L'horloger de Saint-Paul,* which underlines the conflict between the individual and the oppressive forces of society, the noises in the novel as well as in the film version of *Le chat* are used to much better effect to parallel the conflict between the two elderly people. Also, the tearing down of the old buildings to make way for the new is symbolic of the impending decline of the protagonists into old age, the end of the demolition a harbinger of death.

Throughout the film there are flashbacks, from both his and her point of view, which go backward and forward in time. Through filmy camera lens covers, they appear as young romantic lovers, and then they are shown as they rent their dream house on what was then a idyllic street in Paris, a city that was at that time an agglomeration of small provincial towns. In sharper, more defined flashbacks, we see the youthful Clémence, a circus acrobat, and the fall from a trapeze that ended her career and left her with a limp, probably giving impetus to the alcoholism that typifies her film persona.

The cat in the novel, a common alley cat, embodied everything Marguerite detested in Emile, his vulgarity, his snoring, his masculine sexual presence, and was a symbol of the irreconcilable class differences between the two. But, in the film, the cat becomes a rival for the husband's affections. The wife is jealous of his love for the cat, and, in a rage, chases and shoots her rival to death.[11] She externalizes her feelings, shouting out her frustration at her physical deterioration and the loss of her husband's love. Julien, too, speaks freely about his dislike of his wife, both to a friend and to his occasional sex partner, the owner of a disreputable hotel. He says that he stays with her to make sure she doesn't drink too much. In the novel, the reasons for his remaining are more complicated and never fully explicated, for Simenon's fictional characters are unable to formulate their feelings, much less verbalize them. Similarly, we are never told directly what Marguerite is thinking—we know only what Emile assumes she is thinking.

In the last scene of the film, the couple sits silently opposite one another in front of the fireplace, she drinking, smoking, and coughing, he watching her carefully. The sight of the empty cat's bed prompts him to flick a note into her lap—THE CAT, she reads. He then gets up, slams the door, and goes outside to smoke. She goes upstairs grasping the note, pulls out a box of similar notes from under her bed, and then, in an explosive "film moment," clutches her heart and falls to the ground, knocking over a lamp. He sees the lamp crash to the floor, rushes back into the house, takes the dying woman into his arms, and exhales a sigh of grief as she dies. Then, as a huge garbage truck slowly and ominously approaches the house, he swallows a handful of sleeping pills and sits in a chair opposite her body while the sound of the truck gives way to the siren of the ambulance and fades in to the opening scene in the hospital and the nurse's question about the spelling of Bouin. When asked why she needs to know how Bouin is spelled, she replies that it is for his death certificate.

Le chat is a film that comes close to Simenon's universe of solitude and alienation. Despite certain changes, concessions to the stars Simone Signoret and Jean Gabin and to the cinema's need for action, the film retains Simenon's haunting story of old age, of obsession, and of the inevitable blighting of a human relationship.

Le voyageur de la Toussaint, the most faithful film adaptation of a Simenon novel, successfully captures its dreamlike atmosphere.[12] In the opening chapter of the book, on a cold, cloudy eve of All Saints' Day, Gilles Mauvoisin, the 19-year-old son of itinerant third-rate music hall performers, arrives secretly by boat in the city of La Rochelle from which his parents had eloped many years before. Gilles's parents have just died accidentally during a tour of Norway and Gilles has only their native city and the relatives they left behind to fall back on. He discovers that he is heir to the fortune of his recently deceased uncle—who had been one of the wealthiest and most detested citizens of the city—with the proviso that he live in his uncle's house and permit his young widow, Colette, to remain there. His uncle has also left him the key to a safe containing mysterious contents but not the combination. Gilles must find it himself, just as he must find the key to his own destiny.

Gilles takes over his uncle's business, marries, has a son, and lives in a manner commensurate with his vast wealth. The citizens of La Rochelle believe that he has become one of them because "he sits in an office at a set time, makes telephone calls, writes columns of figures, concerns himself with cars and trucks . . . writes up bills, signs checks and bills of exchange, and greets people distractedly in the street" (*Toussaint,* 355). They do not understand that he, like his parents, is a wanderer of the night, and that he must leave the daytime world of bourgeois preoccupations once he has accomplished what he set out to do.

The story now takes on the feel of a first-rate detective novel that can be translated into film without difficulty. When the body of Gilles's uncle is exhumed and he is found to have died of poison, his widow is accused of the murder. To clear his aunt, for whom he feels a great affinity because they share the same humble background, Gilles sets out to discover which one of the many people who detested his uncle had finally poisoned him. His inquiries plunge him into a mass of intrigue and earn him the hostility of "the Syndicate," a small group made up of politicians, bankers, and businessmen, which also includes his mother's sister Gérardine Eloi, who control the economy of the city. Despite their efforts to thwart him, Gilles continues the struggle, motivated by a sense of duty. He succeeds in opening the safe in which his uncle had accumulated compromising documents on all of the prominent citizens of La Rochelle, documents that had permitted him to keep control over them and to amass his wealth. The documents reveal that Gilles's maternal aunt Gérardine Eloi, weighed down with debt, had both the motivation to kill her creditor and the means—rat poison sold in her store. Using the documents as leverage on the authorities, Gilles succeeds in having Colette freed and Gérardine Eloi indicted; she is acquitted because of the power behind her of the "Syndicate." Gilles then destroys the compromising documents.

Gilles has fallen in love with his uncle's widow, Colette, because she is of the same "race of fugitives, of wanderers" as he (*Toussaint,* 358); only she is able to understand that he is being stifled by his inheritance. She represents his only chance to transcend fear and loneliness. As the novel ends, Gilles and Colette leave together to take up in their turn the life of his parents. In so doing, Gilles abandons his wife, child, and fortune. They do not need him, he is sure, and it is imperative that he rescue Colette from solitude and despair. Gilles's actions provide an excellent illustration of the unconventional sense of morality possessed by Simenon's heroes, for whom morality is not an absolute dictated by the intelligence and the will but an individual choice. Judged by conventional moral standards, Gilles is wrong to abandon his family, but Simenon was always detached from conventional morality. True morality for him is very personal and resembles love of sacrifice; it is the response to a call.

Simenon succeeds in making Gilles's choice comprehensible, even admirable, to the reader, but such behavior on the part of a screen hero would be unacceptable. Thus, there is no child in the film, and the wife, whose only fault is her ordinariness, becomes a frivolous, flirtatious young fiancée. There is one other minor deviation from the novel—aunt Eloi is not acquitted in the film but is to stand trial at a future date. Otherwise, the film succeeds admirably in capturing the atmosphere of the book, from the very first moment in which Gilles, a tall, thin young man, almost a boy, lost in an overcoat that is too big for him and wearing a frayed fur hat, seems to materialize out of the fog into the streets of La Rochelle with their covered arcades, the rich-looking, dreary bourgeois houses with their heavy furniture and somber interiors, the badly lit cafés where habitués play cards[13]—darkness and night in a climate of rain and fog.

This atmosphere is captured by the camera in a remarkable play of black and gray, of shadows and darkness, to produce an enthralling visual re-creation of Simenon's novel. Here, for the first and only time, a director was able to remain faithful to the writer's vision, to show with pictures what Simenon suggested with words. "He is our best scriptwriter . . . his books are divided into chapters, each one the length of a reel,"[14] said one film director about Simenon, and, superficially, that would seem to be true. What he and so many others like him fail to understand is that Simenon is obsessed with what cannot be seen, the dark recesses of the human subconscious inaccessible to the camera's lens. Internal novels, those written largely in the voice inside a character's head, have always been a challenge for filmmakers. In Simenon's case, the challenge almost invariably has not been met. "Ceci tuera cela," wrote Victor Hugo in *Notre-Dame de Paris,* ceci, the book, supplanting the visual images of the stained-glass cathedral windows, but for Simenon's works the reverse can never be true, cela, the visual images, will never supplant his words. "Cela ne tuera jamais ceci!"

Conclusion

Simenon's work is unique in modern literature. It is different from the romans-fleuves of Jules Romains and Roger Martin du Gard and other writers of the early twentieth century, who, like Simenon, also depicted their period. Their works, in the tradition of the nineteenth-century novel, were long descriptive novels with recurring characters and elements of plot tying them together. Simenon's methods were different. In hundreds of short separate novels, both Maigrets and romans durs, by means of delicate impressionistic evocations, he re-created the period between the two world wars over much of the globe, most particularly in France, portraying its provinces and cities, its people and customs on a vast canvas that can be compared to Balzac's *Comédie humaine,* while, at the same time, imbuing the characters with a universality that transcends time and geographical boundaries.

We associate Joyce, Flaubert, Cervantes, or Stendhal with a particular work, but Simenon never wrote a major novel. His great novel, he stated, was a mosaic of all of his small novels, because he could not, like other writers, "summarize man in a single volume or in a few sentences." He "needed two hundred and ten volumes to create characters who were . . . fully human" (*Traces de pas,* 85). What Simenon was seeking to portray was men not as they would like to be but as they really are, not "the clothed man, the man on parade," of nineteenth-century novelists, but "the naked man, the one . . . who has no illusions about himself . . . (but who is) no less great in his search for equilibrium, in his thirst for truth, than his ancestors who draped themselves in purple and affected a borrowed serenity."[1]

Simenon's protagonist is the prototypal modern antihero, prey to the feelings of alienation, solitude, guilt, and expatriation to which the works of writers like Camus and Sartre have accustomed us. His characters, too, find themselves alone in a world without transcendent values and without the social structure and hierarchy that in the past gave order, stability, and meaning to life. They are existentialists inadvertently, for they must find in themselves the answers that were formerly supplied by society and religion, they must act instinctively as they encounter each new situation, for nothing in their past dictates their actions.

Yet Simenon's protagonists are in a more desperate plight than those of Sartre and Camus. Unlike the existentialist heroes, Simenon's characters lack lucidity, they are unable to understand their desperate situation as they are carried along by forces they cannot control. Like Kafka's K. (*The Trial*), they are guilty of the crime of existing, and wander in a trance in a strange dreamlike world; like Beckett's characters, they are the object, not the subject, of the dramas in which they are involved. In their perplexity and confusion, they suffer from a strange amnesia, wondering where they were previously and how long they have been in their present situation.[2]

Their bewilderment, Simenon remarks, results from an internal fissure, a rending of the inner being that causes the characters to be led by vague forces. They do not initiate their actions but merely carry them out. As a result, they are not responsible for what they do, a concept that brings with it the concomitant contemporary theme of the banality of evil. Simenon's characters instinctively give in to the violence that was their destiny. Their lack of lucidity, their subservience to blind forces, is perhaps the twentieth century's "mal du siècle," more fatal than the nineteenth-century despair over the divorce between ideals and reality. The type of man portrayed in Simenon's work lacks distinctive characteristics and positive values, which explains why there are no great thoughts, ambitions, or feelings in Simenon's work (Becker, 2504).

Simenon's empathetic portrayal of man with his fears and insecurities, his temptations and his vices, his doubts and discouragements satisfies a need in the reader who finds that others share his frailties. Simenon believes that when the reader discovers that others are like him, he is less ashamed of himself and regains confidence in life (*Roman,* 57). His compassion for all men—which he extends to only two women in his vast oeuvre[3]—and his understanding of the difficulty of existence, coupled with his narrative genius and feeling for place and atmosphere, account for the phenomenal popularity of Simenon's work.

"I saw and felt and heard the world around me and, within my limitations and within my prejudices I wrote down what I saw, felt, and heard." These words, although written by another novelist (John O'Hara) about his own fiction, convey the essence of Simenon's creativity.

Notes and References

All quotations consist of the author's translations from the French editions; all page references are to the works cited in the endnotes and not necessarily to the editions that are listed by date of publication in the bibliography.

Preface

1. Frédéric Dard in Jean-Baptiste Baronian, "Rencontre du premier type," in *Cahiers Simenon 5: Le milieu littéraire* (Brussels: Les Amis de Georges Simenon, 1991), 169.

Chapter 1

1. Pierre Assouline, *Simenon: Biographie* (Paris: Julliard, 1992), 12–13; hereafter cited in text.
2. *Le drame mystérieux des îles Galapagos,* ed. Pierre Deligny (Brussels: Les Amis de Georges Simenon, 1991), 11; hereafter cited in text as *Drame.*
3. Simenon wrote *Je me souviens,* published in 1945. On the advice of André Gide, Simenon rewrote the work in the third person in the form of a novel, titled *Pedigree.*
4. André Parinaud, *Connaissance de Georges Simenon* (Paris: Presses de la Cité, 1957), 376; hereafter cited in text.
5. Lucille Becker, "Georges Simenon," in *European Writers: The Twentieth Century,* ed. George Stade (New York: Charles Scribner's Sons, 1990), 12:2480; hereafter cited in text.
6. John Raymond, *Simenon in Court* (New York: Harcourt Brace & World, 1968), 40.
7. *Pedigree* (Paris: Presses de la Cité, 1978), preface, 6–7; hereafter cited in text as *Pedigree* 1 ("A l'ombre de Saint-Nicolas"); *Pedigree* 2 ("La maison envahie"); *Pedigree* 3 ("Quand les lampes se sont éteintes").
8. Quoted by Maurice Piron, "Georges Simenon et son milieu natal," in *Simenon,* Cistre Essais 10 (Lausanne: Editions l'Age d'Homme, 1980), 38.
9. Quoted by Michel Lemoine, "Traces autobiographiques d'origine liégoise dans l'oeuvre romanesque de Georges Simenon," *Cahiers Simenon 3: Des doubles et des miroirs* (Brussels: Les Amis de Georges Simenon, 1989), 101.
10. Benoît Denis, "Aller voir, ailleurs si j'y suis: Hergé, Simenon, Michaux." *Textyles: Revue des lettres belges de langue française,* no. 12 (November, 1995): 135.
11. Pol Vandromme, *Georges Simenon* (Brussels: Pierre de Méyère, 1962), 15.

12. Denis Tillinac, *Le mystère Simenon* (Paris: Calmann-Lévy, 1980), 96–97.

13. Jacques Dubois, "Statut littéraire et position de classe," in *Lire Simenon: Réalité/Fiction/Ecriture* (Brussels: Editions Labor, 1980), 22.

14. *Je me souviens,* in *Tout Simenon* (Paris: Presses de la Cité, 1993), 26:49; hereafter cited in text as *Souviens.*

15. *Lettre à ma mère* (Paris: Presses de la Cité, 1975), 64–65; hereafter cited in text as *Mère.*

16. Charlotte Wardi, "Les 'petits Juifs' de Georges Simenon," *Travaux de linguistique et de littérature* 12, no. 2 (1974): 233; hereafter cited in text.

17. Maurice Einhorn, "Georges Simenon: Maigret chez les Juifs," *Regards/Bruxelles,* 8–14 January 1982, 19.

18. *Le fou de Bergerac* (Paris: Presses Pocket, 1980), 116; hereafter cited in text as *Fou.*

19. *Les anneaux de Bicêtre* (Paris: Presses de la Cité, 1979), 175; hereafter cited in text as *Bicêtre.*

20. Simenon, interview with Bernard Pivot on television program "Apostrophes," 1982. Also in Simenon, *Un homme comme un autre* (Paris: Presses de la Cité, 1975), 232.

21. *Malempin* (Paris: Gallimard, 1951), 189–90; hereafter cited in text as *Malempin.*

22. *La vérité sur Bébé Donge* (Paris: Gallimard, Collection Folio, 1975), 9; hereafter cited in text as *Bébé.*

23. *Touriste de bananes* (Paris: Gallimard, 1938), 8–9; hereafter cited in text as *Touriste.*

24. Jean-Jacques Tourteau, *D'Arsène Lupin à San-Antonio: Le roman policier français de 1900 à 1970* (Tours: Mame, 1970), 149; hereafter cited in text.

25. Marcel Moré, "Simenon et l'enfant de choeur," in *Simenon,* ed. Francis Lacassin and Gilbert Sigaux (Paris: Plon, 1973), 239–40.

26. *Je suis resté un enfant de choeur,* in *Tout Simenon* (Paris: Presses de la Cité, 1993), 27:1605.

27. *A quoi bon jurer?* in *Tout Simenon* (Paris: Presses de la Cité, 1993), 27:41.

28. *Quand j'étais vieux* (Paris: Presses de la Cité, 1970), 1:125–26; hereafter cited in text as *Vieux* with volume and page number.

29. Henriette Simenon will be called Elise in the text when it is a question of *Pedigree.*

30. Alain Bertrand, *Georges Simenon* (Lyon: La Manufacture, 1988), 65; hereafter cited in text.

31. *La main dans la main,* in *Tout Simenon* (Paris: Presses de la Cité, 1993), 26:1423.

32. *Les quatre jours du pauvre homme* (Paris: Presses de la Cité, 1977), 36; hereafter cited in text as *Quatre jours.*

33. Quoted by Jules Gheude, "Simenon et la femme," in *Simenon un autre regard* (Lausanne: Editions Luce Wilquin, 1988), 119.

34. Jules Bedner, *Simenon et le jeu des deux histoires: Essai sur les romans policiers* (Amsterdam: Institut de Romanistique, 1990), 107.

35. Notably Mme Moncin (*Maigret tend un piège*), Mme Besson (*Maigret et la vieille dame),* and the chilling Mme Serre (*Maigret et la grande perche*), who was prepared to kill her own son for financial security, as she had killed his father before him.

36. *Portrait-souvenir de Balzac,* in Bertrand, 220; hereafter cited in text as *Balzac.*

37. Patrick Marnham, *The Man Who Wasn't Maigret: A Portrait of Georges Simenon* (New York: Farrar, Straus and Giroux, 1992), 32; hereafter cited in text.

38. *Les mémoires de Maigret* (Paris: Presses de la Cité, 1980), 64; hereafter cited in text as *Mémoires.*

39. Interview of 1952 in *Georges Simenon: Vies privées*, prod. and dir. François Wolff and Tristan Bourlard, 1993, documentary.

40. For the term "adventure's failures," see *La mauvaise étoile* (Paris: Gallimard, 1958), 13; hereafter cited in text as *Etoile.*

41. Jacques Lecarme, "Les romans coloniaux de Georges Simenon," *Textyles: Revue des lettres belges de langue française,* no. 6 (November 1989): 187–88.

42. *Le fond de la bouteille* (Paris: Presses de la Cité, 1949), 25; hereafter cited in text as *Bouteille.*

43. *Simenon sur le gril* (Paris: Presses de la Cité, 1968), 16; hereafter cited in text as *Gril.*

44. *Un homme comme un autre,* in *Tout Simenon* (Paris: Presses de la Cité, 1993), 26:485, 565; hereafter cited in text as *Homme.*

45. Interview in *Marie-France* (June 1958) quoted by Tourteau, 150.

46. *Trois chambres à Manhattan, Lettre à mon juge, Le temps d'Anaïs, L'horloger d'Everton, Le grand Bob, En cas de malheur, Le petit homme d'Arkhangelsk, Le veuf,* and *La mort d'Auguste.*

47. Denyse was the spelling she affected for her name. Simenon changed it back to Denise, and she went back to Denyse after their separation.

48. Maurice Piron (with collaboration of Michel Lemoine), *L'univers de Simenon* (Paris: Presses de la Cité, 1983), 374.

49. *Faubourg* (Paris: Gallimard, 1937), 37–38; hereafter cited in text as *Faubourg.*

50. "In 1960, 1961, 1962, for personal reasons, or for reasons I don't know myself, I began feeling old, and I began keeping notebooks. I was nearing the age of sixty" (*Vieux,* preface, 1:i).

51. *Mémoires intimes,* in *Tout Simenon* (Paris: Presses de la Cité, 1993), 27:1136; hereafter cited in text as *Intimes.*

52. *La boule noire, Feux rouges, Antoine et Julie, Le fond de la bouteille, Les volets verts, Betty,* and *Le déménagement.*

53. The eight Simenon novels are: *Le Locataire, La nuit du carrefour, Crime impuni, Les fiançailles de M. Hire, Le petit homme d'Arkhangelsk, Les inconnus dans la maison, Maigret et son mort,* and *Pietr-le-Letton.*

54. *Pietr-le-Letton* (Paris: Presses Pocket, 1977), 107; hereafter cited in text as *Pietr.*

55. The young protagonist appears in *Les noces de Poitiers, L'aîné des Ferchaux, Le testament Donadieu, Les suicidés,* and *Faubourg.* The middle-aged man can be found in *Le bilan Malétras, La fuite de Monsieur Monde,* and *Les anneaux de Bicêtre.*

56. Quoted by Dinitia Smith, "Learning to Love a Lover—Is Casanova's Reputation as a Reprobate a Bum Rap?" *New York Times,* 1 October 1997, B1; hereafter cited in text.

57. *La neige était sale* (Paris: Presses de la Cité, 1951), 214; hereafter cited in text as *Neige.*

58. Brendan Gill, "Profiles: Out of the Dark," *New Yorker,* 24 January 1953, 35.

59. *Les trois crimes de mes amis* (Paris: Gallimard, 1948), 47; hereafter cited in text as *Trois crimes.*

60. Simenon, "Le romancier," *Le roman de l'homme* (Lausanne: Les Editions de l'Aire, 1980), 82; hereafter cited in text as "Romancier."

61. Lucille Becker, "The Significance of Georges Simenon" (keynote address at the National Press Club, Simenon Festival, Washington, D.C., 18 June 1987).

62. Jean-Christophe Camus, *Simenon avant Simenon: Les années de journalisme (1919–1922)* (Brussels: Didier Hatier, 1989), 143; hereafter cited in text.

63. *L'Ane Rouge* (Paris: Fayard, 1933), 182; hereafter cited in text as *Ane.*

64. Leo Schneiderman, "Simenon: To Understand Is To Forgive," *Clues* 7, no. 1 (Spring–Summer 1986): 29.

65. The other three men, as mentioned previously, were Désiré Simenon, Joseph Demarteau of the *Gazette de Liège,* and the Walloon poet Joseph Vrindt.

66. *M. Gallet, décédé; Maigret et les vieillards; L'affaire Saint-Fiacre;* and *Les mémoires de Maigret.*

67. *Pietr-le-Letton, Au rendez-vous des Terre-Neuvas, Les rescapés du "Télémaque," La Marie du port, L'homme de Londres, Le président.*

68. *Les clients d'Avrenos* (Turkey), *Quartier Nègre* (Panama), *Le coup de lune* (Gabon), *45° à l'ombre* (sea route from Matadi to Bordeaux), *L'Aîné des Ferchaux* (Congo, Panama), *Ceux de la soif* (the Galapagos), *Touriste de bananes* (Tahiti), *Long cours* (Panama and Tahiti), *Le passager clandestin* (Tahiti), and *Le blanc à lunettes* (Belgian Congo).

69. *Jour et nuit,* in *Tout Simenon* (Paris: Presses de la Cité, 1993), 27:604.

70. *Le locataire, L'évadé, Le haut mal, Le testament Donadieu, Le Coup-de-Vague, Le voyageur de la Toussaint, Le clan des Ostendais, Le fils,* and *Le train*—and four nearby in the Vendée: *Le fils Cardinaud* and *Les vacances de Maigret* (Les Sables-d'Olonne), *Lettre à mon juge* (La Roche-sur-Yon), and *Le riche homme* (Marsilly).

71. The films were based on two Maigrets—*Picpus* (*Signé Picpus*) and *Cécile est morte*—and six non-Maigrets—*La maison des sept jeunes filles, Annette et la dame blonde, Monsieur la souris, Le voyageur de la Toussaint, L'homme de Londres,* and *Les inconnus dans la maison.*

72. Claude Gauteur, *Simenon à l'écran,* supplement to *Tout Simenon* (Paris: Presses de la Cité, 1992), 25:9, 11.

73. Brendan Gill, "Georges Simenon," in *A New York Life: Of Friends and Others* (New York: Poseidon Press, 1990), 248.

74. *Un nouveau dans la ville, La mort de Belle, L'horloger d'Everton, La boule noire, La main, Maigret à New York, Trois chambres à Manhattan, Feux rouges,* and *Les frères Rico.*

75. *Des traces de pas* (Paris: Presses de la Cité, 1975), 157; hereafter cited in text as *Traces de pas.*

Chapter 2

1. These stories were later published by Fayard under patronymic in 1932 in three volumes titled *Les treize coupables, Les treize énigmes,* and *Les treize mystères.*

2. Claude Menguy and Pierre Deligny, "Les vrais débuts du commissaire Maigret," *Traces 1: Georges Simenon, genèse et unité de l'oeuvre* (Liège: Centre d'Etudes Georges Simenon, 1989): 27–43.

3. Boileau-Narcejac, *Le roman policier* (Paris: Petite Bibliothèque Payot, 1964), 10–12.

4. Michel Butor, *L'emploi du temps* (Paris: Union Générale d'Editions), 214; hereafter cited in text.

5. Fereydoun Hoveyda, *Histoire du roman policier* (Paris: Les Editions du Pavillon, 1965).

6. Stefano Benevenuti and Granni Rizzoni, *The Whodunit: An Informal History of Detective Fiction* (New York: Macmillan, 1979), 13; hereafter cited in text.

7. For example, S. S. Van Dine wrote "Twenty Rules for Detective Stories."

8. "I never think" ("La pipe de Maigret," in *Maigret se fâche* [Paris: Presses de la Cité, 1947], 85); "I never draw conclusions" (*Un crime en Hollande* [Paris: Fayard, 1931], 117).

9. *Une confidence de Maigret* (Paris: Presses de la Cité, 1980), 33; hereafter cited in text as *Confidence.*

10. The quote is taken from *La première enquête de Maigret (1913)* (Paris: Presses de la Cité, 1949), 105.

11. The second series, consisting of six titles, was published by Gallimard from 1942 to 1944.

12. Brigid Brophy, "Jules et Georges," *New Statesman* 67, no. 1726 (10 April 1964): 567; hereafter cited in text.

13. Roger Stéphane, *Portrait-souvenir de Georges Simenon* (Paris: Quai Voltaire, 1989), 105–6.

14. *Le charretier de la "Providence"* (Paris: Fayard, 1931), 14; hereafter cited in text as *Charretier.*

15. *Maigret voyage* (Paris: Presses de la Cité, 1982), 100.

16. *Maigret et le tueur* (Paris: Presses de la Cité, 1969), 25; hereafter cited in text as *Tueur.*

17. *Maigret tend un piège* (Paris: Presses de la Cité, 1981), 6; hereafter cited in text as *Piège.*

18. *Un échec de Maigret* (Paris: Presses de la Cité, 1956), 75; hereafter cited in text as *Echec.*

19. *Maigret au Picratt's* (Paris: Presses de la Cité, 1982), 120.

20. *M. Gallet, décédé* (Paris: Fayard, 1931), 60.

21. *Maigret et le clochard* (Paris: Presses de la Cité, 1982), 90.

22. *Maigret et le marchand de vin* (Paris: Presses de la Cité, 1970), 172; hereafter cited in text as *Marchand.*

23. Thomas Narcejac, *Le cas Simenon* (Paris: Presses de la Cité, 1950), 22.

24. Remarks of French police quoted in the *New York Times,* 2 April 1974, 16.

25. *Maigret aux assises* (Paris: Presses de la Cité, 1960), 78.

26. Dennis Porter, *The Pursuit of Crime: Art and Ideology in Detective Fiction* (New Haven: Yale University Press, 1981), 55; hereafter cited in text.

27. Pierre-Jean Rémy, "Simenon . . . et encore Simenon," *Revue des deux mondes,* no. 11 (November 1989): 129.

28. *L'affaire Saint-Fiacre* (Paris: Fayard, 1933), 50–51; hereafter cited in text as *Saint-Fiacre.*

29. William W. Stowe, "Simenon, Maigret, and Narrative," *Journal of Narrative Technique* 19, no. 3 (Fall 1988): 332.

30. Robert J. Courtine, one of France's leading food writers, published a book of recipes from the fictional kitchen of Madame Maigret, indicating when each dish was mentioned in one of the Maigret novels. It was translated into English under the title *Madame Maigret's Recipes* (New York: Harcourt Brace Jovanovich, 1975).

31. Dino d'Aniguel, "Mais qu'est-ce que Louise peut bien trouver à son Jules?" *Télérama,* Hors-Série, no. 41 (January 1993): 38.

32. Richard Cobb, "Maigret's Paris," in *Tour de France* (London: Duckworth, 1976), 181.

33. C. D. Lewis, "Chez Georges Simenon," *New York Times Book Review,* 12 November 1967, 48.

Chapter 3

1. Those 12 novels are: *Les anneaux de Bicêtre, Le confessionnal, La maison des sept jeunes filles, La mort d'Auguste, Les noces de Poitiers, Le passage de la ligne, Le petit saint, Le président, 45° à l'ombre, Trois chambres à Manhattan, Une vie comme neuve, Les volets verts.* The murder of the cat and the parrot in *Le chat* can be considered murders by proxy.

2. See *Les trois crimes de mes amis* for the genesis of this theme.

3. *Les suicidés* (Paris: Gallimard, 1958), 191.

4. *L'aîné des Ferchaux* (Paris: Gallimard, 1945), 103; hereafter cited in text as *Ferchaux.*

5. Anne Richter, *George Simenon et l'homme désintégré* (Brussels: La Renaissance du Livre, 1964), 75; hereafter cited in text.

6. Arthur Rimbaud, *Une saison en enfer.*

7. *En cas de malheur* (Paris: Presses de la Cité, 1956), 41–42; hereafter cited in text as *Malheur.*

8. Jacques Dubois, "Simenon et la déviance," *Littérature* (University of Paris) 1 (1971): 64.

9. *L'horloger d'Everton* (Paris: Presses de la Cité, 1954), 7; hereafter cited in text as *Horloger.*

10. *Le passage de la ligne* (Paris: Presses de la Cité, 1979), 34; hereafter cited in text as *Passage.*

11. *L'assassin* (Paris: Gallimard, 1937), 173.

12. *Lettre à mon juge* (Paris: Presses de la Cité, 1977), 73–74; hereafter cited in text as *Juge.*

13. *Le bourgmestre de Furnes* (Paris: Gallimard, 1968), 208; hereafter cited in text as *Bourgmestre.*

14. *L'homme qui regardait passer les trains* (Paris: Gallimard, 1938), 34; hereafter cited in text as *L'homme qui regardait.*

15. Léon Thoorens, "Georges Simenon: Romancier de la fuite inutile," *Revue Générale Belge,* 15 March 1954, 781.

16. *La fuite de Monsieur Monde* (Paris: Editions de la Jeune Parque, 1947), 216.

17. *Le bilan Malétras* (Paris: Gallimard, 1948), 80; hereafter cited in text as *Malétras.*

18. Such abandonment is a frequent theme in Simenon's work: *Le fils Cardinaud, L'horloger d'Everton, Il y a encore des noisetiers, La fuite de Monsieur Monde, Le petit homme d'Arkhangelsk, Les anneaux de Bicêtre.*

19. *Les inconnus dans la maison* (Paris: Gallimard, Collection Folio, 1980), 88.

20. *Oncle Charles s'est enfermé* (Paris: Gallimard, 1951), 190; hereafter cited in text as *Charles.*

21. *Les anneaux de Bicêtre* (Paris: Presses de la Cité, 1979), 27; hereafter cited in text as *Bicêtre.*

22. François Mauriac, in *Simenon,* ed. Francis Lacassin and Gilbert Sigaux (Paris: Plon, 1973), 283.

23. *Les volets verts* (Paris: Presses de la Cité, 1979), 45; hereafter cited in text as *Volets.*

24. François Villon, *Le grand testament,* in *Moyen Age,* edited by André Lagarde and Laurent Michard (Paris: Bordas, 1985), 215:

> Quiconque meurt, meurt à douleur
> Telle qu'il perd vent et haleine;
> Son fiel se crève sur son coeur,
> Puis sue, Dieu sait *quel* sueur
> Et n'est qui de ses maux l'allège,
> Car enfant n'a, frère ni soeur,
> Qui lors voulût être son *plège.*
> La mort le fait frèmir, pâlir,
> Le nez courber, les veines tendre,
> Le col enfler, la chair mollir. . . .

25. François Mauriac, *Le romancier et ses personnages,* quoted in Jacques Robichon, *Mauriac* (Paris: Editions Universitaires, 1958), 26.

26. Quoted by Eléonore Schraiber, "Georges Simenon et la littérature russe," in *Simenon,* ed. Francis Lacassin and Gilbert Sigaux (Paris: Plon, 1973), 187.

27. *Les fantômes du chapelier* (Paris: Presses de la Cité, 1954), 134.

28. *Le petit homme d'Arkhangelsk* (Paris: Presses de la Cité), 162; hereafter cited in text as *Arkhangelsk.*

29. *Les fiançailles de M. Hire* (Paris: Presses Pocket, 1976), 12–13; hereafter cited in text as *Hire.*

30. Charles Baudelaire, "Au lecteur," in *Les fleurs du mal.* "Hypocrite lecteur, mon semblable, mon frère." [Hypocritical reader, my fellow man, my brother.]

31. Preface to novel *Traqué* by Arthur Omre (1944), quoted in *Simenon,* ed. Francis Lacassin and Gilbert Sigaux (Paris: Plon, 1973), 371.

32. *Les complices* (Paris: Presses de la Cité, 1978), 5; hereafter cited in text as *Complices.*

33. *La chambre bleue* (Paris: Presses de la Cité, 1978), 189.

34. These five novels are *Le grand Bob, Le clan des Ostendais, Trois chambres à Manhattan, Le blanc à lunettes,* and *Le voyageur de la Toussaint.*

35. *Le veuf* (Paris: Presses de la Cité, 1959), 7; hereafter cited in text as *Veuf.*

36. *Dimanche* (Paris: Presses de la Cité, 1958), 168; hereafter cited in text as *Dimanche.*

37. *La main* (Paris: Presses de la Cité, 1968), 39; hereafter cited in text as *Main*.

38. *La vérité sur Bébé Donge* (Paris: Gallimard, 1945), 187; hereafter cited in text as *Bébé Donge.*

39. *Antoine et Julie* (Paris: Presses de la Cité, 1953), 87; hereafter cited in text as *Antoine.*

40. *La fenêtre des Rouet* (Paris: Presses de la Cité, 1976), 88; hereafter cited in text as *Rouet.*

41. *Le petit saint* (Paris: Presses de la Cité, 1965), 69; hereafter cited in text as *Saint.*

Chapter 4

1. *Le coup de lune* (Paris: Presses Pocket, 1975), 10–11; hereafter cited in text as *Lune.*

2. "L'heure du Nègre," in *A la recherche de l'homme nu: Mes apprentissages 2,* ed. Francis Lacassin and Gilbert Sigaux (Paris: Union Générale d'Editions, 1976), 68–69.

3. "L'Afrique qu'on dit mystérieuse," in *A la rencontre des autres: Mes apprentissages 3,* ed. Francis Lacassin and Gilbert Sigaux (Paris: Union Générale d'Editions, 1989), 159.

4. *Quartier Nègre* (Paris: Gallimard, 1975), 48–49; hereafter cited in text as *Quartier Nègre.*

5. *Le blanc à lunettes* (Paris: Gallimard, 1978), 84–85; hereafter cited in text as *Blanc.*

6. *Ceux de la soif* (Paris: Gallimard, Collection Folio, 1978), 15; hereafter cited in text as *Soif.*

7. Margret Wittmer, *Floreana* (Shropshire: Anthony Nelson, 1989).

8. Names in parentheses are names used in the novel.

Chapter 5

1. "The Mystery Man," interview with Simenon in *Réalités* 190 (November 1961): 26.

2. Henry Anatole Grunwald, "The World's Most Prolific Novelist," *Life* 45 (3 November 1958): 96.

3. Carvel Collins, "The Art of Fiction IX: Georges Simenon," *Paris Review* 9 (Summer 1955): 78.

4. *La mort d'Auguste* (Paris: Presses de la Cité, 1966), 89; hereafter cited in text as *Auguste.*

5. Preface to novel *Traqué* by Arthur Omre (1944), quoted in *Simenon,* ed. Francis Lacassin and Gilbert Sigaux (Paris: Plon, 1973), 371.

6. *Le passager du "Polarlys"* (Paris: Fayard, 1932), 7–8.

7. "Sous peine de mort," in *Trois nouvelles,* ed. Lindsay and Nazzaro (New York: Appleton Century Crofts, 1966), 101; hereafter cited in text as *Peine.*

8. Ralph Messac, "Georges Simenon, 'romancier-nez,' " in *Simenon,* ed. Francis Lacassin and Gilbert Sigaux (Paris: Plon, 1973), 130–38. The article's title is a play on words of *romancier-né*, or born novelist, and *romancier nez,* or novelist-nose, both of which are pronounced the same way.

9. *Maigret et son mort* (Paris: Presses de la Cité, 1948), 181.

10. *Le cercle des Mahé* (Paris: Gallimard, 1946), 42; hereafter cited in text as *Mahé.*

11. *Mon ami Maigret* (Paris: Presses de la Cité, 1980), 151–52.

12. Roger Stéphane, *Le dossier Simenon* (Paris: P. Laffont, 1961), 119.

13. Jean-Christophe Camus, *Simenon avant Simenon: Les années parisiennes (1923–1931)* (Brussels: Didier Hatier, 1990), 233.

14. *Maigret et les vieillards* (Paris: Presses de la Cité, 1960), 7.

15. *La maison du canal* (Paris: Presses de la Cité, 1976), 5.

16. *Le voyageur de la Toussaint* (Paris: Gallimard, 1941), 74; hereafter cited in text as *Toussaint.*

17. *Le clan des Ostendais* (Paris: Gallimard, 1947), 11, 146.

18. *La Jument Perdue* (Paris: Presses de la Cité, 1948), 11.

19. *Les frères Rico* (Paris: Presses de la Cité, 1952), 10.

20. *Maigret et les témoins récalcitrants* (Paris: Presses de la Cité, 1959), 9.

21. *Maigret et l'homme tout seul* (Paris: Presses de la Cité, 1971), 11–12.

22. George Steiner, *Language and Silence* (New York: Atheneum, 1967), 211.

Chapter 6

1. *La boule noire* (Paris: Presses de la Cité, 1955), 212.

2. *Trois chambres à Manhattan* was directed by Marcel Carné in 1965. *Le fruit défendu* was directed by Henri Verneuil in 1952.

3. *Trois chambres à Manhattan* (Paris: Presses de la Cité, 1946), 52; hereafter cited in text as *Chambres.*

4. *La veuve Couderc* (Paris: Gallimard, 1982), 60; hereafter cited in text as *Couderc.*

5. Claude Mauriac, "Georges Simenon et le secret des hommes," in *L'Allitérature contemporaine* (Paris: Editions Albin Michel, 1958), 147.

6. Régis Boyer, "Georges Simenon ou Nous sommes tous des assassins," *Le Français dans le monde,* no. 66 (July–August 1969): 9.

7. In Claude Gauteur, *Simenon à l'écran,* supplement to *Tout Simenon* (Paris: Presses de la Cité, 1992), 25:55.

8. Lucille F. Becker, *Twentieth-Century French Women Novelists* (Boston: Twayne Publishers, 1989), 111.

9. The film *Le chat* was directed by Pierre Granier-Deferre in 1971.

10. *Le chat* (Paris: Presses de la Cité, 1978), 6; hereafter cited in text as *Chat.*

11. There is a similar love triangle in Colette's novel, *La chatte,* where the wife tries to kill her feline rival.

12. *Le voyageur de la Toussaint* was directed by Louis Daquin in 1943.

13. Maurice Dubourg, "Filmographie de Georges Simenon," in *Simenon,* Cistre Essais 10 (Lausanne: Editions l'Age d'Homme, 1980), 171.

14. Maurice Pialat, quoted in Norbert Multeau, "Simenon trahi et servi par le cinéma," *Le spectacle du monde,* no. 327 (June 1989): 72.

Conclusion

1. *Le roman de l'homme* (Lausanne: Les Editions de L'Aire, 1980), 63–64; hereafter cited in text as *Roman.*

2. See Samuel Beckett, *Waiting for Godot* (New York: Grove Press, 1954).

3. These two women are the protagonists of *Tante Jeanne* and *La fenêtre des Rouet.*

Bibliography

Primary Sources

Simenon's complete works

Oeuvres complètes. Edited by Gilbert Sigaux. 72 volumes. One series numbered in Roman numerals from I to XXVIII contains Maigret novels and all of the detective short stories. The other series, numbered in Arabic from 1 to 44, contains the other novels, articles, essays, and autobiographical works. Lausanne: Editions Rencontre, 1967–1973.

Tout Simenon. 27 volumes. Collection "Omnibus." Paris: Presses de la Cité, 1988–1993. Complete works of Simenon.

Published under pseudonyms

[Georges Sim, pseud.]. *Au pont des Arches.* Liège: Bénard, 1921. Reissued under author's name, Paris: Presses de la Cité, 1991.

[Georges Sim, pseud.]. *Jehan Pinaguet: Histoire d'un homme simple.* Written in 1921. Published under name Georges Simenon, Paris: Presses de la Cité, 1991.

Les treize coupables. 1929–30 for magazine *Détective.* Printed under author's name, Paris: Fayard, 1932.

Les treize énigmes. 1928–29 for magazine *Détective.* Printed under author's name, Paris: Fayard, 1932.

Les treize mystères. 1928–29 for magazine *Détective.* Printed under author's name, Paris: Fayard, 1932.

Les introuvables de Georges Simenon. 12 volumes. Paris: Presses de la Cité, 1980. Pulp fiction written under pseudonyms from 1921 to 1932.

Published under the author's name

Works are listed chronologically accompanied by the title, publisher, and date of the English translation. Translations of titles not published in English are given in parentheses.

MAIGRET NOVELS

Pietr-le-Letton. Paris: Fayard, 1931. *Maigret and the Enigmatic Lett.* Harmondsworth: Penguin, 1963.

M. Gallet, décédé. Paris: Fayard, 1931. *Maigret Stonewalled.* Baltimore: Penguin, 1963.

Le pendu de Saint-Pholien. Paris: Fayard, 1931. *Maigret and the Hundred Gibbets.* Harmondsworth: Penguin, 1963.

Le charretier de la "Providence." Paris: Fayard, 1931. *Maigret Meets a Milord.* Harmondsworth: Penguin, 1974.

La tête d'un homme. Paris: Fayard, 1931. *A Battle of Nerves.* In *The Patience of Maigret.* New York: Harcourt Brace & Co., 1940.

Le chien jaune. Paris: Fayard, 1931. *Maigret and the Yellow Dog.* New York: Harcourt Brace Jovanovich, 1987.

La nuit du Carrefour. Paris: Fayard, 1931. *Maigret at the Crossroads.* Baltimore: Penguin, 1964.

Un crime en Hollande. Paris: Fayard, 1931. *A Crime in Holland.* In *Maigret Abroad.* New York: Harcourt Brace & Co., 1940.

Au rendez-vous des Terre-Neuvas. Paris: Fayard, 1931. *The Sailors' Rendez-vous.* Harmondsworth: Penguin, 1970.

La danseuse du Gai-Moulin. Paris: Fayard, 1931. *Maigret at the Gai-Moulin.* New York: Harcourt Brace Jovanovich, 1991.

La Guinguette à deux sous. Paris: Fayard, 1931. *The Guinguette by the Seine.* In *Maigret to the Rescue.* New York: Harcourt Brace & Co., 1941.

Le port des brumes. Paris: Fayard, 1932. *Death of a Harbor Master.* In *Maigret and M. Labbe.* New York: Harcourt Brace & Co., 1942.

L'ombre chinoise. Paris: Fayard, 1932. *Maigret Mystified.* Harmondsworth: Penguin, 1964.

L'affaire Saint-Fiacre. Paris: Fayard, 1932. *Maigret Goes Home.* New York: Harcourt Brace Jovanovich, 1989.

Chez les Flamands. Paris: Fayard, 1932. *The Flemish Shop.* In *Maigret to the Rescue.* New York: Harcourt Brace & Co., 1941.

Le fou de Bergerac. Paris: Fayard, 1932. *The Madman of Bergerac.* In *Maigret Travels South.* London: Routledge, 1940.

Liberty-Bar. Paris: Fayard, 1933. *Liberty-Bar.* In *Maigret Travels South.* London: Routledge, 1940.

L'écluse no. 1. Paris: Fayard, 1933. *The Lock at Charenton.* In *Maigret Sits It Out.* London: Routledge, 1941.

Maigret. Paris: Fayard, 1934. *Maigret Returns.* In *Maigret Sits It Out.* London: Routledge, 1941.

Cécile est morte. In *Maigret revient.* Paris: Gallimard, 1942. *Maigret and the Spinster.* New York: Harcourt Brace Jovanovich, 1977.

Les caves du Majestic. In *Maigret revient.* Paris: Gallimard, 1942. *Maigret and the Hotel Majestic.* New York: Harcourt Brace Jovanovich, 1991.

La maison du juge. Paris: In *Maigret revient.* Paris: Gallimard, 1942. *Maigret in Exile.* New York: Harcourt Brace Jovanovich, 1994.

Signé Picpus. Paris: Gallimard, 1944. *To Any Lengths.* Harmondsworth: Penguin, 1958.

L'inspecteur Cadavre. In *Signé Picpus.* Paris: Gallimard, 1944.

Félicie est là. In *Signé Picpus.* Paris: Gallimard, 1944. *Maigret and the Toy Village.* New York: Harcourt Brace Jovanovich, 1979.

Maigret se fâche, with short story "La pipe de Maigret." Paris: Presses de la Cité, 1947. *Maigret in Retirement.* In *Maigret's Christmas.* New York: Harcourt Brace Jovanovich, 1981. In *Maigret's Pipe: Seventeen Stories.* New York: Harcourt Brace Jovanovich, 1985.

Maigret à New York. Paris: Presses de la Cité, 1947. *Inspector Maigret in New York's Underworld.* New York: New American Library, 1956.

Les vacances de Maigret. Paris: Presses de la Cité, 1948. *No Vacation for Maigret.* New York: Bantam Books, 1959.

Maigret et son mort. Paris: Presses de la Cité, 1948. *Maigret's Special Murder.* London: Hamish Hamilton, 1964.

La première enquête de Maigret (1913). Paris: Presses de la Cité, 1949. *Maigret's First Case.* London: Hamish Hamilton, 1965.

Mon ami Maigret. Paris: Presses de la Cité, 1949. *My Friend Maigret.* In *Maigret Triumphant.* London: Hamish Hamilton, 1969.

Maigret chez le coroner. Paris: Presses de la Cité, 1949. *Maigret at the Coroner's.* New York: Harcourt Brace Jovanovich, 1992.

Maigret et la vieille dame. Paris: Presses de la Cité, 1950. *Maigret and the Old Lady.* In *Maigret Cinq.* New York: Harcourt Brace & World, 1965.

L'amie de Madame Maigret. Paris: Presses de la Cité, 1950. *Madame Maigret's Own Case.* New York: Harcourt Brace Jovanovich, 1990.

Un Noël de Maigret. Paris: Presses de la Cité, 1951. In *Maigret's Christmas.* New York: Harcourt Brace Jovanovich, 1981.

Les mémoires de Maigret. Paris: Presses de la Cité, 1951. *Maigret's Mémoirs.* New York: Harcourt Brace Jovanovich, 1985.

Maigret au Picratt's. Paris: Presses de la Cité, 1951. *Maigret in Montmartre.* New York: Harcourt Brace Jovanovich, 1989.

Maigret en meublé. Paris: Presses de la Cité, 1951. *Maigret Takes a Room.* In *Maigret Cinq.* New York: Harcourt Brace & World, 1965.

Maigret et la grande perche. Paris: Presses de la Cité, 1951. *Maigret and the Burglar's Wife.* New York: Harcourt Brace Jovanovich, 1991.

Maigret, Lognon et les gangsters. Paris: Presses de la Cité, 1952. *Maigret and the Killers.* New York: Harcourt Brace Jovanovich, 1984.

Le revolver de Maigret. Paris: Presses de la Cité, 1952. *Maigret's Revolver.* New York: Harcourt Brace Jovanovich, 1991.

Maigret et l'homme du banc. Paris: Presses de la Cité, 1953. *Maigret and the Man on the Bench.* New York: Harcourt Brace Jovanovich, 1975.

Maigret a peur. Paris: Presses de la Cité, 1953. *Maigret Afraid.* New York: Harcourt Brace Jovanovich, 1983.

Maigret se trompe. Paris: Presses de la Cité, 1953. *Maigret's Mistake.* New York: Harcourt Brace Jovanovich, 1988.

Maigret à l'école. Paris: Presses de la Cité, 1954. *Maigret Goes to School.* In *Five Times Maigret.* New York: Harcourt Brace & World, 1964.

Maigret et la jeune morte. Paris: Presses de la Cité, 1954. *Maigret and the Dead Girl.* In *Maigret Cinq.* New York: Harcourt Brace & World, 1965.

Maigret chez le ministre. Paris: Presses de la Cité, 1955. *Maigret and the Calame Report.* New York: Harcourt Brace & World, 1965.

Maigret et le corps sans tête. Paris: Presses de la Cité, 1955. *Maigret and the Headless Corpse.* New York: Harcourt Brace & World, 1968.

Maigret tend un piège. Paris: Presses de la Cité, 1955. *Maigret Sets a Trap.* New York: Harcourt Brace Jovanovich, Harvest, 1979.

Un échec de Maigret. Paris: Presses de la Cité, 1956. *Maigret's Failure.* London: Hamish Hamilton, 1962.

Maigret s'amuse. Paris: Presses de la Cité, 1957. *Maigret's Little Joke.* In *Maigret Cinq.* New York: Harcourt Brace & World, 1965.

Maigret voyage. Paris: Presses de la Cité, 1958. *Maigret and the Millionnaires.* New York: Harcourt Brace Jovanovich, 1974.

Les scrupules de Maigret. Paris: Presses de la Cité, 1958. *Maigret Has Scrupules.* New York: Harcourt Brace Jovanovich, 1988.

Maigret et les témoins récalcitrants. Paris: Presses de la Cité, 1959. *Maigret and the Reluctant Witnesses.* In *Five Times Maigret.* New York: Harcourt Brace & World, 1964.

Une confidence de Maigret. Paris: Presses de la Cité, 1959. *Maigret Has Doubts.* New York: Harcourt Brace Jovanovich, 1982.

Maigret aux assises. Paris: Presses de la Cité, 1960. *Maigret in Court.* London: Hamish Hamilton, 1961.

Maigret et les vieillards. Paris: Presses de la Cité, 1960. *Maigret in Society.* London: Hamish Hamilton, 1962.

Maigret et le voleur paresseux. Paris: Presses de la Cité, 1961. *Maigret and the Lazy Burglar.* London: Hamish Hamilton, 1963.

Maigret et les braves gens. Paris: Presses de la Cité, 1962. *Maigret and the Black Sheep.* New York: Harcourt Brace Jovanovich, 1976.

Maigret et le client du samedi. Paris: Presses de la Cité, 1962. *Maigret and the Saturday Caller.* New York: Harcourt Brace Jovanovich, 1992.

Maigret et le clochard. Paris: Presses de la Cité, 1963. *Maigret and the Bum.* New York: Harcourt Brace Jovanovich, 1973.

La colère de Maigret. Paris: Presses de la Cité, 1963. *Maigret Loses His Temper.* New York: Harcourt Brace Jovanovich, 1974.

Maigret et le fantôme. Paris: Presses de la Cité, 1964. *Maigret and the Apparition.* New York: Harcourt Brace Jovanovich, 1991.

Maigret se défend. Paris: Presses de la Cité, 1964. *Maigret on the Defensive.* Harmondsworth: Penguin, 1968.

La patience de Maigret. Paris: Presses de la Cité, 1965. *Maigret Bides His Time.* New York: Harcourt Brace Jovanovich, 1985.

Maigret et l'affaire Nahour. Paris: Presses de la Cité, 1967. *Maigret and the Nahour Case.* New York: Harcourt Brace Jovanovich, 1986.

Le voleur de Maigret. Paris: Presses de la Cité, 1967. *Maigret's Pickpocket.* New York: Harcourt Brace & World, 1968.

Maigret à Vichy. Paris: Presses de la Cité, 1968. *Maigret in Vichy.* New York: Harcourt Brace & World, 1969.

Maigret hésite. Paris: Presses de la Cité, 1968. *Maigret Hesitates.* New York: Harcourt Brace Jovanovich, 1970.

L'ami d'enfance de Maigret. Paris: Presses de la Cité, 1968. *Maigret's Boyhood Friend.* New York: Harcourt Brace Jovanovich, 1970.

Maigret et le tueur. Paris: Presses de la Cité, 1969. *Maigret and the Killer.* New York: Harcourt Brace Jovanovich, 1971.

Maigret et le marchand de vin. Paris: Presses de la Cité, 1970. *Maigret and the Wine Merchant.* New York: Harcourt Brace Jovanovich, 1971.

La folle de Maigret. Paris: Presses de la Cité, 1970. *Maigret and the Madwoman.* New York: Harcourt Brace Jovanovich, 1972.

Maigret et l'homme tout seul. Paris: Presses de la Cité, 1971. *Maigret and the Loner.* New York: Harcourt Brace Jovanovich, 1975.

Maigret et l'indicateur. Paris: Presses de la Cité, 1971. *Maigret and the Informer.* New York: Harcourt Brace Jovanovich, 1973.

Maigret et monsieur Charles. Paris: Presses de la Cité, 1972. *Maigret and M. Charles.* London: Hamish Hamilton, 1973.

"ROMANS DURS"

Le Relais d'Alsace. Paris: Fayard, 1931. *The Man from Everywhere.* In *Maigret and M. Labbe.* New York: Harcourt Brace & Co., 1942.

Le passager du "Polarlys." Paris: Fayard, 1932. *The Mystery of the "Polarlys."* In *Two Latitudes.* New York: Harcourt Brace & Co., 1943.

La maison du canal. Paris: Fayard, 1933. *The House by the Canal.* London: Routledge & Kegan Paul, 1948.

Les fiançailles de M. Hire. Paris: Fayard, 1933. *M. Hire's Engagement.* In *The Sacrifice.* London: Hamish Hamilton, 1956.

Le coup de lune. Paris: Fayard, 1933. *Tropic Moon.* In *African Trio.* New York: Harcourt Brace Jovanovich, 1979.

Les gens d'en face. Paris: Fayard, 1933. *The Window Over the Way.* Baltimore: Penguin, 1966.

L'Ane Rouge. Paris: Fayard, 1933. *The Nightclub.* New York: Harcourt Brace Jovanovich, 1979.

Le haut mal. Paris: Fayard, 1933. *The Woman in the Grey House.* In *Affairs of Destiny.* New York: Harcourt Brace & Co., 1944.

Le locataire. Paris: Gallimard, 1934. *The Lodger.* New York: Harcourt Brace Jovanovich, 1983.

Les suicidés. Paris: Gallimard, 1934. *One Way Out.* In *Escape in Vain.* London: Routledge & Kegan Paul, 1943.

L'homme de Londres. Paris: Fayard, 1934. *Newhaven-Dieppe.* In *Affairs of Destiny.* New York: Harcourt Brace & Co., 1944.
Les Pitard. Paris: Gallimard, 1935. *A Wife at Sea.* London: Routledge & Kegan Paul, 1949.
Les clients d'Avrenos (Avrenos's customers). Paris: Gallimard, 1935.
Quartier Nègre (Negro quarter). Paris: Gallimard, 1935.
L'évadé. Paris: Gallimard, 1936. *The Disintegration of J.P.G.* London: Routledge & Kegan Paul, 1937.
Les demoiselles de Concarneau. Paris: Gallimard, 1936. *The Breton Sisters.* In *Havoc by Accident.* New York: Harcourt Brace & Co., 1943.
45° à l'ombre. Paris: Gallimard, 1936. *Aboard the Aquitaine.* In *African Trio.* New York: Harcourt Brace Jovanovich, 1979.
Long cours. Paris: Gallimard, 1936. *The Long Exile.* New York: Harcourt Brace Jovanovich, 1983.
Faubourg. Paris: Gallimard, 1937. *Home Town.* In *On the Danger Line.* New York: Harcourt Brace & Co., 1944.
L'assassin. Paris: Gallimard, 1937. *The Murderer.* New York: Harcourt Brace Jovanovich, 1986.
Le blanc à lunettes. Paris: Gallimard, 1937. *Talatala.* In *African Trio.* New York: Harcourt Brace Jovanovich, 1979.
Le testament Donadieu. Paris: Gallimard, 1937. *Donadieu's Will.* New York: Harcourt Brace Jovanovich, 1991.
Ceux de la soif (Those who thirst). Paris: Gallimard, 1938.
Chemin sans issue. Paris: Gallimard, 1938. *Blind Alley.* New York: Harcourt Brace & Co., 1946.
L'homme qui regardait passer les trains. Paris: Gallimard, 1938. *The Man Who Watched the Trains Go By.* New York: Berkeley Publishing Co., 1958.
Les rescapés du "Télémaque." Paris: Gallimard, 1938. *The Survivors.* New York: Harcourt Brace Jovanovich, 1985.
Monsieur La Souris. Paris: Gallimard, 1938. *The Mouse.* Harmondsworth: Penguin, 1966.
Touriste de bananes ou les dimanches de Tahiti. Paris: Gallimard, 1938. *Banana Tourist.* In *Lost Moorings.* London: Routledge, 1946.
La Marie du port. Paris: Gallimard, 1938. *A Chit of a Girl.* London: Routledge & Kegan Paul, 1949.
Le suspect. Paris: Gallimard, 1938. *The Suspect.* New York: Harcourt Brace Jovanovich, 1991.
Les soeurs Lacroix. Paris: Gallimard, 1938. *Poisoned Relations.* London: Routledge & Kegan Paul, 1950.
Le Cheval Blanc. Paris: Gallimard, 1938. *The White Horse Inn.* New York: Harcourt Brace Jovanovich, 1980.
Chez Krull. Paris: Gallimard, 1939. *Chez Krull.* London: New English Library, 1966.
Le bourgmestre de Furnes. Paris: Gallimard, 1939. *The Burgomaster of Furnes.* London: Routledge & Kegan Paul, 1952.

Le Coup-de-Vague (The hamlet of the Coup-de-Vague). Paris: Gallimard, 1939.

Les inconnus dans la maison. Paris: Gallimard, 1940. *Strangers in the House.* New York: Doubleday, 1954.

Malempin. Paris: Gallimard, 1940. *The Family Lie.* London: Hamish Hamilton, 1978.

Cour d'assises. Paris: Gallimard, 1941. *Justice.* New York: Harcourt Brace Jovanovich, 1983.

La maison des sept jeunes filles (The house of seven girls). Paris: Gallimard, 1941.

L'outlaw. Paris: Gallimard, 1941. *The Outlaw.* New York: Harcourt Brace Jovanovich, 1986.

Bergelon. Paris: Gallimard, 1941. *The Delivery.* New York: Harcourt Brace Jovanovich, 1981.

Il pleut, bergère . . . . Paris: Gallimard, 1941. *Black Rain.* Harmondsworth: Penguin, 1965.

Le voyageur de la Toussaint. Paris: Gallimard, 1941. *Strange Inheritance.* London: Routledge & Kegan Paul, 1970.

Oncle Charles s'est enfermé. Paris: Gallimard, 1942. *Uncle Charles Has Locked Himself In.* New York: Harcourt Brace Jovanovich, 1987.

La veuve Couderc. Paris: Gallimard, 1942. *The Widow.* New York: Doubleday, 1955.

La vérité sur Bébé Donge. Paris: Gallimard, 1942. *The Truth about Bébé Donge.* New York: Harcourt Brace Jovanovich, 1992.

Le fils Cardinaud. Paris: Gallimard, 1942. *Young Cardinaud.* In *The Sacrifice.* London: Hamish Hamilton, 1956.

Le rapport du gendarme. Paris: Gallimard, 1944. *The Gendarme's Report.* London: Routledge & Kegan Paul, 1951.

La fenêtre des Rouet. Paris: Editions de la Jeune Parque, 1945. *Across the Street.* New York: Harcourt Brace Jovanovich, 1992.

L'aîné des Ferchaux. Paris: Gallimard, 1945. *Magnet of Doom.* London: Routledge & Kegan Paul, 1948.

La fuite de Monsieur Monde. Paris: Editions de la Jeune Parque, 1945. *Monsieur Monde Vanishes.* New York: Harcourt Brace Jovanovich, 1977.

Les noces de Poitiers. Paris: Gallimard, 1946. *The Couple from Poitiers.* New York: Harcourt Brace Jovanovich, 1985.

Le cercle des Mahé (The Mahés's circle). Paris: Gallimard, 1946.

Trois chambres à Manhattan. Paris: Presses de la Cité, 1946. *Three Beds in Manhattan.* New York: Doubleday, 1964.

Au bout du rouleau (At the end of your tether). Paris: Presses de la Cité, 1947.

Le clan des Ostendais. Paris: Gallimard, 1947. *The Ostenders.* London: Routledge & Kegan Paul, 1952.

Lettre à mon juge. Paris: Presses de la Cité, 1947. *Act of Passion.* New York: Prentice-Hall, 1952.

Le destin des Malou. Paris: Presses de la Cité, 1947. *The Fate of the Malous.* London: Hamish Hamilton, 1962.

Le passager clandestin. Paris: Editions de la Jeune Parque, 1947. *The Stowaway.* London: Hamish Hamilton, 1957.

Pedigree. Paris: Presses de la Cité, 1948. *Pedigree.* New York: London House, 1963.

Le bilan Malétras. Paris: Gallimard, 1948. *The Reckoning.* New York: Harcourt Brace Jovanovich, 1984.

La Jument Perdue (The Lost Mare ranch). Paris: Presses de la Cité, 1948.

La neige était sale. Paris: Presses de la Cité, 1948. *Stain on the Snow.* Baltimore: Penguin, 1964.

Le fond de la bouteille. Paris: Presses de la Cité, 1949. *The Bottom of the Bottle.* London: Hamish Hamilton, 1977.

Les fantômes du chapelier. Paris: Presses de la Cité, 1949. *The Hatter's Phantoms.* New York: Harcourt Brace Jovanovich, 1976.

Les quatre jours du pauvre homme. Paris: Presses de la Cité, 1949. *Four Days in a Lifetime.* London: Hamish Hamilton, 1977.

Un nouveau dans la ville (A stranger in town). Paris: Presses de la Cité, 1950.

Les volets verts. Paris: Presses de la Cité, 1950. *The Heart of a Man.* London: Hamish Hamilton, 1955.

L'enterrement de Monsieur Bouvet. Paris: Presses de la Cité, 1950. *Inquest on Bouvet.* London: Hamish Hamilton, 1958.

Tante Jeanne. Paris: Presses de la Cité, 1951. *Aunt Jeanne.* London: Routledge & Kegan Paul, 1953.

Le temps d'Anaïs. Paris: Presses de la Cité, 1951. *The Girl in His Past.* New York: Prentice-Hall, 1952.

Une vie comme neuve. Paris: Presses de la Cité, 1951. *A New Lease on Life.* New York: Doubleday, 1963.

Marie qui louche. Paris: Presses de la Cité, 1952. *The Girl with a Squint.* New York: Harcourt Brace Jovanovich, 1978.

La mort de Belle. Paris: Presses de la Cité, 1952. *Belle.* In *An American Omnibus.* New York: Harcourt Brace & World, 1967.

Les frères Rico. Paris: Presses de la Cité, 1952. *The Brothers Rico.* In *An American Omnibus.* New York: Harcourt Brace & World, 1967.

Antoine et Julie. Paris: Presses de la Cité, 1953. *The Magician.* London: Hamish Hamilton, 1974.

L'escalier de fer. Paris: Presses de la Cité, 1953. *The Iron Staircase.* New York: Harcourt Brace Jovanovich, 1977.

Feux rouges. Paris: Presses de la Cité, 1953. *The Hitchhiker.* In *An American Omnibus.* New York: Harcourt Brace & World, 1967.

Crime impuni. Paris: Presses de la Cité, 1954. *Account Unsettled.* London: Hamish Hamilton, 1962.

L'horloger d'Everton. Paris: Presses de la Cité, 1954. *The Watchmaker.* In *An American Omnibus.* New York: Harcourt Brace & World, 1967.

Le grand Bob. Paris: Presses de la Cité, 1954. *Big Bob.* New York: Harcourt Brace Jovanovich, 1981.

Les témoins. Paris: Presses de la Cité, 1955. *The Witnesses.* New York: Doubleday, 1956.

La boule noire. Paris: Presses de la Cité, 1955. *The Rules of the Game.* New York: Harcourt Brace Jovanovich, 1988.

Les complices. Paris: Presses de la Cité, 1956. *The Accomplices.* New York: Harcourt Brace Jovanovich, 1977.

En cas de malheur. Paris: Presses de la Cité, 1956. *In Case of Emergency.* New York: Doubleday, 1958.

Le petit homme d'Arkhangelsk. Paris: Presses de la Cité, 1956. *The Little Man from Archangel.* New York: Harcourt Brace & World, 1966.

Le fils. Paris: Presses de la Cité, 1957. *The Son.* London: Hamish Hamilton, 1958.

Le Nègre. Paris: Presses de la Cité, 1957. *The Negro.* London: Hamish Hamilton, 1958.

Strip-tease. Paris: Presses de la Cité, 1958. *Striptease.* London: Hamish Hamilton, 1959.

Le président. Paris: Presses de la Cité, 1958. *The Premier.* New York: Harcourt Brace & World, 1966.

Le passage de la ligne (Crossing the line). Paris: Presses de la Cité, 1958.

Dimanche. Paris: Presses de la Cité, 1958. *Sunday.* New York: Harcourt Brace Jovanovich, Harvest, 1976.

La vieille. Paris: Presses de la Cité, 1959. *The Grandmother.* New York: Harcourt Brace Jovanovich, 1981.

Le veuf. Paris: Presses de la Cité, 1959. *The Widower.* New York: Harcourt Brace Jovanovich, 1981.

L'ours en peluche. Paris: Presses de la Cité, 1960. *Teddy Bear.* New York: Harcourt Brace Jovanovich, 1972.

Betty. Paris: Presses de la Cité, 1961. *Betty.* New York: Harcourt Brace Jovanovich, 1975.

Le train. Paris: Presses de la Cité, 1961. *The Train.* New York: Harcourt Brace & World, 1966.

La porte. Paris: Presses de la Cité, 1962. *The Door.* New York: Harcourt Brace Jovanovich, 1990.

Les autres. Paris: Presses de la Cité, 1962. *The House on the Quai Notre-Dame.* New York: Harcourt Brace Jovanovich, 1975.

Les anneaux de Bicêtre. Paris: Presses de la Cité, 1963. *The Bells of Bicêtre.* New York: Harcourt Brace & World, 1964.

La chambre bleue. Paris: Presses de la Cité, 1964. *The Blue Room.* New York: Harcourt Brace Jovanovich, Harvest, 1978.

L'homme au petit chien. Paris: Presses de la Cité, 1964. *The Man With the Little Dog.* New York: Harcourt Brace Jovanovich, 1989.

Le petit saint. Paris: Presses de la Cité, 1965. *The Little Saint.* New York: Harcourt Brace & World, 1965.

Le train de Venise. Paris: Presses de la Cité, 1965. *The Venice Train.* New York: Harcourt Brace Jovanovich, 1974.

Le confessionnal. Paris: Presses de la Cité, 1966. *The Confessional.* New York: Harcourt Brace & World, 1968.

La mort d'Auguste. Paris: Presses de la Cité, 1966. *The Old Man Dies.* New York: Harcourt Brace & World, 1967.

Le chat. Paris: Presses de la Cité, 1967. *The Cat.* New York: Harcourt Brace & World, 1967.

Le déménagement. Paris: Presses de la Cité, 1967. *The Move.* New York: Harcourt Brace & World, 1968.

La prison. Paris: Presses de la Cité, 1968. *The Prison.* New York: Harcourt Brace & World, 1969.

La main. Paris: Presses de la Cité, 1968. *The Man on the Bench in the Barn.* New York: Harcourt Brace Jovanovich, 1970.

Il y a encore des noisetiers (There are still some hazel trees). Paris: Presses de la Cité, 1969.

Novembre. Paris: Presses de la Cité, 1969. *November.* New York: Harcourt Brace Jovanovich, 1970.

Le riche homme. Paris: Presses de la Cité, 1970. *The Rich Man.* New York: Harcourt Brace Jovanovich, 1971.

La disparition d'Odile. Paris: Presses de la Cité, 1971. *The Disappearance of Odile.* New York: Harcourt Brace Jovanovich, 1972.

La cage de verre. Paris: Presses de la Cité, 1971. *The Glass Cage.* New York: Harcourt Brace Jovanovich, 1973.

Les innocents. Paris: Presses de la Cité, 1971. *The Innocents.* New York: Harcourt Brace Jovanovich, 1973.

Collections of Short Stories

La folle d'Itteville (The madwoman of Itteville). Paris: Haumont, 1931.

Les sept minutes (Seven minutes). Paris: Gallimard, 1938.

Le petit docteur. Paris: Gallimard, 1943. *The Little Doctor.* New York: Harcourt Brace Jovanovich, 1981.

Les dossiers de l'Agence O (The files of Agency O). Paris: Gallimard, 1943.

Nouvelles exotiques (Exotic stories). Paris: Gallimard, 1954.

Signé Picpus (Signed Picpus). Paris: Gallimard, 1944.

Les nouvelles enquêtes de Maigret. Paris: Gallimard, 1944. *The Short Cases of Inspector Maigret.* New York: Doubleday, 1959.

Maigret et l'inspecteur malchanceux (later *malgracieux*) (Maigret and the unlucky [later boorish] police inspector). Paris: Presses de la Cité, 1947.

Maigret et les petits cochons sans queue (Maigret and the little tailless pigs). Paris: Presses de la Cité, 1949.

Un Noël de Maigret (Maigret's Christmas). Paris: Presses de la Cité, 1951.

Le bateau d'Emile (Emile's boat). Paris: Gallimard, 1954.

La rue aux trois poussins (The street of the three chicks). Paris: Presses de la Cité, 1963.

AUTOBIOGRAPHICAL AND OTHER NONFICTIONAL WORKS

A la conquête de Tigy: Lettres inédites, 1921–24 (Courting Tigy: Previously unpublished letters, 1921–24). Paris: Julliard, 1995. 270 letters written between January 1921 and February 1924 to his fiancée, Régine Renchon (Tigy).

A la découverte de la France: Mes apprentissages 1. Edited by Francis Lacassin and Gilbert Sigaux. Preface and bibliography by Francis Lacassin. Paris: Union Générale d'Editions, 1976. Articles on France published in French newspapers between 1930 and 1934 as well as texte of *La femme en France* without the photographs of the original album.

A la recherche de l'homme nu: Mes apprentissages 2. Edited by Francis Lacassin and Gilbert Sigaux. Preface and bibliography by Francis Lacassin. Paris: Union Générale d'Editions, 1976. Articles on Africa, Tahiti, Latin America, Québec, and the United States published in French magazines between 1932 and 1946.

A la rencontre des autres: Mes apprentissages 3. Edited by Francis Lacassin and Gilbert Sigaux. Preface and bibliography by Francis Lacassin. Paris: Union Générale d'Editions, 1989. Articles on Europe published in French magazines between 1931 and 1934 as well as an article of 1946 omitted from *A la recherche de l'homme nu.*

Carissimo Simenon. Mon cher Fellini. Edited by Claude Gauteur. Preface by Jacqueline Risset. Paris: Editions Cahiers du cinéma, 1999. Correspondence between Georges Simenon and Frederico Fellini.

Le drame mystérieux des îles Galapagos (The mysterious drama of the Galapagos Islands). Preface by Pierre Deligny. Brussels: Les Amis de Georges Simenon, 1991. Seven articles written for *Paris-Soir* in 1935.

Histoires de partout et d'ailleurs (Stories from everywhere). Edited by Pierre Deligny. Brussels: Les Amis de Georges Simenon, 1993. Twelve articles written for the publication *Courrier royal* in 1935 and 1936.

Les trois crimes des mes amis (The three crimes of my friends). Paris: Gallimard, 1938.

La mauvaise étoile (Unlucky star). Paris: Gallimard, 1938. Series of articles, "Les ratés de l'aventure," published in *Paris-Soir* in 1935 and later in book form.

"Honoré de Balzac: Portrait souvenir." In *Georges Simenon,* by Alain Bertrand. Lyon: La Manufacture, 1988. Reprint of a broadcast presented by Roger Stéphane and Roland Darbois.

Lettres sur Balzac. Brussels: Les Amis de Georges Simenon, 1994. Correspondence with André Jeannot.

"L'Aventure." In *Les Etincelles.* Lyon: Editions de Savoie, 1945.

Je me souviens (I remember). Paris: Presses de la Cité, 1945.

"Le romancier." *French Review* 19, no.4 (February 1946): 212–29.

Le roman de l'homme. Paris: Presses de la Cité, 1960. *The Novel of Man.* New York: Harcourt Brace & World, 1964. Speech delivered at Brussels World's Fair, 3 October 1958.

Le roman de l'homme. Lausanne: Editions de l'Aire, 1980. Contains "Le roman de l'homme," "L'Age du roman," "Le romancier," and "Une interview sur l'art du roman" with Carvel Collins.

La femme en France. Paris: Presses de la Cité, 1958. Essay on French women illustrated with photographs by Daniel Frasnay.

Quand j'étais vieux. Paris: Presses de la Cité, 1970. *When I Was Old.* New York: Harcourt Brace Jovanovich, 1971.

Lettre à ma mère. Paris: Presses de la Cité, 1974. *Letter to My Mother.* New York: Harcourt Brace Jovanovich, 1976.

Mémoires intimes suivis du livre de Marie-Jo. Paris: Presses de la Cité, 1981. *Intimate Memoirs.* New York: Harcourt Brace Jovanovich, 1984. Simenon's last work.

"Dictées"

These 21 works were transcribed from Simenon's dictation into tape recorder and published by Presses de la Cité.

Un homme comme un autre. Paris: Presses de la Cité, 1975.

Des traces de pas. Paris: Presses de la Cité, 1975.

Les petits hommes. Paris: Presses de la Cité, 1976.

Vent du nord-Vent du sud. Paris: Presses de la Cité, 1976.

Un banc au soleil. Paris: Presses de la Cité, 1977.

De la cave au grenier. Paris: Presses de la Cité, 1977.

A l'abri de notre arbre. Paris: Presses de la Cité, 1977.

Tant que je suis vivant. Paris: Presses de la Cité, 1978.

Vacances obligatoires. Paris: Presses de la Cité, 1978.

La main dans la main. Paris: Presses de la Cité, 1978.

Au-delà de ma porte-fenêtre. Paris: Presses de la Cité, 1979.

Je suis resté un enfant de choeur. Paris: Presses de la Cité, 1979.

A quoi bon jurer. Paris: Presses de la Cité, 1979.

Point-virgule. Paris: Presses de la Cité, 1979.

Le prix d'un homme. Paris: Presses de la Cité, 1980.

On dit que j'ai soixante-quinze ans. Paris: Presses de la Cité, 1980.

Quand vient le froid. Paris: Presses de la Cité, 1980.

Les libertés qu'il nous reste. Paris: Presses de la Cité, 1980.

La femme endormie. Paris: Presses de la Cité, 1981.

Jour et nuit. Paris: Presses de la Cité, 1981.

Destinées. Paris: Presses de la Cité, 1981.

Television Interviews

Cassettes of these interviews are in the Simenon Centre of Drew University.

Desfons, Pierre. Commentary by Francis Lacassin. "Un siècle d'écrivains—Georges Simenon." October 1997.

Hauduroy, J. F. "Simenon arbre à romans." 1960. Reconstructs writing of novel *Le président*.

Pivot, Bernard. "Apostrophes." Interview with Georges Simenon, 1981.

Wolff, Françoise, and Tristan Bourlard. "Georges Simenon, vies privées." Documentary. 1993.

Ballet

"La chambre." For Roland Petit Ballet Company. Music by Georges Auric, scenery by Bernard Buffet. January 1956.

Theater

Quartier Nègre. Play in three acts and seven tableaux. Music by Maurice Jaubert. Settings by R. Moulaert. First performance at Théâtre Royal des Galeries Saint-Hubert, Brussels, 9 December 1936.

La neige était sale. Play in three acts. Producer Raymond Rouleau. Actors: Daniel Gélin, Lucienne Bogaërt. First performance at Théâtre de l'Oeuvre in Paris, 12 December 1950.

Le flair du petit docteur. "The Man Who Ran Away." England, 1956.

Liberty Bar. Adaptation by Charles Régnier. First performance in Zurich, 1960.

Maigret se trompe. Play in three acts. Adaptation by Arturo Rigel. First performance in Madrid, 1960.

Simenon, by Jean Louvet. Staging by Armand Delcampe. First performance at Théâtre Blocry in Louvain-la-Neuve, l September 1994.

Secondary Sources

Alavoine, Bernard. "Georges Simenon: De l'impressionnisme à la peinture de l'atmosphère." In *Traces 2,* 79–87. Liège: Centre d'Etudes Georges Simenon, 1990.

Assouline, Pierre. *Simenon: Biographie.* Paris: Julliard, 1992. *Simenon: A Biography.* New York: Alfred A. Knopf, 1997. The definitive work on the life of Georges Simenon.

Au revoir, Georges Simenon! Brussels: Les Amis de Georges Simenon, 1989. Festschrift on occasion of Simenon's death.

Bajomée, Danielle. "Le style et l'esthétique." In *Simenon: L'homme, l'univers, la création,* 147–65. Brussels: Editions Complexe, 1993.

Barré, Jean-Luc. "Les fantômes du romancier." *Revue des deux mondes,* no. 10 (Octobre 1992): 193–97.

Becker, Lucille. *Georges Simenon.* Boston: Twayne Publishers, 1977. Comprehensive study of Simenon's work in English. Portions of this work were reprinted in "Georges Simenon," *European Writers: The Twentieth Century,* ed. George Stade, 12: 2479–2510. New York: Charles Scribner's Sons, 1990.

———. "The Significance of Georges Simenon." Keynote address at the National Press Club, Simenon Festival, Washington, D.C., 18 June 1987.

———. "Simenon and the Detective Novel." Paper presented at the International Monetary Fund, Simenon Festival, Washington, D.C., October 1987.

———. "Science and Detective Fiction: Complementary Genres on the Margins of French Literature." In *On the Margins of French Literature.* French Literature Series, 20. Columbia: University of South Carolina Press, 1992. Science fiction of Pierre Boulle—detective fiction of Georges Simenon.

———. " 'L'exotisme n'existe pas'—Paysages intérieurs de Georges Simenon." *Traces 9: Georges Simenon et l'exotisme,* 281–95. Liège: Centre d'Etudes Georges Simenon, 1997. Proceedings of fifth international colloquium in 1996 on exoticism in Simenon's work.

Bedner, Jules. *Simenon et le jeu des deux histoires: Essai sur les romans policiers*. Amsterdam: Institut de Romanistique, 1990. Examines Simenon's Maigrets to determine Simenon's originality in the field of detective fiction.

Benevenuti, Stefano, and Granni Rizzoni. *The Whodunit: An Informal History of Detective Fiction.* Translated by Anthony Eyre. New York: Macmillan, 1979. Comprehensive study of detective fiction.

Bertrand, Alain. *Georges Simenon.* Lyon: La Manufacture, 1988. Critical work on Simenon. Also contains reprints of *Simenon sur le gril*—Simenon interviewed by five doctors—and "Honoré de Balzac: Portrait souvenir," by Simenon.

Boileau-Narcejac. *Le roman policier.* 3rd ed. Paris: Presses Universitaires de France, 1988. Genesis and evolution of the detective novel.

Boisdeffre, Pierre de. "Le secret de Georges Simenon." *La Revue de Paris,* 65e année, no. 1 (January 1958): 173–74. Simenon and modern themes of guilt, expatriation, and solitude.

———. "A la recherche de Simenon." *La Revue de Paris,* 69e année, no. 9 (September 1962): 96–107.

Boussart, Jean-Denys. *Itinéraire Simenon: Promenade dans le Liège de Simenon,* suivi de *L'itinéraire Simenon en photos* (with the collaboration of the Liège tourist office). Illustrated by François Walthery. Liège: Noir Dessin Production, 1994. Guidebook to Simenon's Liège.

Boutry, Marie-Paule. *Les 300 vies de Simenon.* Paris: Editions de l'Arsenal, 1994. Excellent study of the major themes in Simenon's novels.

Boyer, Régis. "Georges Simenon ou Nous sommes tous des assassins." *Le Français dans le monde,* no. 64 (April–May 1969): 13–17; no. 66 (July–August 1969): 9–15. Explores Simenon's thesis that all men are capable of murder if driven to their limit.

———. *"Le chien jaune" de Georges Simenon.* Paris: Hachette, 1973. Detailed study of *Le chien jaune.*

Brophy, Brigid. "Jules et Georges." *New Statesman* 67, no. 1726 (10 April 1964). Article on *Le train.*

Cahiers Simenon 1: Simenon et le cinéma. Brussels: Les Amis de Georges Simenon, 1988. Articles on cinema and filmography.

Cahiers Simenon 2: Les lieux de la mémoire. Brussels: Les Amis de Georges Simenon, 1988. Articles on cities that figure prominently in Simenon's novels.

Cahiers Simenon 3: Des doubles et des miroirs. Brussels: Les Amis de Georges Simenon, 1989. Autobiographical elements in Simenon's works.

Cahiers Simenon 4: Du petit reporter au grand romancier. Brussels: Les Amis de Georges Simenon, 1990. Simenon, reporter and journalist.

Cahiers Simenon 5: Le milieu littéraire. Brussels: Les Amis de Georges Simenon, 1991. Evaluation of Simenon's place in the history of twentieth-century literature.

Cahiers Simenon 6: Le nouvelliste et le conteur. Brussels: Les Amis de Georges Simenon, 1993. Simenon's novellas and short stories.

Cahiers Simenon 7: Le roman d'une amitié. Brussels: Les Amis de Georges Simenon, 1993. Correspondence between Georges Simenon and Gilbert Sigaux, 1954–1982.

Cahiers Simenon 8: Boire et manger. Brussels: Les Amis de Georges Simenon, 1994. Importance of food, particularly in the Maigrets.

Cahiers Simenon 9: Traversées de Paris. Brussels: Les Amis de Georges Simenon, 1996. Paris in Simenon's oeuvre.

Cahiers Simenon 10: Dix ans d'Amérique. Brussels: Les Amis de Georges Simenon, 1997. The United States in Simenon's oeuvre.

Cahiers Simenon 11: D'Afrique et d'ailleurs. Brussels: Les Amis de Georges Simenon, 1998.

Camus, Jean-Christophe. *Simenon avant Simenon: Les années de journalisme (1919–1922).* Brussels: Didier Hatier, 1989. Interesting work on Simenon's early years as a journalist in Liège.

———. *Simenon avant Simenon: Les années parisiennes (1923–1931).* Brussels: Didier Hatier, 1990. Simenon's initial eight years in Paris.

Chastenet, Patrick, and Philippe Chastenet. *Simenon, album de famille: Les années Tigy.* Paris: Presses de la Cité, 1981.

Cobb, Richard. *Tour de France.* London: Duckworth, 1976. Includes "Maigret's Paris," 179–84; "The Geography of Simenon," 185–89; "Simenon on Simenon," 190–94; and "Maigret retired," 195–199. Excellent articles.

———. *People and Places.* New York: Oxford University Press, 1985. Includes "Simenon at Eighty," 93–101; and "Simenon's Mother," 102–5.

Collins, Carvel. "The Art of Fiction IX: Georges Simenon." *Paris Review* 9 (Summer 1955): 71–90. Interesting interview with Simenon on his technique and ideas.

Courtine, Robert. J. *Le cahier de recettes de Madame Maigret.* Paris: Robert Laffont, 1974. Recipes from the fictional kitchen of Madame Maigret. Translated into English under the title *Madame Maigret's Recipes.* New York: Harcourt Brace Jovanovich, 1975.

———. *Simenon et Maigret passent à table.* Paris: Laffont, 1992.

Debray-Ritzen, Pierre. *Psychologie de la littérature et de la création littéraire.* Paris: Retz-C.E.P.L., 1977.

———. *Georges Simenon: Romancier de l'instinct.* Lausanne: Editions Favre, 1989. Revision and update of his *Simenon: Avocat des hommes,* written under the pseudonym Quentin Ritzen. Simenon as spokesman for Everyman.

Decaudin, Michel. "Topographie et imaginaire chez Simenon." *La Licorne,* no. 12 (1986): 37–45.

Deguy, Jacques. "Simenon, Signoret, Cinéma (*La veuve Couderc*)." *Nord,* no. 7 (June 1986): 21–26.

Delbouille, Paul. "Notes pour une étude du récit de paroles." *Traces 1: Georges Simenon, genèse et unité de l'oeuvre,* 157–67. Liège: Centre d'Etudes Georges Simenon, 1989.

Deligny, Pierre, and Claude Menguy. "Les vrais débuts du commissaire Maigret." *Traces 1: Georges Simenon, genèse et unité de l'oeuvre,* 27–44. Liège: Centre d'Etudes Georges Simenon, 1989. Early pseudonymous novels in which Maigret appeared.

———. Preface to *Le drame mystérieux des îles Galapagos.* Brussels: Les Amis de Georges Simenon, 1991. Collection of Simenon's articles on Galapagos adventures.

Desonay, Fernand. "Georges Simenon: Romancier et académicien." *Le Flambeau,* 35e année, no. 2 (1953); continued in no. 3. Biographical details, analysis, study of *Les trois crimes des mes amis* and several Maigrets.

Drysdale, Dennis. "Simenon and Social Justice." *Nottingham French Studies* 13, no. 2 (October 1974): 85–97.

Dubois, Jacques. "Simenon et la déviance." *Littérature* (University of Paris) 1 (1971): 62–72. One of the best studies of Simenon's work. Analysis of six novels that deal with the theme of deviance from the norm. The deviant, in sociological terms, is one who transgresses the norms of the group to which he belongs and thus provokes hostile reactions on the part of the majority of the group.

———. "Statut littéraire et position de classe." In *Lire Simenon: Réalité/Fiction/Ecriture,* 17–45. Brussels: Editions Labor, 1980. Significance of class in Simenon's work.

———. *Le roman policier ou la modernité.* Brussels: Editions Nathan, 1992. Comprehensive study of the detective novel with important chapter on Simenon.

Dubourg, Maurice. "Maigret et cie ou les détectives de l'agence Simenon." *Ellery Queen Magazine* (December 1964): 108–18.

———. "Filmographie de Georges Simenon." In *Simenon,* 157–200. Cistre Essais 10. Lausanne: Editions l'Age d'Homme, 1980.

Dumortier, Jean-Louis. *Georges Simenon—Un livre: Le bourgmestre de Furnes. Une oeuvre.* Revised, enlarged edition. Brussels: Editions Labor, 1991. Detailed study of the novel *Le bourgmestre de Furnes.*

Einhorn, Maurice. "Georges Simenon: Maigret chez les Juifs." *Regards/Bruxelles* 8–14 January 1982, 18–19. Anti-Semitism in Simenon's work.

Eisinger, Erica M. "Maigret and Women: *La Maman and La Putain." Journal of Popular Culture* 12, no. 1 (Summer 1978): 52–60.

Eskin, Stanley. *Simenon: A Critical Biography.* Jefferson, N.C.: McFarland & Co., 1987. Interesting study in English of Simenon's life and work.

Fabre, Jean. *Enquête sur un enquêteur, Maigret: Un essai de sociocritique.* Montpelier: Editions du CERES, 1981. Biography of Simenon and influence of his life on his work.

———. "Simenon et Maigret à l'ère du soupçon." *L'Esprit créateur* 26, no. 2 (Summer 1986): 82–92.

Fallois, Bernard de. *Simenon.* Paris: Gallimard, 1961. Updated version, Lausanne: Editions Rencontre, 1971. Comprehensive study of Simenon's work.

Feyder, Vera. *Liège.* Paris: Editions Champs Vallon, 1992. Fascinating portrayal of Liège—its history, customs, artists, and writers. Omnipresence of the city in the work of Simenon.

Forest, Jean. *L'affaire Maigret.* Montreal: Les Presses de l'Université de Montréal, 1994. The Maigret cycle as Simenon's "comédie humaine."

———. *Les archives Maigret.* Montreal: Les Presses de l'Université de Montréal, 1994. Detailed analysis of 107 Maigrets in chronological order.

Franck, Frederick. *Simenon's Paris.* New York: Dial Press, 1970. Beautiful, nostalgic collection of Franck's illustrations of Paris accompanied by appropriate texts from Simenon's works.

Gauteur, Claude. *Simenon au cinéma.* Brussels: Didier Hatier, 1990. Texts on Simenon and the cinema collected and presented by Gauteur. The best work on Simenon and film.

———. *Simenon à l'écran,* supplement to *Tout Simenon,* vol. 25. Paris: Presses de la Cité, 1992. Films based on Simenon's novels from 1932 to 1992.

Gelernter, David. *Drawing Life: Surviving the Unabomber.* New York: Free Press, 1997. The fallacy of refusing to pass judgment on the guilty.

Gill, Brendan. "Profiles: Out of the Dark." *New Yorker,* 24 January 1953, 35–45. Valuable study of Simenon's life and work until 1953.

———. "Georges Simenon." In *A New York Life: Of Friends and Others,* 231–52. New York: Poseidon Press, 1990.

Gothot-Mersch, Claudine: "Simenon et la gestion de l'écriture romanesque." *Etudes: Art et Littérature* (University of Jerusalem) 15 (Fall 1988): 57–77.

———. "Simenon et le souvenir." *Bulletin de l'Académie royale de langue et de littérature françaises* 68, nos. 1–2 (1990): 53–65.

Grella, George. "Simenon and Maigret." *Adam International Review* (1970): 54–61.

Henry, Gilles. *La véritable histoire du commissaire Maigret.* Condé-sur-Noireau: Editions Corlet, 1989. Biography of Commissaire Maigret taken from more than 100 short stories and novels devoted to Simenon's legendary hero.

Jour, Jean. *Simenon et "Pedigree."* Liège: Editions de l'Essai, 1963. Themes and characters of Simenon's novels in *Pedigree.*

Lacassin, Francis. *Mythologie du roman policier.* Paris: Union Générale d'Editions, 1987. Update of work of 1974 on the detective novel.

———. *Conversations avec Simenon.* Geneva: La Sirène/Alpen, 1990.

———. *La vraie naissance de Maigret.* Monaco: Editions du Rocher, 1992. Creation and development of Maigret.

Lacassin, Francis, and Gilbert Sigaux, eds. *Simenon.* Paris: Plon, 1973. Collected essays and studies of Simenon's work by prominent critics including the editors, selected texts by Simenon, selections from correspondence between Simenon and André Gide.

Lecarme, Jacques. "Les romans coloniaux de Georges Simenon." *Textyles: Revue des lettres belges de langue française,* no. 6 (November 1989): 178–89.

Lemoine, Michel. *Index des personnages de Simenon.* Brussels: Editions Labor, 1985. Index of all characters in Simenon's oeuvre.

———. "Georges Simenon: approche biographique et littéraire." *Les cahiers des paralittératures,* no. 1 (1989): 167–200.

———. *Liège dans l'oeuvre de Simenon.* Liège: Université de Liège Faculté Ouverte, 1990. Persistence of youthful impressions of Liège in Simenon's work.

———. *L'autre univers de Simenon.* Liège: Editions du C.L.P.C.F., 1991. Complete guide to early popular novels written under pseudonyms.

———. "Quand Sim préparait Simenon." *La revue nouvelle* (October 1991): 71–79. Simenon's early years.

Lire Simenon: Réalité/Fiction/Ecriture. Brussels: Editions Labor, 1980. Includes essays by Jacques Dubois, Danièle Racelle-Latin, Claudine Gothot-Mersch, Jean-Marie Klinkenberg, and Christian Delcourt. Studies of various aspects of Simenon's work in a festchrift dedicated to Maurice Piron, founder of the Centre d'Etudes Georges Simenon, Liège, Belgium.

Louvet, Jean. *Simenon.* Brussels: Editions Lansman, 1994. A play inspired by Simenon's life and work.

Marnham, Patrick. *The Man Who Wasn't Maigret: A Portrait of Georges Simenon.* New York: Farrar, Straus and Giroux, 1992. Good biographical study.

Mathonet, Anne. *Regard et voyeurisme dans l'oeuvre romanesque de Simenon.* Liège: Editions du C.E.F.A.L., 1996. Voyeurism in Simenon's work.

Menguy, Claude. "Ostrogoth-sur-Seine ou A la recherche de *La Guinguette à deux sous.*" *Traces 7: Les lieux de l'écrit,* 191–224. Liège: Centre d'Etudes Georges Simenon, 1995. Sites in the novel *La Guinguette à deux sous.*

Mercier, Paul. Postface to *La mort de Belle.* Paris: Belfond, 1996. Good analysis of the novel.

Messac, Ralph. "Georges Simenon, 'romancier-nez.' " In *Simenon,* ed. Francis Lacassin and Gilbert Sigaux, 130–38. Paris: Plon, 1973. Simenon and olfactory images.

Monnoyer, Maurice. *Trois heures avec Simenon.* Montpelier, Fr.: the author, 1989. Interviews.

Moré, Marcel. "Simenon et l'enfant de choeur." *Dieu Vivant* 19 (1951): 39–69. Reprinted in *Simenon,* ed. Francis Lacassin and Gilbert Sigaux, 227–63. Paris: Plon, 1973. Stresses importance of Simenon's early Catholic formation on his work.

Multeau, Norbert. "Simenon trahi et servi par le cinéma." *Le spectacle du monde,* no. 327 (June 1989): 69–73. Simenon and cinema.

Narcejac, Thomas. *Le cas Simenon.* Paris: Presses de la Cité, 1950. *The Art of Simenon.* London: Routledge & Kegan Paul, 1952. Excellent study of Simenon's techniques, themes, atmosphere, as well as his view of humanity.

Parinaud, André. *Connaissance de Georges Simenon.* Paris: Presses de la Cité, 1957. Places writer and work within his period. Detailed analysis of *Pedigree* and relationship of Simenon's life to his work, followed by an interview originally broadcast over the radio in October and November 1955.

Piron, Maurice (with collaboration of Michel Lemoine). *L'univers de Simenon.* Paris: Presses de la Cité, 1983. Indispensable guide to the novels and short stories (1931–1972) of Simenon.

Porter, Dennis. *The Pursuit of Crime: Art and Ideology in Detective Fiction.* New Haven: Yale University Press, 1981. Study of the crime novel.

Radine, Serge. *Quelques aspects du roman policier psychologique.* Geneva: Editions du Mont-Blanc, 1960. Discusses Simenon as a moralist in the tradition of classic novel of psychological analysis.

Raymond, John. *Simenon in Court.* New York: Harcourt Brace & World, 1968. Early study in English of Simenon's work.

Richard, Jean-Pierre. "Petites notes sur le roman policier." *Le Français dans le monde* 50 (July–August 1967): 23–28. Historical study of the detective novel.

Richter, Anne. *Simenon malgré lui.* Brussels. Les Amis de Georges Simenon, 1993. Update of *Georges Simenon et l'homme désintégré.* Brussels: La Renaissance du Livre, 1964. Seeks to reveal the real Simenon hidden behind the words he used to create his own legend.

Ritzen, Quentin. *Simenon: Avocat des hommes.* Paris: Le Livre Contemporain, 1961. Updated in Pierre Debray-Ritzen, *Georges Simenon: Romancier de l'instinct.* Analyzes Simenon's work in terms of Simenon as spokesman for Everyman.

Rolo, Charles J. "Simenon and Spillane: The Metaphysics of Murder for the Millions." In *New World Writing,* 234–45. New York: New American Library of World Literature, 1952. Study of the problem of evil and the mystery story defined as modern man's passion play.

Rutten, Mathieu. *Simenon: Ses origines, sa vie, son oeuvre.* Nandrin: Eugène Wahle, 1986. Explores relationship between Simenon's origins, his destiny, and his psychological and literary evolution.

Schneiderman, Leo. "Simenon: To Understand Is To Forgive." *Clues* 7, no. 1 (Spring–Summer 1986): 19–37.

Simenon. Cistre Essais 10. Lausanne: Editions l'Age d'Homme, 1980. Literary criticism as well as an unpublished interview with Georges Simenon.

Simenon: L'homme, l'univers, la création. Brussels: Editions Complexe, 1993. Commemorative volume of 1993 exposition "Tout Simenon."

Simenon sur le gril. Paris: Presses de la Cité, 1968. Simenon interviewed by five doctors.

Simenon Travelling (collective work). Catalog of the eleventh international festival of the novel and film noir. Grenoble, October 1989.

Simenon un autre regard. Lausanne: Editions Luce Wilquin, 1988. Collections of texts by Simenon specialists to celebrate his eighty-fifth birthday.

Simont, Juliette. "La passion de l'être selon Georges Simenon." *Annales de l'Institut de philosophie et de sciences morales de l'Université de Bruxelles* (1985): 89–93.

Stéphane, Roger. *Le dossier Simenon.* Paris: Laffont, 1961. Particularly good in study of sensuality and imagery.

———. *Portrait-souvenir de Georges Simenon.* Paris: Quai Voltaire, 1989. Interviews.

Stowe, William W. "Simenon, Maigret, and Narrative." *Journal of Narrative Technique* 19, no. 3 (Fall 1988): 331–42.

Sureau, François. "Le puits des âmes: A propos de Georges Simenon." *Commentaire,* no. 48 (Winter 1989–1990): 825–30.

Swings, Christine. "Etapes d'une vie et d'une carrière." In *Simenon un autre regard.* Lausanne: Editions Luce Wilquin, 1988. Stages in Simenon's life and work.

Tauxe, Henri Charles. *Georges Simenon: De l'humain au vide.* Paris: Buchet/Castel, 1983. The author attempts to explain the "profound psychic impact" of Simenon's novels by "micropsychoanalysis," an offshoot of Freudian psychoanalysis. Second part devoted to interviews with Simenon.

Télérama. "Maigret, ce phénomène." Hors-Série, no. 41 (January 1993). Articles on various televised Maigret series.

Thoorens, Léon. "Georges Simenon: Romancier de la fuite inutile." *Revue Générale Belge,* 15 March 1954, 781–98. Studies theme of flight in several of Simenon's novels.

———. *Qui êtes-vous Georges Simenon?* Verviers: Marabout Flash, 1959.

Tillinac, Denis. *Le mystère Simenon.* Paris: Calmann-Lévy, 1980. Good study of Simenon's work.

Tourteau, Jean-Jacques. *D'Arsène Lupin à San-Antonio: Le roman policier français de 1900 à 1970.* Tours: Mame, 1970. Description of methods and techniques used by French authors of detective and espionage novels from 1900 to 1970. Section on Simenon provides keys to his work.

Traces 1: Georges Simenon, genèse et unité de l'oeuvre. Liège: Centre d'Etudes Georges Simenon, 1989. Proceedings of first international colloquium in 1988 on Simenon and his work. All issues of *Traces* contain in-depth studies of Simenon's work by Simenon authorities.

Traces 2. Liège: Centre d'Etudes Georges Simenon, 1990. Articles on Simenon's work followed by catalog of manuscripts of novels published by Simenon between 1931 and 1972.

Traces 3: Simenon et son temps. Liège: Centre d'Etudes Georges Simenon, 1991. Proceedings of second international colloquium in 1990 on Simenon and his work.

Traces 4. Liège: Centre d'Etudes Georges Simenon, 1992. Articles on Simenon's work.

Traces 5: Simenon et la biographie. Liège: Centre d'Etudes Georges Simenon, 1993. Proceedings of third international colloquium in 1992 on biographical elements in Simenon's work.

Traces 6. Liège: Centre d'Etudes Georges Simenon, 1994. Articles on Simenon's work.

Traces 7: Les lieux de l'écrit. Liège: Centre d'Etudes Georges Simenon, 1995. Proceedings of fourth international colloquium in 1994 on places in Simenon's work.

Traces 8. Liège: Centre d'Etudes Georges Simenon, 1996. Articles on Simenon's work followed by list of novellas and short stories signed with pseudonyms.

Traces 9: Georges Simenon et l'exotisme. Liège: Centre d'Etudes Georges Simenon, 1997. Proceedings of fifth international colloquium in 1996 on exoticism in Simenon's work.

Traces 10. Liège: Centre d'Etudes Georges Simenon, 1998. Articles on Simenon's work, followed by résumés of articles that appeared in *Traces 1 to 10.*

Vandromme, Pol. *Georges Simenon.* Brussels: Pierre de Méyère, 1962.

———. "Simenon ou le style de l'humanité moyenne." *Défense de l'occident* 21 (March–April 1962): 43–52. Study of disintegration of Simenon's heroes and their lack of comprehension of the forces that destroy them.

Vanoncini, André. "Du roman policier au roman de l'homme: *La nuit du carrefour* de Georges Simenon." *Cahiers de l'Association internationale des études françaises,* no. 40 (May 1988): 183–96.

———. *Simenon et l'affaire Maigret.* Paris: Librairie Honoré Champion, 1990. Importance of Maigret in Simenon's work.

Vareille, Jean-Claude. "Roman de la recherche et recherche du roman: L'exemple de Simenon." *Richesses du roman populaire,* no. 2 (October 1983): 181–94.

———. "Culture savante et culture populaire." *Annales*, no. 23 (1986): 5–19.

Veirard, M. *"L'Affaire Saint-Fiacre" de Georges Simenon.* Paris: Editions Pédagogie Moderne, 1982.

Veldmann, Hendrik. *La tentation de l'inaccessible: Structure narrative chez Simenon.* Amsterdam: Rodopi, 1981. Systematic analysis of the ensemble of Simenon's work in an effort to evaluate the laws governing his fictional world.

Wardi, Charlotte. "Les 'petits Juifs' de Georges Simenon." *Travaux de linguistique et de littérature* 12, no. 2 (1974): 231–42. The Jew in Simenon's work.

Weisz, Pierre. "Simenon and 'Le Commissaire.' " In *Essays on Detective Fiction,* 174–84. London: Macmillan Press, 1983.

Filmography

The following is derived in large part from Claude Gauteur, *Simenon au cinéma* (Paris: Didier Hatier, 1991), as well as from Ariane Sulzer, Administration de l'Oeuvre de Georges Simenon, S.A., Lausanne, Switzerland. Only French and English titles are given.

For theatrical distribution

Description includes date of film; title (with title of book or short story if different from film title); director; principal actors.

1932 *La nuit du carrefour*; Jean Renoir; Pierre Renoir.

Le chien jaune; Jean Tarride; Abel Tarride.

1933 *La tête d'un homme*; Julien Duvivier; Harry Baur and Valéry Inkijinoff.

1942 *La maison des sept jeunes filles*; Albert Valentin; Jean Tissier.

Annette et la dame blonde; Jean Dréville; Louise Carletti.

Les inconnus dans la maison; Henri Decoin; Raimu.

Monsieur La Souris; Georges Lacombe; Raimu.

1943 *Picpus* (from *Signé Picpus*); Richard Pottier; Albert Préjean and Jean Tissier.

Le voyageur de la Toussaint; Louis Daquin; Jean Desailly, Simone Valère, and Assia Noris.

L'homme de Londres; Henri Decoin; Fernand Ledoux and Jules Berry.

1944 *Cécile est morte;* Maurice Tourneur; Albert Préjean.

1945 *Les caves du Majestic;* Richard Pottier; Albert Préjean and Suzy Prim.

1947 *Panique* (from *Les fiançailles de M. Hire*); Julien Duvivier; Michel Simon and Viviane Romance.

Dernier refuge (from *Le locataire*); Marc Maurette; Raymond Rouleau.

1948 *Temptation Harbour* (English from *L'homme de Londres*); Lance Confort; Robert Newton, Simone Simon, and William Hartnell.

1950 *The Man on the Eiffel Tower* (English from *La tête d'un homme*); Burgess Meredith; Charles Laughton and Franchot Tone.

La Marie du Port; Marcel Carné; Jean Gabin and Nicole Courcel.

Midnight Episode (English from *Monsieur La Souris*); Gordon Parry; Stanley Holloway.

1952 *La vérité sur Bébé Donge;* Henri Decoin; Jean Gabin and Danielle Darrieux.

Le fruit défendu (from *Lettre à mon juge*); Henri Verneuil; Fernandel and Françoise Arnoul.

Brelan d'as (from *Le témoignage de l'enfant de choeur*); Henri Verneuil; Michel Simon.

1953 *The Man Who Watched the Trains Go By* (English from *L'homme qui regardait passer les trains*); Harold French; Claude Rains.

1954 *La neige était sale;* Luis Saslavsky; Daniel Gélin and Valentine Tessier.

1955 *A Life in the Balance* (English from "Sept petites croix dans un carnet"); Harry Horner; Ricardo Montalban, Lee Marvin, and Anne Bancroft.

1956 *Maigret dirige l'enquête* (from three Maigret stories); Stany Cordier; Maurice Manson.

The Bottom of the Bottle (English from *Le fond de la bouteille*); Henry Hathaway; Van Johnson, Joseph Cotten, and Ruth Roman.

Le sang à la tête (from *Le fils Cardinaud*); Gilles Grangier; Jean Gabin.

1958 *Maigret tend un piège;* Jean Delannoy; Jean Gabin, Annie Girardot, and Jean Desailly.

Le passager clandestin; Ralph Habib; Martine Carol, Arletty, and Serge Reggiani.

The Brothers Rico (English from *Les frères Rico*); Phil Karlson; Richard Conte.

En cas de malheur; Claude Autant-Lara; Jean Gabin, Brigitte Bardot, and Edwige Feuillère.

1959 *Maigret et l'affaire Saint-Fiacre* (from *L'affaire Saint-Fiacre*); Jean Delannoy; Jean Gabin, Valentine Tessier, and Michel Auclair.

1960 *Le baron de l'écluse* (from short story "Le baron de l'écluse," in collection *Le bateau d'Emile*); Jean Delannoy; Jean Gabin and Micheline Presle.

1961 *Le président;* Henri Verneuil; Jean Gabin and Bernard Blier.

La mort de Belle; Edouard Molinaro; Jean Desailly.

1962 *Le bateau d'Emile* (short story in collection *Le bateau d'Emile*); Denys de la Patellière; Annie Girardot, Pierre Brasseur, Lino Ventura, and Michel Simon.

1963 *Maigret voit rouge* (from *Maigret, Lognon et les gangsters*); Gilles Grangier; Jean Gabin and Françoise Fabien.

L'aîné des Ferchaux, Jean-Pierre Melville; Jean-Paul Belmondo and Charles Vanel.

1965 *Trois chambres à Manhattan;* Marcel Carné; Annie Girardot and Maurice Ronet.

1967 *Le commissaire Maigret à Pigalle* (from *Maigret au Picratt's*); Mario Landi; Gino Cervi and Lila Kedrova.

A Stranger in the House (English from *Les inconnus dans la maison*); Pierre Rouve; James Mason and Geraldine Chaplin.

1968 *Maigret fait mouche* (from *La danseuse du Gai-Moulin*); Alfred Weidenmann; Heinz Rühmann.

1971 *Le chat;* Pierre Granier-Deferre; Jean Gabin and Simone Signoret.

La veuve Couderc; Pierre Granier-Deferre; Simone Signoret and Alain Delon.

1973 *Le train;* Pierre Granier-Deferre; Romy Schneider and Jean-Louis Trintignant.

1974 *L'horloger de Saint-Paul* (from *L'horloger d'Everton*); Bertrand Tavernier; Philippe Noiret and Jean Rochefort.

1982 *L'Etoile du Nord* (from *Le locataire*); Pierre Granier-Deferre; Simone Signoret and Philippe Noiret.

Les fantômes du chapelier; Claude Chabrol; Michel Serrault and Charles Aznavour.

1983 *Equateur* (from *Le coup de lune*); Serge Gainsbourg; Francis Huster and Barbara Sukowa.

1989 *Monsieur Hire* (from *Les fiançailles de M. Hire*); Patrice Leconte; Michel Blanc and Sandrine Bonnaire.

1992 *Betty;* Claude Chabrol; Marie Trintignant and Stéphane Audran.

Un étranger dans la maison (from *Les inconnus dans la maison*); Georges Lautner; Jean-Paul Belmondo and Renée Faure.

1994 *L'ours en peluche;* Jacques Deray; Alain Delon.

1998 *En plein coeur* (from *En cas de malheur*); Pierre Jolivet; Gérard Lanvin and Carole Bouquet.

Films of romans durs made for television (in alphabetical order)

IN FRENCH

Les anneaux de Bicêtre, Antoine et Julie, Le blanc à lunettes, Le bourgmestre de Furnes, Ceux de la soif, Chez Krull, Les complices, Cour d'assises, Crime impuni, Les demoiselles de Concarneau, L'enterrement de M. Bouvet, Les fantômes du chapelier, La fenêtre des Rouet, Feux rouges, Le fils Cardinaud, Les gens d'en face, L'homme au petit chien, L'homme de Londres, Il y a encore des noisetiers, Long cours, La main, La maison du canal, La mort d'Auguste, Un nouveau dans la ville, Novembre, L'ours en peluche, Le passager clandestin, Le petit docteur (13 episodes), *Quartier nègre, Le rapport du gendarme, Le riche homme, Les soeurs Lacroix, Strip-Tease, Le temps d'Anaïs, Le testament Donadieu, Le train de Venise, Le veuf, Les volets verts.*

IN ENGLISH

L'assassin, Chemin sans issue, Cour d'assises, Le destin des Malou, L'évadé, Les fiançailles de M. Hire, Les gens d'en face, Le haut mal, L'horloger d'Everton, Le locataire, La prison, Les rescapés du "Télémaque," Les témoins, Le veuf, Le voyageur de la Toussaint.

Maigret Series

FRANCE

TV France-Europe—ORTF *Liberty Bar*
Antenne 2/Maigret: Jean Richard (63 titles)
Société DUNE/Maigret: Bruno Cremer (30 titles)

ENGLAND

Granada Television/ Maigret: Michael Gambon (12 titles)
BBC/ Maigret : Rupert Davies (52 titles)

UNITED STATES

"Le témoignage de l'enfant de choeur," "Stan le tueur,"
La vieille dame de Bayeux

CANADA

Maigret et la grande perche

Index

The Author

Lucille Frackman Becker is a Drew University Professor Emerita of French. She received a B.A. from Barnard College, where she was elected to Phi Beta Kappa; a Diplôme d'Etudes Françaises from the University of Aix-Marseille, where she studied under a Fulbright grant; and an M.A. and Ph.D. from Columbia University. Her articles and reviews have appeared in numerous publications, among them *Montherlant vu par des jeunes de 17 à 27 ans, The Nation, Collier's Encyclopedia, Yale French Studies, Romanic Review, World Literature Today, Encyclopedia of World Literature in the 20th Century,* and *Contemporary World Writers.* Her books include *Henry de Montherlant* (Southern Illinois University Press, 1970), as well as *Louis Aragon* (1971), *Georges Simenon* (1977), *Françoise Mallet-Joris* (1985), *Twentieth-Century French Women Novelists* (1989), and *Pierre Boulle* (1996), which were published in Twayne's World Authors Series. Dr. Becker has lectured on modern French literature at universities in Thailand, Australia, New Zealand, Hong Kong, People's Republic of China, Sri Lanka, India, and Nepal. She was the keynote speaker at the National Press Club and at the International Monetary Fund during the 1987–1988 Georges Simenon Festival in Washington, D.C.

The Editor

David O'Connell is professor of French at Georgia State University. He received his Ph.D. in 1966 from Princeton University, where he was a National Woodrow Wilson Fellow, the Bergen Fellow in Romance Languages, and a National Woodrow Wilson Dissertation Fellow. He is the author of *The Teachings of Saint Louis: A Critical Text* (1972), *Les Propos de Saint Louis* (1974), *Louis-Ferdinand Céline* (1976), *The Instructions of Saint Louis: A Critical Text* (1979), and *Michel de Saint Pierre: A Catholic Novelist at the Crossroads* (1990). He has edited more than 60 books in the Twayne World Authors Series.